Distributive Principles
of Criminal Law

Distributive Principles
of Criminal Law

Who Should Be Punished How Much?

PAUL H. ROBINSON

Oxford University Press, Inc., publishes works that further Oxford University's objective of excellence in research, scholarship, and education.

Oxford New York
Auckland   Cape Town   Dar es Salaam   Hong Kong   Karachi   Kuala Lumpur   Madrid
Melbourne   Mexico City   Nairobi   New Delhi   Shanghai   Taipei   Toronto

With offices in
Argentina   Austria   Brazil   Chile   Czech Republic   France   Greece   Guatemala
Hungary   Italy   Japan   Poland   Portugal   Singapore   South Korea   Switzerland
Thailand   Turkey   Ukraine   Vietnam

Library of Congress Cataloging-in-Publication Data

Robinson, Paul H., 1948-
   Distributive principles of criminal law : who should be punished how much? /
Paul H. Robinson.
      p. cm.
   Includes bibliographical references and index.
   ISBN 978-0-19-536575-7 (alk. paper)
   1. Punishment—Philosophy. 2. Criminal liability—Philosophy.
3. Crime prevention—Philosophy. 4. Distributive justice. I. Title.
   K5103.R628 2008
   345'.04—dc22

                                                                2008022256

1 2 3 4 5 6 7 8 9
Printed in the United States of America on acid-free paper

Note to Readers
This publication is designed to provide accurate and authoritative information in regard to the subject matter covered. It is based upon sources believed to be accurate and reliable and is intended to be current as of the time it was written. It is sold with the understanding that the publisher is not engaged in rendering legal, accounting, or other professional services. If legal advice or other expert assistance is required, the services of a competent professional person should be sought. Also, to confirm that the information has not been affected or changed by recent developments, traditional legal research techniques should be used, including checking primary sources where appropriate.

(Based on the Declaration of Principles jointly adopted by a Committee of the American Bar Association and a Committee of Publishers and Associations.)

You may order this or any other Oxford University Press publication by
visiting the Oxford University Press website at www.oup.com

To Sarah McAlpine Robinson
my spouse, my love, my best friend

TABLE OF CHAPTERS

TABLE OF CONTENTS

ACKNOWLEDGMENTS

This project has been in the works for two decades or more, and many people have stimulated my thinking about punishment theory over that time. My greatest intellectual debt is to John Darley, Warren Professor of Psychology at Princeton. He and I have coauthored several articles that make up the foundation for several chapters in this book, in particular Chapters 3 and 8. Many of the ideas contained in those chapters originated with him. I am also indebted to law students in my punishment theory seminars at the University of Pennsylvania Law School, who provided both original ideas and a challenge to me to better develop and express my own. Special thanks go to Scott Kaplan, of the University of Pennsylvania Law School Class of 2009, who provided enormously helpful research assistance in the production of this book. Finally, I repeat my now well-worn thanks for the support of Sarah McAlpine Robinson, my spouse, my love, my best friend.

— PHR

SELECTED ROBINSON BIBLIOGRAPHY

Selected articles by Robinson related to the subject matter of this book are listed below. A complete bibliography of Robinson's articles, together with their download links, is available at http://ssrn.com/author=47441.

Competing Conceptions of Modern Desert: Vengeful, Deontological, and Empirical, 67 Cambridge Law Journal 145–175 (2008).

Concordance & Conflict in Intuitions of Justice, 91 Minnesota Law Review 1829–1893 (2007) (with Robert Kurzban).

Intuitions of Justice: Implications for Criminal Law and Justice Policy, 81 Southern California Law Review 1–67 (2007) (with John Darley).

Restorative Processes & Doing Justice, 3 University of St. Thomas Law Review 421–429 (2007).

The Role of Moral Philosophers in the Competition Between Philosophical and Empirical Desert, Symposium Issue, 48 William & Mary Law Review 1831–1843 (2007).

How Psychology Has Changed the Punishment Theory Debate, in Current Legal Issues 2006: Law & Psychology 94–104 (B. Brooks-Gordon & M. Freeman, eds., Oxford 2006).

Does Criminal Law Deter? A Behavioural Science Investigation, 24 Oxford Journal of Legal Studies 173–205 (2004) (with John Darley).

The A.L.I.'s Proposed Distributive Principle of "Limiting Retributivism": Does It Mean In Practice Pure Desert? 7 Buffalo Criminal Law Review 3–15 (2004).

The Role of Deterrence in the Formulation of Criminal Law Rules: At Its Worst When Doing Its Best, 91 Georgetown Law Journal 949–1002 (2003) (with John Darley).

The Virtues of Restorative Processes, the Vices of Restorative Justice, in Symposium on Restorative Justice, 2003 Utah Law Review 375–388 (2003).

Why Do We Punish? Deterrence and Just Deserts as Motives for Punishment, 83 Journal of Personality and Social Psychology 284–299 (2002) (Robinson as coauthor after Kevin Carlsmith and John Darley).

Punishing Dangerousness: Cloaking Preventive Detention as Criminal Justice, 114 Harvard Law Review 1429–1455 (2001).

The Ex Ante Function of the Criminal Law, 35 Law and Society Review 165–189 (2001) (Robinson as coauthor after John Darley and Kevin Carlsmith).

Incapacitation and Just Deserts as Motives for Punishment, 24 Law and Human Behavior 659–683 (2000) (Robinson as coauthor after John Darley and Kevin Carlsmith).

Why Does the Criminal Law Care What the Lay Person Thinks is Just? Coercive vs. Normative Crime Control, 86 Virginia Law Review 1839–1869 (2000).

The Utility of Desert, 91 Northwestern University Law Review 453–499 (1997) (with John Darley).

The Criminal-Civil Distinction and the Utility of Desert, 76 Boston University Law Review 201–214 (1996).

The Severity of Intermediate Penal Sanctions: A Psychophysical Scaling Approach for Obtaining Community Perceptions, 11 Journal of Quantitative Criminology 71–95 (1995) (Robinson as coauthor after Robert E. Harlow and John M. Darley).

The Criminal-Civil Distinction and Dangerous Blameless Offenders, 83 Journal of Criminal Law and Criminology 693–717 (1993).

Hybrid Principles for the Distribution of Criminal Sanctions, 82 Northwestern University Law Review 19–42 (1987).

CHAPTER 1

Distributing Criminal Liability and Punishment

This book is not about the justification of the institution of punishment but rather about how punishment should be distributed once that institution is established. A long and elaborate literature is found within moral philosophy and criminal law theory about the former. While the question of justifying the institution of punishment is important and interesting, it is nonetheless academic. Every known organized society has, and probably must have, some system by which it punishes those who violate its most important prohibitions.

A variety of reasons may be given to justify the institution of punishment. The traditional account distinguishes retributivist justifications—giving deserved punishment as an end in itself—from utilitarian justifications—giving punishment to advance some future good, such as to reduce future crime. But the point is that each of these traditional justifications leads to the same conclusion: support of an institution of punishment. Having a system of punishment can do justice and can avoid future crime (by deterring potential offenders, by providing the opportunity to rehabilitate and/or incapacitate dangerous offenders, by harnessing the power of social influence).

This book assumes that one can justify the *institution* of punishment and examines how one might justify one or another *distribution* of punishment. The latter question is of more than philosophical significance. How should criminal liability and punishment be distributed within a punishment system? Who should be punished how much? These are the questions that every criminal justice system designer must answer, whether giving instructions to criminal code drafters, sentencing guideline drafters, or individual judges exercising discretion in interpreting the code or in sentencing offenders.

One can imagine using any of the justifications or "purposes" of punishment as a distributive principle. That is, one could set liability and punishment distribution rules in a way that would maximize efficient deterrence, for example, or maximize rehabilitation or incapacitation of the dangerous, or maximize doing justice. As will become clear later in these discussions, each purpose of punishment when used as a distributive principle gives a quite different distribution of punishment. (In contrast, when used to justify the institution of punishment, the alternative "purposes" work together toward a unanimous conclusion in support of punishment.) Because each distributes liability and punishment differently, we must decide which of the competing distributive principles should prevail when they conflict.

One might initially suspect that the issue of the *distribution* of criminal liability and punishment is as academic an inquiry as the justification of the *institution* of punishment, for the two debates have commonly been combined into one. But the truth is that setting the criminal justice system's distributive principle is of enormous practical importance. Indeed, it is the single most important decision in constructing a criminal justice system. It is the means by which the legislature, the most democratic branch, can provide needed guidance on fundamental principles to criminal code and sentencing guideline drafting commissions. And an articulated principle is essential to guide the exercise of discretion by individual judges.[1] Research has shown that different judges each have their own personal liability and punishment philosophy. One survey of federal sentencing judges, for example, revealed that "While one-fourth of the judges thought rehabilitation was an extremely important goal of sentencing, 19 percent thought it was no more than "slightly" important;

---

1 *See* Paul H. Robinson & Barbara Spellman, Sentencing Decisions: Matching the Decisionmaker to the Decision Nature, 105 Col. L. Rev. 1124–1161 (2005).

conversely, about 25 percent thought "just deserts" was a very important or extremely important purpose of sentencing, while 45 percent thought it was only "slightly important or not important at all."[2] Research also confirms that these differences in philosophy do indeed translate into different sentences.[3] An articulated distributive principle increases the likelihood that an offender's punishment will be a product of what he has done and his personal characteristics rather than a product of the judge he happens to draw for sentencing.

Many documents purport to give decision makers the guidance of principle. For example, the original Model Penal Code section 1.02 gives judges a list of purposes to guide the interpretation of criminal code provisions and the exercise of sentencing discretion:

(1) The general purposes of the provisions governing the definition of offenses are:

    (a) to forbid and prevent conduct that unjustifiably and inexcusably inflicts or threatens substantial harm to individual or public interests;

    (b) to subject to public control persons whose conduct indicates that they are disposed to commit crimes;

    (c) to safeguard conduct that is without fault from condemnation as criminal;

    (d) to give fair warning of the nature of the conduct declared to constitute an offense;

    (e) to differentiate on reasonable grounds between serious and minor offenses.

---

2 S. Rep. No. 98-225, at 41 n.18 (1983) (Senate Report for Sentencing Act of 1984) (citing INSLAW/Yankelovich, Skelly & White, Inc., Federal Sentencing at III-4 (1981)).

3 One study done by the judiciary gave 50 judges the same 20 cases to sentence. The differences in sentences were staggering. In one extortion case, for example, sentences ranged from twenty years' imprisonment and a $65,000 fine to three years' imprisonment and no fine. *Id.* at 44 n.23; *see also id.* at 42–43 (citing Anthony Partridge & William Butler Eldridge, The Second Circuit Sentencing Study (1974)). This same disparity in sentencing is reflected in the sentences given in real cases every day. One study compared the sentences imposed in the different federal circuits. For forgery, as an example, the average sentence ranged from 30 months in the Third Circuit to 82 months in the District of Columbia. For interstate transportation of stolen motor vehicles, the extremes in average sentences were 22 months in the First Circuit and 42 months in the Tenth Circuit. *Id.* at 41 & n.21 (citing Whitney North Seymour, 1972 Sentencing Study: Southern District of New York, 45 N.Y.S. Bar J. 163 (1973)). *See* generally Marvin Frankel, Criminal Sentences: Law Without Order (1973).

(2) The general purposes of the provisions governing the sentencing and treatment of offenders are:

(a) to prevent the commission of offenses;

(b) to promote the correction and rehabilitation of offenders;

(c) to safeguard offenders against excessive, disproportionate or arbitrary punishment;

(d) to give fair warning of the nature of the sentences that may be imposed on conviction of an offense;

(e) to differentiate among offenders with a view to a just individualization in their treatment;

Similarly, the Sentencing Reform Act of 1984, which created the United States Sentencing Commission, provides:

The court shall impose a sentence sufficient, but not greater than necessary, to comply with the purposes set forth in paragraph (2) of this subsection. The court, in determining the particular sentence to be imposed, shall consider—

(1) the nature and circumstances of the offense and the history and characteristics of the defendant;

(2) the need for the sentence imposed—

(A) to reflect the seriousness of the offense, to promote respect for the law, and to provide just punishment for the offense;

(B) to afford adequate deterrence to criminal conduct;

(C) to protect the public from further crimes of the defendant; and

(D) to provide the defendant with needed educational or vocational training, medical care, or other correctional treatment in the most effective manner;[4]

But, as Chapter 2, Section C makes clear, these kinds of statements of purpose are more facade than guiding principle. Each of the alternative purposes listed in a subsection above is likely to give a different distribution of liability and punishment than those listed in other subsections. The now elderly former Nazi concentration camp torturer may no longer be dangerous, and therefore no longer in need of incapacitation, but may

---

4 18 U.S.C. 3553(a).

well deserve substantial punishment. The mentally ill offender may so lack any substantial capacity to understand the nature of his conduct as to be blameless for it and therefore deserving of complete excuse, yet nonetheless may be seriously dangerous and in need of incapacitation and, if possible, rehabilitation.

And the conflicts among the alternative principles are not limited to the adjudication or sentencing of specific cases. Consider decisions in the formulation of a criminal code, such as whether the code should give significance to resulting harm—whether, for example, an inchoate offense should be punished the same as or less than the substantive offense. An incapacitation distributive principle might punish an inchoate offense as severely as its substantive counterpart on the theory that a completed attempt to commit an offense demonstrates as much dangerousness as a successful completion if the reason for the failure has little to do with the offender's lack of dangerousness and everything to do with police competence or good luck. On the other hand, a deterrence-based system would certainly want to punish the completed offense more, if for no other reason than to assure that some additional punishment remains as a continuing deterrent threat after the offender has reached the point where his conduct constitutes a criminal attempt. Moral philosophers, in contrast, disagree among themselves about whether resulting harm ought to be significant to criminal liability, suggesting that deontological desert as a distributive principle would have difficulty resolving the issue. Yet, laypersons almost universally believe in the significance of resulting harm in assessing deserved punishment and therefore believe that justice unequivocally demands a rule that gives greater punishment for the completed offense that for the inchoate. Hence, a distributive principle based upon shared lay intuitions of justice ("empirical desert," as it is called in Chapter 7) would give great deference to resulting harm.

This natural conflict between alternative distributive principles means that the "laundry list" approach of the Model Penal Code, the Sentencing Reform Act of 1984, and most of such existing statements of guiding principle are seriously inadequate. If one distributive principle is to prevail, drafters and judges must be told which one and when. If more than one principle is to be relied upon as a distributive principle, such a hybrid distributive principle must articulate the interrelation among the different purposes. Without an articulation of the interrelation, the "laundry list" provides more illusion than guidance. It leaves the decisionmaker free to decide issues ad hoc and privately, and inconsistently, while portraying the decision making as being constrained by principle. One could argue that a criminal justice system would be better off without such "guiding principles" as these, for at least then the lack of a principled basis for decisions would be more apparent and therefore more likely to prompt reform. Chapter 2 says more about the danger of unarticulated hybrid distributive principles, Chapter 11 discusses how a principled hybrid that defines the interrelation among the different principles might be constructed, and Chapter 12 proposes a specific hybrid distributive principle.

There is reason to be hopeful that the dangerousness of the unarticulated "laundry list" approach is gaining recognition. The first change to the Model Penal Code in the forty-five years since its promulgation is a reformulation of the Code section 1.02 quoted above. The revised version attempts to do more to articulate the interrelation among alternative purposes. Though the proposed section has its flaws (discussed in Chapter 11, Section B), it nonetheless provides an important improvement in clarity and consistency over the present Code language. One would wish that the purposes governing the United States Sentencing Guidelines would similarly have their interrelation defined. Indeed, one would wish for such legislative direction in all jurisdictions in the form of an articulated distributive principle that can assure rationality and internal consistency in drafting penal codes and sentencing guidelines and in the exercise of judicial discretion in interpreting statutes and imposing specific sentences.

The goal of this book is to encourage movement toward that end and to help people think more clearly about how this can be done. The book's general plan is this: After a preliminary discussion that makes clear the criterion that guides each alternative distributive principle and that demonstrates the natural conflict among them in Chapter 2, each alternative distributive principle is examined in turn to understand its strengths and weaknesses in Chapters 3 through 9. Then, stepping back, these strengths and weaknesses are summarized and compared in Chapter 10 and, with this background, Chapter 11 discusses how a hybrid distributive principle might be constructed, an exercise illustrated in Chapter 12.

Even if the specific proposal in Chapter 12 does not persuade the reader—many aspects of the determination of a distributive principle depend upon one's value judgments—it is hoped that the process leading up to that proposal can help the reader think through for herself the distributive principle that she might prefer, perhaps gaining insights from the critique of strengths and weaknesses of each alternative.

CHAPTER 2

The Need for an Articulated Distributive Principle

Each of the justifications for punishment, or "purposes" as they are often called, might be used as a distributive principle for criminal liability and punishment. As preparation for the coming examination of each of these alterative distributive principles, Section A describes what is meant when one speaks of each. Because each principle follows a different distributive criterion, the different principles suggest different results, as Section B illustrates, and this conflict among principles, Section C explains, is a serious challenge to reaching the goal of providing real guidance to drafters and judges.

A. The Criterion for Each Alternative Distributive Principle

Consider the specific criterion that each principle would use in distributing criminal liability and punishment. Most of the discussion below simply confirms what is meant by one distributive principle or another. It is more terminological than substantive and is also an opportunity to sketch a brief introduction to the basic operation of each principle for those who may be unfamiliar with punishment theory. It shows what the criterion for each distributive principle means in practical terms—which factors have influence and which factors do not. This sets up the discussion in Section B, which demonstrates that different distributive principles conflict with one another in whom they would punish how much. In addition to this overview, each distributive principle is discussed in greater detail in the subsequent chapters of this book.

1. Deterrence General and Special

One might set the distribution of punishment to most efficiently deter future offenses. When the aim is to deter other potential offenders, it is referred to as "general deterrence"; when the aim is to deter the offender at hand, it is "special deterrence."

Both distributive principles make the amount of punishment proportional to the seriousness of the offense, all other things being equal. The greater the harm or evil threatened, the greater the investment in punishment that can be justified. Intentional killing calls for greater punishment than intentional bodily injury, which in turn calls for greater punishment than intentional property destruction, all other things being equal.

Deterrence's preference for punishment proportional to the offense harm or evil also is supported by its operational challenge. One might initially think that deterrence would frequently impose the harshest sentence allowed to maximize the potential cost of a criminal act. However, if during a course of criminal conduct an actor thinks that no additional punishment can be received, then a deterrent effect is lost. If attempted murder is punishable by death, for example, then the actor who has failed in an attempt to murder might as well try again as there will be no greater penalty for the completed killing than for the penalty the offender already faces.

General and special deterrence also are similar in that both increase punishment to compensate for offenses with low capture rates. That is, if the probability of punishment for an offense is lower than average, the amount of punishment threatened must be correspondingly higher to maintain the overall deterrent threat (probability × amount).

In other respects, however, general deterrence and special deterrence may rely on somewhat different factors. General deterrence would impose greater punishment in cases of greater media coverage, for example, because these cases would give a greater general deterrent payoff for the punishment cost investment. Special deterrence, in contrast, has less reason to care about media coverage. The target audience is the offender at hand who will know the liability and punishment even if there is no media coverage.

For another example, general deterrence would not support excuse doctrines such as the insanity defense, while special deterrence would. The threat of sanctions cannot deter persons who do not or cannot take account of the consequences of a violation. Thus, if the goal is to deter the offender at hand, the punishment is wasted if that offender's mental illness prevents a deterrent effect. However, punishment of a mentally ill person can be quite useful in deterring others. Indeed, if a person is incapable of appreciating the nature of his conduct and is still punished, it may send a useful message to other persons (who are sane) that there is little means by which one can escape liability. This unattractiveness of an insanity defense under a general deterrence principle is only one illustration of a larger point: Any failure to punish an actor who has violated a prohibition tends to undermine the effectiveness of the prohibition, for it shows potential offenders the possibility that they can offend yet escape punishment even if caught.

2. Incapacitation of the Dangerous

The most direct means of preventing future offenses is through incapacitation of offenders by imprisoning, executing, or in some other way making impossible their commission of another offense. One can imagine quiet dramatic methods: Castrating a potential rapist or cutting off the hand of a potential pickpocket could prevent a repeat offense. Liberal democracies tend to bar such punishments as in conflict with other important values and, with some important exceptions, such as the death penalty, tend to limit incapacitative means to incarceration.

If the dangerousness of two people is the same—the same probability of the same harm predicted to last for the same period of time—the degree of incarceration justified under a purely incapacitative rationale would be the same. Thus, to use the example offered in Chapter 1, under a distributive principle of incapacitation, many if not most completed attempts would be punished the same as the completed offense because they typically demonstrate the offender's dangerousness in the same way that a completed offense would.

Under an incapacitation distributive principle, logically punishment would not need to wait until after the commission of an offense; a reliable prediction of future criminality would provide adequate justification. (Of course, a society might have other interests, beyond crime control, that would conflict with such a practice.) And conversely, an incapacitation distributive principle would decline to impose any punishment, no matter how serious the wrongdoing, if there remained no risk of a repeat offense. For example, if a husband kills his spouse of fifty years because he believes she is dying of cancer and wants them to die together, there would be no justification to punish him if it was clear that the circumstances provoking him to kill would never arise again. Under a purely incapacitative distribution, then, he would receive no punishment.

3. Rehabilitation

Rehabilitating or reforming an offender is another means by which future offenses can be avoided. Rehabilitation takes away the offender's desire or need to engage in criminal conduct. Medical treatment, psychological counseling, drug treatment, and education and training programs are the most common forms of rehabilitation. However, anything designed to minimize the actor's desire to engage in conduct that is criminal (other than intimidation by deterrent threat of official punishment) typically is included within the label of rehabilitation.

The distribution of liability and punishment under this distributive principle will depend upon a person's predicted future criminality, the ability of existing rehabilitation programs to rehabilitate this kind of offender, the availability of those programs, and the ability of the programs to determine when a person under treatment is in fact rehabilitated. As with incapacitation, the effectiveness of this mechanism does not require that rehabilitative treatments wait until after the potential offender has committed an offense. Nothing in this crime prevention mechanism requires that the potential offender agrees with or approves of the changes that are made to him. (For some people, this raises ethical issues not present in other distributive principles, at least where rehabilitation involves changing the nature of the offender, because such can involve serious intrusion on personal autonomy not just the coercive imposition of suffering.)

4. Deontological Desert

Standing as an alternative to these instrumentalist distributive principles to reduce crime is "just desert," which aims instead only to do justice. Under a distributive principle of "deontological desert" (a term used to distinguish it from "empirical desert," discussed below), the sole criterion for punishment is the actor's moral blameworthiness, a matter of moral philosophy. A person is punished if and only if the person is blameworthy and is punished strictly according to the degree of his or her blameworthiness, no more, no less. The degree of an offender's blameworthiness depends upon both the seriousness of the violation and the extent of the person's moral accountability for it.

5. Empirical Desert

An alternative to relying on moral philosophers can be found in the social science research suggesting that average people, no matter their training or level of education, hold strong intuitive views of an offender's blameworthiness for wrongdoing. Indeed, the studies suggest that an astounding level of agreement across demographics regarding the relative blameworthiness of different offenders exists, at least with respect to the core of wrongdoing (physical aggression, taking of property, and deception in exchanges). Thus, one could adopt a distributive principle of "desert" based upon the community's shared intuitions of justice rather than based upon philosophical notions of desert.

Though they both look to the offender's blameworthiness, such an "empirical desert" distribution is likely to be different from a "deontological desert" distribution. For example, while philosophers are seriously split as to whether blameworthiness should take account of resulting harm—for example, whether attempted murder should be punished the same as murder—laypersons almost universally see resulting harm as central in assessing blameworthiness and would punish attempted murder less than murder.

People do not share a sense of the absolute amount of punishment that is deserved for an offense. Some tend to be harsher in their punishment tastes than others. Rather, what people share is a sense of the relative blameworthiness of different cases. What this means, however, is that, given the large number of cases of distinguishable blameworthiness to be placed on a limited continuum of punishment, once a society establishes the endpoint of its punishment continuum, as all societies must do—be it the death penalty, life imprisonment, or fifteen years imprisonment—then each offender's blameworthiness relative to other offenders will place the person at a specific point on the punishment continuum and thereby produce a specific sentence. (If the continuum endpoint were changed, the punishment amounts for each offender along the continuum would also change.) If empirical desert were the sole distributive principle, it would distribute liability and punishment according to rules that tracked the community's shared intuitions of justice. That is, social science research would determine how average people assessed the relative blameworthiness of an offender based on the offense committed, and the offender would then be punished at the proper level based on where the offense fell along the continuum of punishment.

B. Conflicts Among Distributive Principles

As Chapter 1 has already noted, because each of these alternative distributive principles relies upon a different distributive criterion, it is inevitable that they conflict with one another in how they would distribute criminal liability and punishment. But the importance of this point, and the fact that it has been commonly denied,[5] suggests that a more detailed explication is needed. Factors highly influential in determining liability and punishment for one distributive principle may be irrelevant to another. Reliance upon a factor that advances one principle can undermine another. The liability or sentencing rules suggested by one distributive principle will be different from those suggested by another. Consider a few illustrations.

1. Deterrence General and Special

If deterrence were the distributive principle, a potential offender's perception of the probability of apprehension would be highly relevant.[6]

---

5 *See*, e.g., Gordon Bazemore, The Expansion of Punishment and the Restriction of Justice: Loss of Limits in the Implementation of Retributive Policy, 74 Social Research 651 (2007) (arguing that "restorative justice is compatible with many goals and assumptions of other justice approaches/philosophies, including crime control (deterrence; incapacitation), rehabilitation, and libertarian/due process models").

6 *See*, e.g., Steven Shavell, Criminal Law and the Optimal Use of Nonmonetary Sanctions as a Deterrent, 85 Colum. L. Rev. 1232, 1235–1236 (1985).

To maintain an effective deterrent threat, offenses with a perceived low probability of apprehension should be graded higher and punished more severely. Further, a deterrence principle would base liability upon the extent of the publicity that a punishment receives in a particular case. Just as an advertising executive would pay more to place an ad that reaches more people, a deterrence-based criminal justice system would spend more (i.e., impose a greater penalty at a greater cost) if the punishment would be widely communicated. Thus, news coverage should aggravate the grade or sentence for an offense. Taking account of such factors as media coverage or probability of apprehension obviously would conflict with a desert distributive principle, as it would with incapacitation or rehabilitation principles, for neither of the factors correlate with either blameworthiness or dangerousness.

A deterrence program also would produce a different set of criminal code liability rules. Any liability rule that makes conviction more difficult and, therefore, punishment less likely, would be disfavored because it could undermine the credibility of the deterrent threat. Thus, culpability and proximate cause requirements, for example, might well be dispensed within a general deterrence program. As long as the prohibited harm came about, and the defendant's conduct was a "but for" cause, punishment of the offender provides a useful deterrent threat against future conduct that might cause the result.

Similarly, general deterrence also would tend to ignore excusing conditions external to the defendant, such as duress or coercion, that might be highly relevant under desert, incapacitation, and rehabilitation principles. The latter principles would excuse the actor because he was a blameless and nondangerous, but general deterrence would take these conditions as signaling a need for an increased rather than a reduced deterrent threat to counterbalance the increased inclination of a person in such situations to commit an offense. If the pressure to commit an offense is so great as to be essentially irresistible, special deterrence might accept an excuse or mitigation because such punishment would be futile and thus an inefficient expenditure. Nonetheless, a general deterrent value in imposing punishment remains. In *Regina v. Dudley & Stephens*,[7] for example, the sailors who killed and drank the blood of the sick cabin boy to stay alive until they could be rescued were hardly shown to be dangerous people (as long as they stayed off boats that would be adrift for

---

7 14 Q.B.D. 273 (1884).

weeks), and their blameworthiness was significantly reduced because of the life-threatening conditions. However, the court concluded that punishing the offenders would serve a useful function in reaffirming the prohibition against killing innocent nonaggressors and sentenced the men to death. Bowing to public pressure, the Crown later commuted the sentences.

Conflict also arises in applying mitigating principles, such as heat of passion, provocation, and mistake as to self-defense by battered spouses. In these cases, an otherwise normal person reacts less than admirably when confronted with a difficult situation. Such an actor is not as dangerous or as blameworthy as an actor who kills absent the mitigating conditions, but, as with instances of duress, coercion, and nonjustified necessity, there is a need for an increased deterrent threat in these situations to serve as a counter to the increased inclination to offend.

At the extreme, general deterrence would justify punishment of the innocent. As long as the public believes the "offender" to be guilty, the deterrent goal would be served. Obviously, this and many of the other implications of a deterrence-based system noted above would conflict with a desert principle and sometimes other principles.

2. Incapacitation and Rehabilitation

Incapacitation and rehabilitation as distributive principles similarly would rely upon factors that are irrelevant to and inconsistent with distributive principles of desert or deterrence. The former would give great importance to the probability of recidivism, for example. Thus, offenders would be sentenced on the basis of backgrounds and characteristics having little or no connection to their crimes. If past employment history is highly relevant in predicting recidivism, then unemployment for the preceding years might aggravate the grade of an offense or increase the sentence imposed. If gender, age, or family situation are predictors of future criminality, they too would become the basis for increasing or decreasing liability and punishment.

Indeed, the nature of the crime committed might be of little relevance. The Model Sentencing Act from 1962, which relies heavily upon incapacitation and rehabilitation principles, proudly points out:

> The [Act] diminishes the major source of [sentencing] disparity—
> sentencing according to the particular offense. Under [the Act]
> the dangerous offender may be committed to a lengthy term;

the non-dangerous offender may not. It makes available, for the first time, a plan that allows the sentence to be determined by the defendant's make-up, his potential threat in the future, and other similar factors, with a minimum of variation according to the offense.[8]

These differences in relevant factors and distributive criterion inevitably would produce different liability and sentencing rules. For example, as noted previously, the focus on dangerousness would have an inchoate offense punished the same as the substantive offense where the failure to complete the offense is due to factors other than the offender's choice or competency. Similarly, incapacitation and rehabilitation distributive principles would have little reason for keeping traditional causation rules, which are careful to ensure a sufficient causal relation between the defendant's conduct and the prohibited result. It is not the offender's causal accountability for the present harm that is relevant but only what his present conduct says about future dangerousness.

Consider how different distributive principles also can produce different punishment procedures. To further incapacitative and rehabilitative goals, fully indeterminate sentences were imposed in the recent past.[9] The length of the sentence was to be determined by the length of time that the offender remained dangerous, which could not be determined at the time of conviction because it did not depend upon the offense facts. The offender remained in prison until she was rehabilitated. In contrast, a deterrence distributive principle would find indeterminate sentencing objectionable because of its tendency to undermine the clarity of the deterrent threat. A desert distributive principle also would prefer determinate sentences. Almost without exception, all factors relevant to desert are fully known at the time a sentence is imposed. If the sentence is influenced by a factor that becomes known only after sentencing, that influence is likely to be something inconsistent with desert. (Although some desert theorists argue that genuine remorse is an exception to this rule.)

---

8 Model Sentencing Act art. 1, §1 comment (National Council on Crime and Delinquency 1st ed. 1962), reprinted in 9 Crime & Delinq. 337, 346 (1963).

9 *See*, e.g., National Congress on Penitentiary and Reformatory Discipline, Declaration of Principles, Transactions of the National Congress on Penitentiary and Reformatory Discipline 541–547 (1871); *see also* Model Sentencing Act §1 (National Council on Crime and Delinquency rev. ed. 1972) ("[D]angerous offenders shall be identified, segregated, and correctively treated in custody for long terms as needed. . . . Persons convicted of crime shall be dealt with in accordance with their potential for rehabilitation.").

At the extreme, incapacitation and rehabilitation as distributive principles would give little reason for waiting until an offense is committed. It would be more efficient to screen the general population for dangerous persons and "convict" them of being dangerous and in need of rehabilitation or, failing that, incapacitation.

Incapacitation and rehabilitation overlap with one another as distributive principles because they both begin their analysis by asking whether a person is dangerous. However, they also conflict with one another. Most fundamentally, if rehabilitation were the sole distributive principle, it would take criminal justice jurisdiction only over those cases for which rehabilitation is possible, releasing offenders for whom it is not possible, even if they are dangerous. (It is primarily because of this peculiarity that Chapter 11 concludes that rehabilitation would be unsuitable as a sole distributive principle and that it logically operates best in conjunction with another distributive principle, such as incapacitation.)

3. Deontological and Empirical Desert

That desert can conflict with deterrence, incapacitation, and rehabilitation has already been shown. A desert principle would insist on excuse doctrines like the insanity defense and the voluntary act requirement, which acquit blameless offenders even though they may be dangerous and even though their punishment might serve a general deterrent function. For a reverse example, the Model Penal Code's defense for inherently unlikely attempts acquits offenders because of a lack of dangerousness though they may be morally blameworthy.[10]

Obviously, the major source of conflict between deontological desert, on the one hand, and the instrumentalist crime-control distributive principles, on the other, arises from their obvious difference in focus. The instrumentalist distributive principles are calculated to efficiently reduce

---

10 An example of an inherently unlikely attempt is one that occurs when an actor sticks pins in a voodoo doll representing the victim, honestly believing that this will cause the victim's death or injury. The Model Penal Code provides: "If the particular conduct charged to constitute a criminal attempt, solicitation or conspiracy is so inherently unlikely to result or culminate in the commission of a crime that neither such conduct nor the actor presents a public danger warranting the grading of such offense under this Section, the Court shall . . . enter judgment and impose sentence for a crime of lower grade or degree or, in extreme cases, may dismiss the prosecution." Model Penal Code §5.05(2) (1985).

future crime. Deontological desert has no interest in either reducing crime or doing it efficiently; its only concern is deserved punishment for a past offense. Such a desert distributive principle might impose punishment that has no preventive effect or that costs more than the crime that it would prevent.

Empirical desert, in contrast, as Chapters 7 and 8 explain, does not share deontological desert's fundamental conflict with these instrumentalist distributive principles. Its distributive rules are fundamentally consistent with instrumentalist crime-control goals. By tracking community views of justice, it builds the criminal justice system's moral credibility, which thereby allows the system to harness the crime-control power of social and norm influence. As has already been shown, however, while empirical desert is instrumentalist in nature, its focus on offender blameworthiness means that it conflicts with the other traditional instrumentalist principles that do not.

Deontological and empirical desert also conflict with one another where moral philosophy generates distributive principles in conflict with lay intuitions of justice, as occurs, for example, in the context of the significance given to resulting harm, noted previously. Moral philosophers are quite divided over whether resulting harm aggravates blameworthiness, but lay views almost universally supports such a role. The former principle seeks rules that do justice; the latter only seeks rules that do what is perceived as justice.

C. The Problem of Unarticulated Combinations of Distributive Principles

Most criminal codes, and most criminal law courses, begin with the "familiar litany" of the traditional alternative distributive principles— just punishment, deterrence, incapacitation of the dangerous, and rehabilitation. We often train and direct our lawyers, judges, and legislators to use these as guiding principles for the distribution of criminal liability and punishment and to guide the drafting and interpretation of criminal statutes and sentencing guidelines and the exercise of discretion in individual cases.

The principles frequently conflict, however, as Section B demonstrates. Conflicts arise because each principle requires consideration of different criteria. A fact may suggest one statutory formulation or sentence under one principle but a different formulation or sentence under another principle. The drafters or decision makers must adopt one or another of the alternative formulations or sentences, yet, when faced with such conflicts, judges, legislators, and sentencing-guideline drafters have no guide for their decision as to which principle to follow and which to sacrifice or how to otherwise resolve the conflict.

In the absence of a guiding principle in selecting among competing principles, the choices made are, at best, unpredictable and commonly internally inconsistent. For example, most state criminal codes maintain an insanity defense because it exculpates the blameless (and thus furthers just punishment even though it sacrifices general deterrence and incapacitation). Yet, instead of consistently following this just desert principle, the same codes often sacrifice just punishment in favor of increasing deterrence by adopting strict liability offenses—for example, imposing strict liability for having sex with a minor. In turn, these codes frequently abandon deterrence when it is perhaps needed most to advance desert by recognizing the offender's reduced blameworthiness. This is true in cases of provocation, for example, where deterrence would suggest greater punishment to counteract the greater inclination to commit the crime. In other words, code drafters have chosen to follow different principles in different contexts but offer no explanation as to what might guide the choice.

At worst, the absence of a guiding principle fosters arbitrariness and helps hide prejudice. This can occur most easily in individual sentencing decisions. Rehabilitation might be the best means of avoiding future crime by a young African American addict caught selling drugs to support his habit, for example, but a judge also might rationally forgo rehabilitation and impose a long prison term to better further general deterrence. When the next case is a young bank teller who embezzled money from her cash drawer, the same judge might decide to sacrifice the general deterrent value of a long prison term and put her on probation, under an incapacitative theory—she is no longer dangerous because she will never again be placed in a position of trust. But how can we know whether the judge's choice of distributive principle is the product of some rational, yet unarticulated, principle or the product of conscious or unconscious bias—perhaps his personal or family history has given him a soft spot for female offenders or a hard spot for black addicts. In both cases, either a short or a long sentence might be justified under one or another principle, but if no articulable principle for following one principle over another exists, then the choice can as easily be the product of arbitrariness or bias.

Why do we not define for code and sentencing-guideline drafters and sentencing judges the interrelation among alternative distributive principles to direct their choices in situations of conflicting principles? A cynic may conclude that the use of unarticulated combinations of principles is a convenient means of rationalizing results for which the decision maker has another, undisclosed reason. This suspicion—that the "litany" of principles are popular as a method of guidance precisely *because* they offer hidden flexibility—is fueled by the almost universal failure to articulate a guiding principle.

The Model Penal Code, for example, quoted in Chapter 1, gives the traditional "litany" of principles and directs judges to use them in interpreting the provisions of the Code and in fashioning sentences under the Code but provides no more guidance in cases of conflict than to urge in commentary that the principles be "just[ly] harmoniz[ed]."[11] Others urge that the competing interests be "balance[d],"[12] "blend[ed],"[13] "accommodate[d],"[14] "taken account of,"[15] or "deal[t] with [such that] the public interest will be served,"[16] but with no indication of how this is to be done.

Are these urgings cynical obfuscation or simply a failure of the theorists? Is it that decision makers would love to have an articulated governing principle but simply cannot figure out how one can feasibly be fashioned? People with this view should be greatly heartened by Chapter 11, which demonstrates several mechanisms by which a workable, articulated hybrid distributive principle can be constructed.

---

11 Model Penal Code §1.02 commentary at 4 (Tent. Draft No. 2, 1954). This same lack of rigor is apparent when the drafters of §7.01 (Criteria for Withholding Sentence of Imprisonment and for Placing Defendant on Probation) explain that "the reasons for imprisonment are usually obvious." *Id.* §7.01 commentary at 34.

12 Stanley A. Cohen, An Introduction to the Theory, Justifications and Modern Manifestations of Criminal Punishment, 27 McGill L.J. 73, 81 (1981).

13 Solicitor General, Report of the Canadian Committee on Corrections—Toward Unity: Criminal Justice and Corrections 188 (1969) (known as the Ouimet Report).

14 Cohen, *supra* note 12, at 73.

15 Herbert Wechsler, Sentencing, Corrections, and the Model Penal Code, 109 U. Pa. L. Rev. 465, 468 (1961).

16 State v. Ivan, 33 N.J. 197, 201, 162 A.2d 851, 853 (1960) (Weintraub, C.J.). Chief Justice Weintraub concluded that one should arrive at a "composite judgment, a total evaluation of all the facets, giving to each [crime prevention method] the weight, if any, it merits in the context."

CHAPTER 3

Does Criminal Law Deter?

Would deterrence make a good distributive principle? Its attractiveness lies in part in what seems like the enormous potential of general deterrence in particular to deter future crime. By punishing the offender at hand, the system can dissuade many others from committing that and other offenses. On the other hand, there is reason to be skeptical about whether distributing criminal liability and punishment to optimize deterrence would in fact have such influence on potential offenders. This chapter examines that fundamental question of whether criminal law deters.[17] With that background, the next chapter returns to the question of whether deterrence would make a desirable distributive principle.

Having a criminal justice system that imposes liability and punishment for violations does deter. Allocation of police resources or the use of enforcement methods that dramatically increase the capture rate can deter. However, it seems likely that manipulating *criminal law*—the substantive rules governing the distribution of criminal liability and punishment—commonly does not materially effect deterrence, contrary to what

---

17 Much of this chapter is drawn from Robinson & Darley, Does Criminal Law Deter? A Behavioral Science Investigation, 24 Oxford Journal of Legal Studies 173–205 (2004).

law and policy makers have assumed for decades. The claim here is not that criminal law formulation can never influence behavior but rather that the conditions under which it can do so are not typical. By contrast, as the next chapter documents, criminal lawmakers formulate criminal law rules on an assumption that their formulation will have the intended deterrent effect. And it is that working assumption that is so disturbing and so dangerous.

Skepticism of criminal law's deterrent effect is derived in large part from a behavioral science research critique of the alleged path of influence from doctrinal manipulation to behavioral response. This critique finds that the transmission of influence faces so many hurdles and is so unlikely to clear them all that it will be the unusual instance in which the doctrinal manipulation can ultimately influence conduct. Yet, this is a startling conclusion because it contradicts the common wisdom and standard practice of lawmakers and scholars. If, as appears to be the case, doctrinal formulation does not affect conduct, then most of the criminal analysis of the past forty years has been misguided. It may be that where doctrine has been formulated to optimize deterrence, overriding other goals such as doing justice, that frustration of other goals begets little or no deterrent benefit.

To briefly sketch the line of analysis: Potential offenders commonly do not know the legal rules, either directly or indirectly, even those rules that have been explicitly formulated to produce a behavioral effect. Even if they know the legal rules, potential offenders commonly cannot or will not use such knowledge to guide their conduct in their own best interests, such failure stemming from a variety of social, situational, or chemical influences. And even if they know the rules and do rationally calculate what is in their best interests, the cost-benefit analysis that potential offenders perceive—which is the only cost-benefit analysis that matters—commonly leads to a conclusion suggesting violation rather than compliance, either because the perceived likelihood of punishment is so small, or because it is so distant as to be highly discounted, or for a variety of other or combination of reasons. Even if none of these three hurdles is fatal to law's behavioral influence, their cumulative effect commonly is. Section A reviews the behavioral science evidence.

But some might argue that, although a behavioral science analysis of criminal law's action path says doctrinal formulation can rarely influence conduct, it might in fact do so in some mysterious way presently beyond the understanding of human knowledge. We can test this argument by looking at the effect of specific doctrinal formulations on the crime rates they are intended to lower.

The available studies of what one might call "aggregated effects"— that is, studies that do not concern themselves with how a deterrent effect might come about but look strictly to whether an effect of doctrine on crime rate can be found—are consistent with the conclusion above. A majority of these studies finds no discernible deterrent effect of doctrinal formulation. Others claim to find such an effect and these results require explanation. Even if the mechanism of transmission from doctrinal formulation to behavioral influence is unknown, finding such a connection may be inconsistent with some of the claims made here and must be dealt with, especially because many deterrence advocates will speculate that the causal mechanism in the "black box" is deterrence.

Some aggregated-effect studies are simply poorly done and cannot reliably support a conclusion that doctrine affects crime rates. Others seem undeniably to have found an effect on crime rate, but one may suspect that much if not most of this is the result of incapacitative rather than deterrent effects. Increasing prison terms, for example, could be taken as a means of providing a greater deterrent threat, but a resulting reduction in crime may be the result of the isolating effect of longer incarcerations rather than their greater deterrent effect. But even if one concludes that some of these studies show a deterrent effect from doctrinal formulation, the specific circumstances of those studies serve generally to affirm the points about the prerequisites of deterrence. That is, these studies involve rules and target audiences that do what is rarely done: to satisfy the prerequisites to deterrence. The circumstances of these studies only serve to illustrate that the existence of such prerequisites are not typical. Section B reviews these aggregated-effect studies.

After this sobering view of deterrence effectiveness, Section C considers whether reforms might produce a greater deterrent effect. There are possibilities for reform that might increase the situations in which deterrence might be effective, but there are also serious limitations, due in large part to the sacrifices such reforms would require: in greater financial cost, in infringing interests of privacy and freedom from governmental intrusion, in compromising basic notions of procedural fairness, and in doing injustice and failing to do justice. Within the realm of plausible reforms, one could increase the situations in which the conditions exist where doctrinal manipulation could have a deterrent effect, but such conditions would remain the exception rather than the rule.

A. The Prerequisites to Deterrence

Can doctrinal formulation influence conduct? For criminal law to have an effect on a potential offender's conduct choices, the following three questions must all be answered in the affirmative:

1. Does the potential offender know, directly or indirectly, and understand the implications for him of the law that is meant to influence him?
2. If he does know, will he bring such understanding to bear on his conduct choices at the moment of making his choices?
3. If he does know the rule and is able and willing to be influenced in his choices, is his perception of his choices such that he is likely to choose compliance with the law rather than commission of the criminal offense? That is, do the perceived costs of noncompliance outweigh the perceived benefits of the criminal action so as to bring about a choice to forgo the criminal action?

1. The Legal Knowledge Hurdle

Does the potential offender know, directly or indirectly, and understand the implications for him of the law that is meant to influence him? One study tested the knowledge of residents in five different states with regard to four legal rules, each of which involves a situation in which an ordinary person might find herself: rules concerning their duty to assist a stranger in danger, the use of deadly defensive force in situations where the victim can safely retreat, their duty to report a known felony, and the use of deadly force in protection of property.[18] Each of these rules was written with the expectation that it would guide a person's conduct in the situation at hand. States take different positions on each of these rules, and each state in the study took a minority view toward at least one of the rules. Yet, the study found that both the residents of states adopting a minority position on a rule and the residents of states adopting a majority position on the same rule had essentially identical beliefs about the law's rule. The actual legal rule apparently had no effect on their belief. Interestingly, their belief in the law's commands did not always match the

---

18 John M. Darley, Kevin M. Carlsmith & Paul H. Robinson, The Ex Ante Function of the Criminal Law, 35 Law & Soc. Rev. 165 (2001).

majority view; rather, it closely matched their own judgments of what the law *should* be, suggesting that they were using their own moral intuitions to predict the legal rule, rather than any real knowledge of the legal code's rules.[19]

It might be argued that knowledge of criminal law by the general population provides unclear evidence of the knowledge among that subset of the population likely to commit crimes, that the deterrence's "target population" of potential offenders may have more accurate knowledge of criminal law rules. A recent study measured actual criminals' knowledge of the penalties assigned by criminal codes and found them not very precise. Males who had been imprisoned for a felony were tested—persons who, given their time in prison and their interest in the question, one would assume had both the motivation and the opportunity to learn the comparative magnitudes of sentences. However, only 22 percent of criminals thought that they knew "exactly what the punishment would be" for the crime they committed (although they may have been wrong), while 18 percent reported that they had no idea of the penalty, and another 35 percent reported that, as to the punishment for the offense they committed, "I didn't even think about it."[20] And for those who reported that they *thought* they knew the exact punishment for the crime they committed, there is ample reason to believe that a good number of them were, in fact, wrong about the penalties assigned by the code.[21]

To sum up, people rarely know the criminal law rules, even when those rules are formulated under the express assumption that they will

---

19 *Id.* at 181. *See also* John M. Darley, Catherine Sanderson & Peter LaMantia, Community Standards for Defining Attempt: Inconsistencies With the Model Penal Code American Penal Code, 39 Amer. Behav. Sci. 405 (1996) (study of attempt suggests they used their own moral intuitions to predict the magnitude of punishment rather than having any real knowledge of law).

20 David Anderson, The Deterrence Hypothesis and Picking Pockets at the Pickpocket's Hanging, 4 Amer. L. & Econ. Rev. 295 (2002). *See also* Andrew Hochstetler, In With a Bad Crowd: An Analysis of Criminal Decision-making in Small Groups 23–29 (Ph.D. dissertation submitted to the Department of Sociology, University of Tennessee, Knoxville, December, 1999, UMI Microform 9962267).

21 Daniel Bailis et al., Community Standards of Criminal Liability and the Insanity Defense, 19 Law & Human Behavior 425 (1995). *See also* Robert MacCoun et al., Do Citizens Know Whether Their State Has Decriminalized Marijuana? A Test of the Perceptual Assumption in Deterrence Theory (Apr. 15, 2003) (unpublished manuscript, *available at* http://papers.ssrn.com/sol3/papers.cfm?abstract_id=1120930) (finding that the percentage of people who believe they could be jailed for marijuana possession is quite similar in both states that have removed those penalties and those that have not).

influence conduct. Apparently, people commonly assume the law to be as they think it should be, so they assume the existence of criminal law rules that correspond to their own intuitions of justice. Thus, when the legal rule deviates from the community's shared intuitions of justice, the system has a greater burden to make the law known, and a failure to make a special effort to announce the counterintuitive rule will increase the likelihood that potential offenders will not know of the rule. As noted, potential offenders have a greater incentive than others to know the details of the law's rules and policies, but in fact their knowledge also is relatively poor.

This is not meant as an all-encompassing generalization. It is likely that some legal rules are widely known. For example, it is probably well known that dramatically greater penalties for all offenses are imposed once a juvenile reaches the age of majority and thereby comes under the jurisdiction of the adult criminal justice system rather the more rehabilitation-based juvenile justice system. And, thus, it should be no surprise to see that crime rates by juveniles drop off when they reach that age, albeit a temporary drop off.[22] But such well-known rules are the exception rather than the rule.

Of course, a potential offender need not "know the law" in an intellectual sense to be influenced by it. Even rats can be deterred by a perceived threat. They react to the conditions that they experience, such as electric shocks when they pull the lever that previously had given food. In the same way, a potential offender may know nothing about the law per se, yet may through his experience and that of others of which he hears indirectly come to understand, perhaps even subconsciously, the conditions of criminal liability or punishment that the criminal law sets out.

This may frequently be the case with regard to policing practices. When the potential offender sees three times as many police cruisers pass by as before, he may perceive a greater risk of capture for purse snatching. But will this same method of education effectively communicate the substantive criminal law rules that lawmakers have justified on deterrence grounds? It is unlikely. The imposition of criminal liability is not a

---

22 Steven Levitt, Juvenile Crime and Punishment, 106 J. Pol. Econ. 1156 (abstract) (1998) ("Juvenile offenders are at least as responsive to criminal sanctions as adults. Sharp drops in crime at the age of majority suggest that deterrence (and not merely incapacitation) plays an important role.").

common or contemporaneous event; it does not influence the potential offender in the immediate manner as does a police cruiser drive-by.

Perhaps more importantly, the application of the criminal law rules is difficult, if not impossible, for a potential offender to separate from the large number of variables at work in determining a given case disposition. Variations in investigative resources, in police efficiency, in prosecutorial policies and exercise of discretion, in witness availability, in the exercise of judicial sentencing discretion, and in an almost infinite variety and combinations of other factors will influence every case disposition. When the rat gets electrically shocked upon pulling the food bar, it is not hard for it to sort out the cause and effect. But given the low capture and prosecution rates (see below), it seems highly unrealistic to think that the potential criminal can do an intuitive multiple-regression analysis to divine the applicable liability rules and their meaning for her.

Indeed, the "indirect communication" of experience and gossip often generates inaccurate information about criminal law rules. The insanity defense, for example, is commonly thought to be offered in a large number of cases and is commonly successful. One study found that people thought that 38 percent of all defendants charged with crime pled not guilty by reason of insanity.[23] In reality, an insanity plea is exceedingly rare, raised in less than one 1 percent of even felony cases.[24] In addition, the public perception is that it is commonly granted,[25] but the reality is that, even in the rare cases in which the insanity defense is sought, the defense is usually not granted.[26] The point is, if citizens have this level of ignorance about the operation of a well-publicized criminal law rule, it seems unrealistic to think that they could accurately divine through "indirect" means the difference between one criminal law formulation and another for the host of rules at work in each case.

---

23 *See* Valerie P. Hans, An Analysis of Public Attitudes Toward the Insanity Defense, 24 Criminology 393, 406 (1986); *see also* Eric Silver et al., Demythologizing Inaccurate Perceptions of the Insanity Defense, 18 Law & Hum. Behav. 63, 67–68 (1994).
24 *See* Lisa A. Callahan et al., The Volume and Characteristics of Insanity Defense Pleas: An Eight-State Study, 19 Bull. Am. Acad. Psychiatry & L. 331, 334 (1991).
25 *See*, e.g., Hans, *supra* note 23, at 406 (reporting a study indicating that the public believes more than 36% of all NGRI claims result in NGRI verdict, which would translate to roughly 14% of criminal prosecutions);
26 One study reports that the average acquittal rate for an insanity plea is 26%. *See* Callahan et al., *supra* note 24, at 334. Pasewark and McGinley report a success rate of 15% of pleas. *See* Richard A. Pasewark & Hugh McGinley, Insanity Plea: National Survey of Frequency and Success, 13 J. Psychiatry & L. 101, 106 (1985).

2. The Rational Choice Hurdle

Assume the potential offender understands the law's implications for him. Can he and will he bring such understanding to bear on his conduct choices? Behavioral scientists who study the decision-making patterns of people now realize that being able to demonstrate that a person has some knowledge of various facts that could be relevant to a decision does not mean that those facts are recalled and mobilized appropriately by the decision maker. Much depends on the momentary context in which the need for the decision arises or on the particular interpretations that the decision maker puts on the facts as they are relevant to him. Effects due to the particular personalities of the crime-prone actor and the circumstances in which the decisions arise make rational decision making about crime doing difficult.

Available evidence suggests that potential offenders as a group are less inclined to think at all about the consequences of their conduct or to guide their conduct accordingly.[27] They often are risk seekers, rather than risk avoiders[28] and as a group are more impulsive than the average.[29] Further, alcohol and drug intake commonly alter conduct decisions. In one study's sample, an astounding 66 percent of those interviewed reported that "recent drug use" contributed to the commission of the crime.[30]

A number of other temporary states of mind are likely to drive out rational considerations of punishment, such as desires for revenge or retaliation and suddenly induced rages or angers, the duration of which

---

27 Anderson, *supra* note 20, at abstract.

28 Marianne Junger, Robert West & Reinier Timman, Crime and Risky Behavior in Traffic: An Example of Cross-Situational Consistency, 38 J. Res. in Crime & Delinq. 439 (2001). A second way of being a high risk taker is by perceiving various risks as lower risk than they actually are. The following studies find that criminals are also prone to this error. *See* Eleanora Gullone, Jacqueline Paul & Susan M. Moore, A Validation Study of the Adolescent Risk-taking Questionnaire, 17 Behavior Change 143 (2000).

29 David P. Farrington, Human Development and Criminal Careers, in Oxford Handbook of Criminology 361, 384 (Mike Maguire, Rod Morgan & Robert Reiner eds., 2nd ed. 1997).

30 Anderson, *supra* note 20, at Table 2. In the National Crime Victimization Survey, victims of violence were asked to describe whether they perceived the offender to have been drinking or using drugs. About 28% of the victims of violence perceived the offender as under the influence of drugs, alone or in combination with alcohol. (Another 42% of the victims reported that they could not tell if the offender was using alcohol or drugs at the time of the crime.) Bureau of Justice Statistics, US Dep't of Justice, Drug Use and Crime, *available at* http://www.ojp.usdoj.gov/bjs/dcf/duc.htm (last modified May 9, 2002).

can extend from minutes to days. Other states of mind can be in place for longer durations and also can induce flawed reasoning. For instance, paranoia—feelings that others are immediate and overwhelming threats—is known to cycle over the course of months. When it is acute, it is likely that the degree of threat felt will override considerations of the deterrent weight of possible punishments.[31] The grandiose component of manic-depression, which occurs when the manic-depressive cycles into the manic phase, can give the person experiencing it a feeling of incredible brilliance that is likely to cause him to underestimate the likelihood of the not-so-brilliant forces of law ever catching and convicting him.[32]

These examples are of actors with diagnosable mental difficulties, but a good many personality differences exist that do not cause us to regard a person as "mentally ill" yet have implications for the degree to which the person will process deterrence considerations at the moment of contemplating a crime. To the degree that these characteristics are permanent and continuously displayed, they will constantly affect the behavior of the individual. Some persons, for instance, are characterized by a relatively low ability to delay gratification, and they are disproportionately likely to give in to temptation in the present.[33] In fact, a prominent theory about the personality characteristics of criminals, set forth by Gottfredson and Hirschi, makes the lack of self-control central to their theory.[34]

Even absent mental abnormalities that distort reasoning, a variety of contextual effects, some of which have been touched on above, can influence both the ability and the motivation to make the calculations required for deterrence;. Perhaps the most important of these stems from the fact that groups often commit crimes. When offenders commit crimes in street gangs, for instance, several effects can temporarily reduce the possible influence of a threatened future prison term on current law-breaking activities: an "arousal effect" leads to sprees and reduced sensitivity to risk,[35] and an increase in the immediate rewards can arise

31 Timothy Fjordbak, Clinical Correlates of High Lie Scale Elevations Among Forensic Patients, 49 J. Person. Assess. 252 (1985).
32 For a general characterization of the manic state, *see* Ronald Comer, Abnormal Psychology 262–265 (3rd ed. 1988).
33 Janet Metcalfe & Walter Mischel, A Hot/Cool System Analysis of Delay of Gratification: Dynamics of Willpower, 106 Psych. Rev. 3 (1999).
34 Michael R. Gottfredson & Travis Hirschi, A General Theory of Crime (1990).
35 Paul F. Cromwell, James N. Olson & D'Aunn Wester Avary, Breaking and Entering: An Ethnographic Analysis of Burglary, 8 St. in Crime, Law & Just. 69–70 (1991).

from an increase in esteem in which the group holds the member who boldly breaks the law.

Differential association is an exacerbating effect. As Gottfredson and Hirschi point out, those predisposed toward crime "end up in the company of each other and . . . [t]he individuals in such groups will therefore tend to be delinquent, as will the group itself."[36] This means that the crime-prone individual, already disposed to downplay the long-term punishment consequences, has those around him expressing the same neglect of those consequences, thus reinforcing the decision to commit the crime. Interviews with criminals consistently show that the individual feels "led to" the commission of the crime by the confidence expressed by other gang members that "they will not get caught."[37] Many report that they "got involved primarily because of partners."[38] Behavioral scientists recognize this as an instance of the well-known "risky shift" phenomenon, in which a group that comes to a collective decision after discussion comes to a decision that is often more risky than the average of the decisions that individuals held prior to the discussion. Therefore, the group tends to badly underestimate the risk of being caught and punished.

Yet another process likely to lead groups toward crime commission is the phenomenon called "deindividuation" in which the individual "is lost in a crowd"; he perceives a loss of accountability for his individual actions when those actions are taken in a crowd or mob and thus engages in many more antisocial acts.[39] The effect is illustrated most dramatically by gangs of teenagers or soccer crowds who sweep through neighborhoods, breaking windows, assaulting those unlucky enough to be in their paths, and is at work in most groups of potential offenders.

Available data suggests that offenders in groups commit a significant proportion of offenses.[40] Except in cases of murders and rapes without

---

36 Gottfredson & Hirschi, *supra* note 34, at 158.
37 Cromwell et al., Breaking and Entering, *supra* note 35.
38 Floyd Feeny, Robbers as Decision-Makers, in The Reasoning Criminal: Rational Choice Perspectives on Offending 58 (David Cornish & Ronald Clarke, eds., 1986).
39 Leon Mann, James W. Newton & J. M. Innes, A Test Between Deindividuation and Emergent Norm Theories of Crowd Aggression, 42 J. Person. & Soc. Psych. 260 (1982).
40 Estimated percent distribution of violent victimizations by lone offenders (1999), Table 3.29, Sourcebook of Criminal Justice Statistics 2001, at http://www.albany.edu/sourcebook/1995/pdf/t329.pdf; and Estimated percent distribution of violent victimizations by multiple offenders, Table 3.31, *id.*, *available at* http://www.albany.edu/sourcebook/1995/pdf/t331.pdf (last visited May 16, 2003) (approximately 20% of 1999 violent crimes were committed by offenders in a group).

theft, which are crimes in which offenders usually know their victim, "the majority of offenders commit their offenses with accomplices."[41]

In summary, individuals who commit crimes are likely to have certain individual patterns of thought characterized by impulsivity and risk-seeking behavior and to be under the influence of alcohol or drugs at the time they decide to commit crimes. Their individual pathologies are likely to be extended and amplified by the fact that the decision to commit a crime is often a group rather than an individual decision, and the group processes shift its members toward taking more risky actions and deindividuates them, thus facilitating the commission of destructive behaviors. To fit this with the image of a person guided by complex rational deterrence calculations is difficult.

A further gap between the reality and the assumption of legal-rule influence on conduct is the unrealistic extent to which lawmakers think they can micromanage conduct. Consider, for example, the situation where one perceives that one is under immediate attack and is considering various options for using force in self-defense. It seems near silly to think that such a person—even a criminal law professor who has been teaching criminal law for decades—would be able to look to the detailed legal rules set out to guide her conduct. Is it realistic, for example, to think that when under attack, a person would or could apply the terms of the two-page Model Penal Code section 3.04, the most common self-defense formulation? Even if one had instant familiarity with these detailed rules, their application depends on the actor's resolution of factual issues that may be difficult, if not impossible, in the split second the actor has to make a decision on the use of defensive force. Is retreat possible, or has the attacker crossed a threshold that no longer requires retreat? What exactly is the level of threat or force conveyed by the hand of the attacker moving menacingly toward a pocket? As the next chapter makes clear, despite the implausibility of a person being able to apply the law's rules, the lawmakers debate and formulate such rules as if the formulation they decide upon really will guide conduct.

---

41 Andrew Hochstetler, In With a Bad Crowd: An Analysis of Criminal Decision-making in Small Groups 3 (Ph.D. dissertation submitted to the Department of Sociology, University of Tennessee, Knoxville, December, 1999, UMI Microform 9962267).

3. The Perceived Net Cost Hurdle

Assume the potential offender, at the time of the offense, understands the law's implications for him and is able to use this knowledge to govern his conduct. Do the perceived costs of noncompliance outweigh its perceived benefits? This prerequisite to deterrent effect has two components, which shall be examined separately: the perceived "cost"—the threatened punishment and the weight the potential offender gives to it—and the perceived "benefit"—what he expects to gain from the offense.

a. The Perceived Cost: Probability, Amount, and Delay

Famously, Jeremy Bentham suggested three aspects of the penalty that need to be taken into account in calculating the resulting weight of the penalty. These are, in a modern terminology, the probability of incurring the penalty, the total amount of the punishment threatened, and, although this is often omitted from deterrence calculations, the delay with which the penalty will or might follow the crime.[42]

For Bentham, the importance of these various aspects of the punishment was intuitively obvious, and it appears that his intuitions were correct. That is, below is evidence about how variations in each of these aspects of punishment affect the weight given to the punishment in serving as a deterrent. However, as will become clear, the current understanding of these issues has outstripped standard deterrence thinking. Available empirical studies suggest that, first, these issues are more complex than standard deterrence analysis assumes and, second, that the dynamics at work often conflict with the principles that traditional deterrence analysis has used in setting today's liability and punishment schemes.

For reasons that can be easily realized, researchers have been ethically hesitant to impose punishments of the magnitudes associated with prison sentences on human beings participating in research studies. (With the consent of human research participants, however, punishments of moderate intensity have been inflicted on those participants and those studies will be reviewed.) But there is a vast experimental literature in which higher magnitudes of punishments have been inflicted on animals, characteristically rats, pigeons, or dogs. Part of the analysis below draws upon

---

42 Jeremy Bentham, The Rationale of Punishment (R. Heward, ed., 1830) at ch. VI.

this literature and deserves a special preliminary note. Obviously, one wants to generalize to humans the patterns discovered using infrahuman subjects with considerable caution. Nevertheless, one reviewer of the animal behavior data asks, "Are the effects of intense punishment on humans the same as those observed on animals?" His reply: "[F]or obvious reasons, the data on this point are limited, but what evidence we do have suggests a number of similarities."[43]

(1) *Probability.* The conditioning literature gives reason to be concerned about the effectiveness of a deterrent threat under the current criminal justice system. Research has been done that varies the likelihood of punishment from its being certain—that is, punishment following every transgression—to a likelihood of only a probability of 0.1 percent. For subjects at a 50 percent punishment rate, the punishment considerably decreased the subsequent response rate, by approximately 30 percent, from the no-punishment rate. But at a 10 percent punishment rate, almost no suppression was observed.[44] This suggests that the response rate will be fairly sensitive to a drop off in the punishment rate. Of course, for comparisons with the criminal justice process, one would be less interested in these fixed-rate studies and more interested in variable-rate studies, in which the punishment occurs on the *average of,* say, one punishment in every ten actions but has a random one-in-ten chance of occurring in response to any of those ten actions. Surprisingly, relatively few such studies are found in the behavioral literature but those available support similar conclusions. In a review of these studies, Lande concludes that as the rates move toward lower probabilities of punishments, they become less effective in suppressing responses.[45] A shock intensity that is an effective suppressant when delivered with certainty after a response, declines in suppression effectiveness as it becomes less probable. When the probability of the shock declines to rates that approximate the arrest rates for various crimes,[46] their behavior suppressive effects are quite low.

---

43 David Lieberman, Learning, Behavior, and Cognition 257 (2nd ed. 1993).
44 Nathan Azran et al., Fixed Ratio Punishment, 6 J. Exper. Anal. Behav. 141 (1963).
45 Stephen Lande, An Interresponse Time Analysis of Variable-Ratio Punishment, 35 J. Exper. Anal. Behav. 55 (1981).
46 *See* Estimated number of arrests (2000), Table 4.1, Sourcebook of Criminal Justice Statistics 2001, *available at* http://www.albany.edu/sourebook/1995/pdf/t41.pdf (listing total number of arrests by offense charged for most major crimes).

In Lande's own study, an interesting additional effect is shown that has rather ominous implications for behavior control via punishments. If the punishments are given on a variable-rate schedule such that the animal is producing a reduced but still present rate of response, the animal shows what are called "response bursts" immediately after receiving a punishment. That is, it is as if the animal is reasoning that it is highly improbable that a second punishment will follow immediately on the first, and it thus produces a high rate of response during the period immediately following punishment. One can imagine a criminal, just released from prison, reasoning that it is highly improbable that he would be caught for the very first crime he next commits. The point here is that the dynamics of deterrence are in fact quite complex, more so than present deterrence analysis acknowledges.

Consider this picture of the effect of reduced probability of punishment in light of the known rates of arrest and conviction for various crimes. The overall average of conviction for criminal offenses committed is 1.3%[47]—with the chance of getting a prison sentence being 100-to-1 for most offenses.[48] Even the most serious offenses, other than homicide, have conviction rates in the single digits. Although no very precise comparisons can be made with the animal research on schedules of punishment, it can be expected that these low rates of conviction and punishment

---

47 Compare U.S. Department of Justice, Bureau of Justice Statistics, Criminal Victimization in the United States, 2000 Statistical Tables, Table 91, *available at* http://www.ojp.usdoj.gov/bjs/pub/pdf/cvus00.pdf; with Disposition of cases terminated in U.S. District Courts (2000), Table 5.17, Sourcebook of Criminal Justice Statistics 2001, *available at* http://www.albany.edu/sourcebook/1995/pdf/t517.pdf (listing federal convictions by offense); and Felony convictions in State courts (1998), Table 5.42, Sourcebook of Criminal Justice Statistics 2001, *available at* http://www.albany.edu/sourcebook/1995/pdf/t542.pdf (listing state convictions by offense). *See* generally Table 1 *available at* http://www.law.upenn.edu/fac/phrobins/OxfordDeterrenceAppendix.pdf (providing a comparison of commissions, reports, arrests, convictions and sentences for various crimes, and including the average length of sentence imposed and served in both the federal and state systems).

48 Compare U.S. Department of Justice, Bureau of Justice Statistics, Criminal Victimization in the United States, 2000 Statistical Tables, *supra* note 47, with Defendants sentenced in U.S. District Courts (2001), Table 5.25, Sourcebook of Criminal Justice Statistics 2001, *available at* http://www.albany.edu/sourcebook/1995/pdf/t525.pdf (listing number of defendants sentenced, by offense, in federal courts); and Felony sentences imposed by State courts (1998), Table 5.43, *available at* http://www.albany.edu/sourcebook/1995/pdf/t545.pdf (providing percentages of defendants sentenced, by offense, in state courts). *See* generally, Table 1, *available at* http://www.law.upenn.edu/faculty/phr/OxfordDeterrenceAppendix, *supra* note 47.

will have a seriously damaging effect on deterrent effect of the threatened punishment.

One suspects that most citizens would be shocked at how low the punishment rates are, which suggests that the perception of detection rates tends to be higher than the rates actually are. Luckily for deterrence, people tend to overestimate the occurrence of rare events.[49] This error is useful because it is the perceived rate of punishment rather than the actual rate that counts for deterrent effect. Probably the best summary is that the average person's perception of punishment rates is low but at least higher than the reality.[50]

On the other hand, the group of persons who are the most likely offenders—those who have already committed an offense account for the majority of future crimes[51]—have a greater incentive than other people to learn the actual punishment rates. Thus, the career criminals—just the persons at whom one would wish to aim the deterrent threat of punishment—are the persons most likely to realize how low the punishment rates really are and, therefore, to perceive a lower chance of punishment than noncrime prone people.

Some evidence shows that many offenders tend to overestimate their own ability to avoid the mistakes that have led others to be caught. This is likely to be an exaggerated form of a tendency that most people show—a perception that they are smarter or more capable than they in fact are. Recent research shows that this is particularly true of persons who are low on the characteristic being rated. For instance, in one study, subjects in the bottom quartile of a test on logic grossly overestimated their logical skills, estimating them on the average as at the 62nd percentile when they were in fact at the 12th percentile.[52]

---

49 Richard J. Zeckhauser & W. Kip Viscusi, Risk Within Reason, in Judgment and Decision Making: An Interdisciplinary Reader 465 (2nd ed., T. Connolly, H. R. Arkes & K. R. Hammond, eds., 2000).

50 Lance Lochner, A Theoretical and Empirical Study of Individual Perceptions of the Criminal Justice System, Figure 5: Average Perceived Probability of Arrest and Official Arrest Rate Over Time, Rochester Ctr. for Econ. Research Working Paper No. 483 (June 2001).

51 Mortimer Zuckerman, War on Crime, By the Numbers, 116 U.S. News & World Rpt. 68 (Jan. 17, 1994) (reporting that 7% of criminals commit 2/3 of all violent crimes); Note: Selective Incapacitation: Reducing Crime Through Predictions of Recidivism, 96 Harv. L. Rev. 511 (1982) ("'career criminals' are responsible for a vastly disproportionate number of crimes committed each year.").

52 Justin Kruger & David Dunning, Unskilled and Unaware of It: How Difficulties in Recognizing One's Own Incompetence Lead to Inflated Self-Assessments, 77 J. Pers. & Soc. Psych. 1121 (1999).

The net effect is that most criminals do not think they will be caught and punished. In the Anderson study noted above, for example, when asked about the risk of being caught, it was found that "76 percent of active criminals and 89 percent of the most violent criminals either perceive no risk of apprehension or have no thought about the likely punishments for their crimes,"[53] perhaps explaining why increasing sentencing severity has limited effect in increasing deterrent effect.

(2) *Punishment Amount.* An effective deterrent system must be able to impose punishments that will be perceived as having punitive "bite." That in itself is not difficult. A term of imprisonment will be perceived as a punishment. However, an effective deterrence system would not impose imprisonment, and certainly not the same term of imprisonment, for every rule violation it wished to deter. First, such action would not be cost effective. The societal harm of only some offenses can justify the high costs of this punishment. More importantly, an effective deterrent system must modulate its punishment to achieve its program. For example, it may want to tie punishment amount to the degree of offense seriousness to provide a continuing disincentive for offenders to commit a more serious offense. That is, if rape automatically triggered the most serious penalty, every rapist would have nothing to lose and something to gain—eliminating the primary witness—by killing his victim. Further, there is a range of other factors—from difficulty of detection to level of publicity—that an efficient deterrence system would want to take into account in setting the optimum level of punishment. In other words, the challenge for an effective deterrent system is not just to threaten punishment with a perceived bite but to modulate the amount of punishment it threatens with sufficient accuracy and in sufficiently discrete units to carry out its deterrent program. As with the probability studies, the studies relating to punishment amount suggest both greater complexity than current deterrence analysis seems to comprehend and dynamics inconsistent with modern deterrence practices.

The first finding of the relevant animal studies is unremarkable: the degree to which the administration of punishment suppresses later actions depends heavily on the amount of the punishment. In one study in which the punishment consisted of electric shocks delivered

---

53 Anderson, *supra* note 20, at 1 (abstract); *see id.* at Table 1.

immediately after the animal pressed a bar (an action that had previously led to reward), the punishment hardly suppressed later bar pressings at all if the shocks were mild in intensity but achieved a great deal of behavior suppression, close to complete suppression, if they were very high in intensity.[54] (It is important to remember that the punishment is delivered immediately and after each and every "transgressive" response, a set of conditions that is not likely to be achieved in instances of human criminal transgressions.)

The second finding of these studies is more remarkable: There is an interesting "adaptation to intensity" effect. In one study, a pigeon was shocked for pecking a key that had previously delivered and continued to deliver a reward.[55] A shock level of 80 volts produced total response suppression when administered as punishment for the animal's first response. When the shock level was slightly below that, at 60 volts, it had little behavior suppression effect. However, if the shock level started at the undeterring 60 volts, then gradually increased, the pigeons continued with the punished response, even up to 300 volts, far beyond the 80 volt "complete deterrence" level!

The application of this to punishments within the criminal justice system is unsettling because it is often the case that the punishment for first offenses is rather low, frequently consisting of short sentences, probation, or suspended sentences. What this suggests is that we may inadvertently be creating offenders who, like the pigeon, learn to tolerate punishment levels that, if administered earlier, would have deterred the punished action.

The data regarding sentences for first offenders, and particularly young offenders, suggests that the problem may be a real one. Forty-five percent of *all felony* offenders without a prior conviction are not given an incarcerative sentence.[56] Sixty-six percent of *all felony* offenders under the ago of 20 receive a probation sentence.[57] One occasionally sees newspaper articles about a youthful offender who has committed some horribly violent offense and who does receive a prison sentence, but the news

---

54 E. Boe & Russell Church, Permanent Effects of Punishment During Extinction, 63 J. Comp. & Physiol. Psych. 486 (1967).

55 Azran, Fixed-Ratio Punishment, *supra* note 44, at 141.

56 Bureau of Justice Statistics, U.S. Dep't of Justice, Felony Defendants in Large Urban Counties—1998, Table 35 (2001).

57 Bureau of Justice Statistics, U.S. Dep't of Justice, State Court Sentencing of Convicted Felons—1998, Table 3.11 (2001).

coverage is probably a testimony to how rare it is to sentence young offenders to prison.

From several perspectives, this is an acceptable, even good, outcome: judges often do not send youthful offenders to prison because the experience may increase their future likelihood of committing criminal offenses.[58] They also may experience appalling treatment by older convicts.[59] However, from the deterrence perspective, it may bring about the "hardening to punishment" effect observed in animals, in which an escalating series of punishments, if it begins at a level that is ineffective in controlling the initial transgression, simply conditions the person to tolerate the increasing punishments, without reducing the rate of transgressions.

Another finding of recent empirical work may be even more unsettling. Deterrence analysis classically uses variation of prison terms as the metric by which punishment severity is adjusted. This is not strictly true, of course: for more minor offenses, probation or community service might be assigned, and for some offenses, the death penalty is available. However, for a variety of crimes, with wide ranges of severity, duration of prison term is the way in which we fit the punishment to the crime.

The simplest assumption to use in equating length of prison term to offense severity is to assume that severity of punishment is linear with the duration of the sentence. So, for instance, a ten-year sentence produces twice the punishment bite as does a five-year sentence. Assuming a constant intensity of 1, which continues at the same level for, say, 100 days, the total amount of punishment—the total punitive "bite"—is the area within the bar below. Call it 100 punishment units.

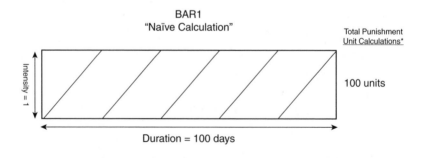

BAR1
"Naïve Calculation"

Total Punishment
Unit Calculations*

Intensity = 1

100 units

Duration = 100 days

---

58 Dennis Stevens, The Depth of Imprisonment and Prisonization: Levels of Security and Prisoners' Anticipation of Future Violence, 33 How. J. Crim. Just. 137–157 (1994); Dennis Stevens, The Impact of Time-Served and Regime on Prisoners' Anticipation of Crime: Female Prisonization Effects, 37 How. J. Crim. Just. 188–205 (1998).

59 Zvi Eisikovits & Michael Baizerman, "Doin' Time": Violent Youth in a Juvenile Facility and in an Adult Prison, 6 J. of Off. Counsel. Serv. & Rehab. 5 (1982).

In a famous paper, Brickman and Campbell introduced the idea of the "hedonic treadmill."[60] The essence of the notion is that over time, people who move to a markedly better, or markedlyworse, situation that initially produces great pleasure or discomfort, will adapt to that new set of circumstances and return to seeing it as a neutral state. They essentially readjust their baseline in assessing how good or bad their situation is. The examples here are of a person who wins the lottery or moves from some place with dreadful weather to California and initially is euphoric but over time reverts to his or her previous neutral level of affect. The same adaptive effect has been found to work in the other direction. Just as those winning the lottery adjust, those suffering accidents making them paraplegics also adjust to their new circumstances, treating them as their new neutral state of affect.[61]

Applying this to the present argument, one sees that the duration of the sentence might not have the deterrent effect that one might attribute to it. Two kinds of adaptation to the prison environment may take place. First, the prisoner, who initially found his seven-foot cell horribly cramped, comes to regard it as the evaluatively neutral condition. His adaptation level shifts, and one consequence of this is that there are now prison experiences that would previously be experienced as nearly as negative as his seven-foot cell that now become above adaptation level experiences and therefore positive—an hour in the exercise yard or a move to a nine-foot cell for instance. On this account, the prisoner who has adapted to prison, experiences it as affectively neutral on the average and is likely to have some positive and some negative experiences during the duration of his sentence, not greatly unlike the experiences of a person who is not confined to prison. Whatever systematic negativity the prison experience has for the prisoner is caused by the initial time in prison during which adaptation takes place. Supporting this view, a study finds

---

60 P. Brickman & D. Campbell, Hedonic Relativism and Planning the Good Society, in Adaptation-level Theory: A Symposium 287–302 (M. H. Appley, ed., 1971). This review draws on the chapter by Shane Frederick & George Loewenstein, Hedonic Adaptation, in Well-Being: The Foundations of Hedonic Psychology 302–329 (Daniel Kahneman, Ed Deiner & Norbert Schwarz, eds., 1999).

61 Shelly Taylor, Adjustment to Threatening Life Events: A Theory of Cognitive Adaptation, 38 Amer. Psych. 1161 (1983); Ronnie Janoff-Bulman & Camille Wortman, Attributions of Blame and Coping in the "Real World": Severe Accident Victims React to Their Lot, 35 J. Person. & Soc. Psych. 351 (1977).

that 50 percent of the suicides that occur in prison occur during the first twenty-four hours of imprisonment.[62]

A second kind of adaptation is a general desensitization to the unpleasant experiences that prison can deliver to the prisoner. The prisoner becomes "hardened" to the prison experience and not only regards it as affectively neutral but also does not experience much negativity when the prison experience temporarily gets worse. To understand this concept, assume that there is a natural fluctuation in the hedonic intensity of the stimuli experienced in prison. Some days are affectively worse, others neutral, others better. The key notion here is that the prisoner's sensitivity to change decreases over time. This "hardening" or becoming "jaded" means that the change in felt affect is damped from the changes in objective circumstances. Thus, when the objective situation gets much worse, it is experienced as only a little worse, and much better is experienced as a little better.[63] Applying this notion and the more general concept of hedonic adaptation to the context of prison incarceration, Fredrick and Loewenstein recently concluded that "although incarceration is designed to be unpleasant, most of the research on adjustment to prison life points to considerable adaptation" over time, citing studies that show improvements in "deviance, attitude and personality measures," and decreases in dysphoria, stress-related problems and boredom among inmates, including those in solitary confinement.[64]

To sum, several empirically supported conclusions in behavioral science suggest that our society's major means of modulating the punitive bite of the punishment felt by a convicted individual, which is by manipulating the duration of the prison sentence, is not going to be as effective as what one might call the "naive calculation system" assumes. Compare Bar 1 above with Bar 2 below.

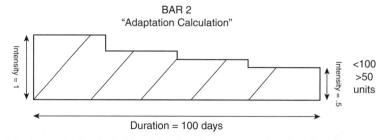

BAR 2
"Adaptation Calculation"

Duration = 100 days

* Punishment unit calculation = Intensity x Duration = total area within the bar

62 L. M. Hayes, "And Darkness Closed In": A National Study of Jail Suicides, 10 Criminal Justice and Behavior 461–484 (1983).

63 Frederick & Loewenstein, *supra* note 60, at 304–305.

64 *Id.* at 311.

This aspect of adaptation to punishment also is problematic because it means that imprisonment becomes increasingly less cost-efficient as punishment increases. Each additional unit of prison time will have a near constant cost, but the punitive bite of each unit will become increasingly less.

Still, it is important to see that what remains common to both of these representations of punishment effect is that the *duration* of the negative experience is a strong determinant of the negative quality of the experience that the punished individual retains in her mind. More specifically, the duration of the punishment interacts multiplicatively with its intensity to produce the total punishment amount of the prison experience. This general assumption of the approximate multiplicative effect of the duration of punishment is the conventional wisdom.

Recent psychological research, however, presents a radical challenge to the role of duration in the experience of punishment. This recent work separates the total remembered pain (or pleasure) of an experience from the moment-by-moment intensity of the experience throughout the duration of the experience. The results are startling. They suggest that duration does not play anything like the major role that intuition gives it in determining punishment amount.[65] Instead, in these experiments, the amount contributed by duration to the remembered experience of pain was small.[66]

One can take this startling finding about "duration neglect" further. In other experiments, participants were led to experience a shorter period of intense pain or a longer period that began with an intense pain of the exact duration of the one in the shorter period, and then, without the subjects becoming aware of it, added a period of less-intense pain.[67] (Thus, whether the subjects had experienced the shorter or longer sequence,

---

65 Daniel Kahneman, Objective Happiness, in Well-Being: The Foundations of Hedonic Psychology 4 (Daniel Kahneman, Ed Deiner & Norbert Schwartz, eds., 1999).

66 D. Redelmeier & Daniel Kahneman, Patients' Memories of Painful Medical Treatments: Real Time and Retrospective Evaluations of Two Minimally Invasive Procedures, 116 Pain 3 (1996). The effect of increasing the duration of, for instance, a painful medical procedure, on the later reported aversiveness of that event, Kahneman summarizes as follows: "A consistent finding of these experiments was that duration always combined additively with other determinants of global evaluation and participants appeared to use it as a minor extra feature (used to evaluate the painfulness) of each trial, as if they were telling themselves 'this episode is painful and is also rather long,' or 'this episode is painful but it is short.'" Daniel Kahneman, Evaluation by Moments, Past and Future, in Choices, Values and Frames 693, 698 (Daniel Kahneman & Amos Tversky, eds., 2000).

67 *Id.* at 701.

they perceived both as being a single experience.) They were then led to believe that they would need to repeat one but not both of the previous experiences of pain and chose which they would suffer for the second time. A strong majority of respondents chose to repeat the longer experience! If duration were given the weight that conventional wisdom assumes, the subjects would have chosen to repeat the shorter pain experience. But they did not.

Kahneman suggests that people retain a "snapshot" of the negative experience that pools by averaging two aspects of the painful episode: the affective value of the most extreme pain experienced during the episode and the affective value of the pain experienced near its end. This rule accounted for more than 90 percent of the variance in pain judgments in the experiments mentioned above. Duration of the experience, again, added only a slight upward boost in pain that is remembered.

What does this mean for our standard duration-linked means of regulating the amount of punishment? Consider again the most plausible version of punishment noted above, which includes the duration of the punishment as a multiplicative determinant of its total pain. Compare this with the remembered punishment amount registered under a "duration neglect" calculation of perceived punishment bite, which is the average of the sum of the maximum intensity and the end intensity. See Bar 2 below. Under the duration-influenced punishment calculation, for the sentence in Bar 2, which lasted 100 days, the punishment effect is less than 100 and more than 50, depending on the precise extent and timing of the adaptation step-downs in intensity. But the remembered punishment amount registered under the "duration neglect" calculation of Bar 2 is the average of the sum of the maximum intensity (1, at the start) and the end intensity (.5), giving a total remembered punishment amount of 75+.

Compare this with a much shorter sentence, which is likely to have a greater chance of being as aversive at its end as at its beginning, as shown

BAR 2
"Standard Duration Calculation"

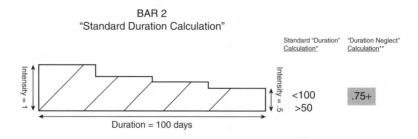

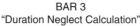

BAR 3
"Duration Neglect Calculation"

25   1.0

Duration = 25 days

* Standard "duration"
  calculation: Intensity x Duration (total area within the bar)

** "Duration Neglect"
  calculation: $\frac{\text{Maximum Intensity + End Intensity}}{2}$ (memory of a longer duration is a minor extra feature, represented by a "+")

in Bar 3 above. The startling realization is that this short sentence will be experienced as more aversive than a much longer sentence that is equally aversive at the beginning but less so at the end! There are two reasons for this. The first is that, under the duration neglect account, the much longer duration of the long sentence contributes little or nothing to the reconstructed negativity of the remembered sentence. The second reason is that the "endpoint intensity" of the short sentence comes before it has had an opportunity to decay, while the endpoint intensity of the longer sentence is reduced at the end. The point here is that lengthening sentences may actually reduce their recalled negative character if the end experiences are relatively less aversive!

All of this is bad news for the standard deterrence practice, which relies on sentence duration to adjust the magnitude of the punishment imposed by a prison term. Realistically, the most unpleasant peak experience of pain of the imprisonment is likely to occur relatively early in the prison experience. As the duration of the sentence is extended, it may not increase remembered negativity. Indeed, if the final days of the term are markedly less aversive, as one would expect, the increase in duration is having a subtractive effect on the remembered negativity of the prison experience! It is, of course, possible to conceive of a punishment that can be inflicted in a period of short duration, that is of high intensity, and that is most intense at the end of the punishment period. These are the sorts of punishments that are usually referred to as "torture."

One might argue that the duration-neglect effect creates problems only for the deterrence program as it is applied to persons who have already been imprisoned and, therefore, have the problematic memory that even a long prison term "isn't so bad." But there is what might be called the "leakage of the truth" that prison is "not so bad" into the communities of people who are at risk of committing crimes but have not yet experienced a prison term. The reality is that the communities within which they grow up and currently exist are socializing that group. To mention a socially repugnant fact, it is unlikely that an African American male child in a poor neighborhood, growing up among a community of elders of whom a significant number have served prison time, is unaware of their view that prison is "not so bad." Any criminological theory of differential association emphasizes the transmission of criminal behavior and criminal thinking within the groups within which the person exists, and transmission of knowledge about the relative "bite" of "jail time" is likely to be a large component transmitted. The evidence suggests that new criminals disproportionately emerge from groups in which other criminals are prominent.[68] The problems of duration neglect and adaptation-to-intensity are simply one more piece of a larger mosaic of general deterrence difficulties.

Before closing the discussion of amount-of-punishment problems, note a few other ways in which the perceived threat of prison is likely to be degraded and complicated, at least regarding persons likely to offend. Potential offenders may come from social groups in which the threat of stigma for being convicted as a felon may not be as high as it is for other persons. In fact, for many offenders, conviction and imprisonment may lead to very little, if any, loss of status and respect in the communities within which they function.[69] Similarly, it is likely that potential offenders as a group live a more deprived existence than the average person,[70] thus the threat of prison, with its provision for meals and shelter, is not so worse an alternative to their current existence as it would be for the more

---

68 *See*, e.g., Kevin Johnson, For Many of USA's Inmates, Crime Runs in the Family, USA Today, Jan. 28, 2008 (detailing patterns of criminality across generations).

69 D. S. Nagin, Deterrence and Incapacitation, in The Handbook of Crime and Punishment 345 (M. H. Tonry, ed., 1998); S. A. Venkatesh, The Gang in the Community, in Gangs in America 241 (2nd ed., C. R. Huff, ed., 1996). But a corollary to this is that, for those people who care a good deal about social approval of persons with traditional values, even very low probability of criminal conviction may produce a deterrent effect because its cost is viewed as so high. S. Klepper & D. Nagin, Tax Compliance and Perceptions of the Risks of Detection and Criminal Prosecution, 23 Law & Soc. Rev. 209 (1989).

70 Bureau of Justice Statistics, U.S. Dep't of Justice, Profile of Jail Inmates 1996, *available at* <www.ojp.usdoj.gov/bjs/pub/pdf/pji96.pdf> (last visited July 24, 2002) (of jail inmates in 1996: 36% were unemployed at time of last arrest; 46% had less than a high school education; 46% had monthly income less than $600; 60% did not live with both parents while growing up; 22% belonged to a family that received welfare while growing up; 46% had a family member incarcerated while growing up; 47% of female inmates were physically or sexually abused prior to most recent incarceration; 36% had a physical or mental disability).

well-to-do person. Indeed, county jails often serve as places of refuge for vagrants during the winter months in cities in cold climates.[71]

The ultimate conclusion here, which evidence strongly supports, is that the threat of punishment amount under current practices is at best unpredictable and at worst unreliable in modulating the threatened amount of punishment, an incapacity that in itself will frustrate a deterrence scheme. And this, in turn, damages the effectiveness of a criminal punishment system that seeks to achieve behavior control by distributing liability and punishment upon a deterrence analysis.

(3) *Delay.* The psychological research literature is similarly unsupportive of our current deterrence practice with regard to the matter of delay of punishment. It is a classic finding that the effects of punishment in deterring behavior drop off rapidly as the delay increases between the transgression and the administration of punishment for that transgression. The rapidity of the drop-off is quite striking. In one study, hungry dogs were given a 10-minute opportunity to eat from a dish of highly preferred or unpreferred food.[72] Then, upon being given the opportunity again, they were punished by a conspicuously present experimenter (1) after 15 seconds or (2) after 5 seconds or (3) immediately, for eating from the preferred food dish, and not punished for eating from the unpreferred dish. All dogs learned to avoid eating from the preferred dish. Next, they were repeatedly returned to the test room, with the experimenter now conspicuously absent. The dogs from (1) the 15-second delay group returned to eating the preferred food in about 3 minutes of the first day, (2) the 5 second delay dogs resisted for 8 days, and (3) the immediately punished dogs resisted for about two weeks![73]

These are remarkable differences to be produced by variations between 0 and 15 seconds of punishment delivery. In criminal cases, the delay that intervenes between the offense and the punishment may be significant. Available data regarding state courts suggest that the average

---

71 Jennifer Stenhauer, A Jail Becomes a Shelter, and Maybe a Mayor's Albatross, N.Y. Times B1 (Aug. 13, 2002).

72 R. L. Solomon, L. H. Turner & M. S. Lessac, Some Effects of Delay of Punishment on Resistance to Temptation in Dogs, 8 J. Person. & Soc. Psych. 233 (1968).

73 *Id.* at 235–238.

time from arrest to sentencing for felony cases ranges from 7.2 months for a guilty plea to 12.6 months for a jury trial.[74]

The deterrent effect of a threat of punishment sometime in the future also is hurt by the findings of recent experimental work showing that humans place less weight on events in the future as compared with events in the present. The research paradigm developed by researchers on human judgment is simple in form. A person is given a choice of, for instance, $100 delivered immediately or $X dollars delivered in, say, one month, and the person is asked to set X such that he is indifferent between the $100 dollars today and the $X dollars one month in the future. He thus is willing to let the experimenter toss a coin to determine which outcome happens. The general finding is that X is set at a startlingly high amount. In one study, subjects were indifferent between receiving $10 immediately and $21 in one year, and also indifferent between receiving $100 immediately and $157 in a year.[75] As a comparison of the two pairs suggests, the discounting rate for higher sums was lower but was still extremely high as compared with the sorts of interest rates that are on offer from banks. (There are no banks offering 110% or 57% interest per year on no-risk investments.) It appears that the same discounting effect appears for future losses as compared to immediate losses, specifically in this study subjects were indifferent between losing $100 right now and $133 in one year's time.[76] That suggests that consequences in the future are given less weight than are consequences in the present, and this remains true when those consequences are negative, such as prison sentences.

Drugs or alcohol use exacerbate this discount of future consequences, which we saw earlier was common among criminal offenders. Recent experimental work has examined the decision-making processes of persons

---

74 Mean and median number of days between arrest and sentencing for felony cases disposed by state courts (1998), Table 5.48, Sourcebook of Criminal Justice 2001, *available at* http://www.albany.edu/sourcebook/1995/pdf/t548.pdf (last visited May 16, 2003). Available data regarding federal district courts suggest that the median time from filing to disposition is 6 months, ranging from 2.3 months for a bench trial, 4.7 months for dismissal, 6 months for a guilty plea, to 11.1 months for a jury trial. Median amount of time from filing to disposition of criminal defendants in U.S. District Courts (2001), Table 5.41, *supra* note 47, *available at* http://www.albany.edu/sourcebook/1995/pdf/t541.pdf.

75 A review of the temporal discounting literature can be found in George Loewenstein, Out of Control: Visceral Influences on Behavior, 65 Org. Behav. & Human Dec. Proc. 272–279 (1996).

76 *Id.* at 277.

under the influence of alcohol and summarizes the results as "alcohol myopia."[77] While under the influence of what were only moderate levels of alcohol, the study respondents showed a general tendency to reduce the weight they gave to more distant consequences. In some research, the decision in question was whether to engage in sexual intercourse, and the distant consequences that discounted were the possibilities of contracting a sexually transmitted disease or causing pregnancy. These findings are consistent with the view that alcohol intoxication restricts attentional capacity so that people are highly influenced by the most salient cues in their present environment. For a crime-prone individual under the influence of alcohol, the salient environmental cues are likely to be the emotionally arousing temptations to rob or burglarize, rather than the not-present reminders of the possibility of distant imprisonment. Under alcohol-or drug-induced myopia, it is reasonable to conclude that the threat of arrest and conviction, and eventually, of prison, is not given much weight in the decisional process.

b. The Perceived Benefit

The same kinds of factors relevant to assessing the perceived threat of punishment are relevant in determining the perceived benefit of a crime: The probability of attaining the benefit, its value, and its immediacy all play a role. However, while the "cost" analysis showed many factors tending to degrade the perceived cost, the benefit analysis suggests little such degradation in valuing the perceived benefit.

Typically, the perceived benefit of the contemplated offense is immediate or at least quite near: with regard to theft, for example, it is the immediate possession of money or property and the choices and possibilities they immediately bring; with regard to assault, the immediate satisfaction of the revenge, anger, or whatever motivation drives the offender. Even if the motivating benefit is delayed—the stolen property must be traded for drugs to feed an addiction—the offender's expectation typically is satisfaction before too long. There will be some offenses for which the benefit is delayed, of course, as in elaborate fraud schemes, and in

---

77 Tara K. MacDonald, Geoff MacDonald, Mark P. Zanna & Geoffrey T. Fong, Alcohol, Sexual Arousal, and Intentions to Use Condoms in Young Men: Applying Alcohol Myopia Theory to Risky Sexual Behavior, 19 Health Psych. 290, 290 (2000).

these cases, the weight of future benefit may be discounted just as future punishment is. As a whole, however, the criminal justice system reflects a picture of a threat of delayed punishment pitted against the attraction of immediate benefits of crime.

As to the value of the benefit, the effects of addiction frequently seriously exaggerate that value. The National Crime Victimization Survey reports that in 1999, about 11 percent of violent crimes and 24 percent of property crimes were committed to raise money to obtain drugs.[78] Consider this in light of experiments on addictive effects. Some studies consider addiction in the context of health-risking behaviours such as smoking and drug use, which produce immediate pleasure but serious long-term health consequences such as painful deaths from lung diseases. Several studies have demonstrated that alcoholics,[79] heroin users,[80] and substance abusing gamblers[81] have higher discounting rates than do normals and that is true when money is the gain in the present or the future. But it is even truer when the gain in the present is the alcohol or drug to which they are addicted. What these studies on normals and addicts imply is that all persons are prone to take immediate gains even if it costs them future consequences, and addicts, even more than normal individuals, are highly driven by the pleasures on offer in the moment and less affected by what might be risked in the future.

4. Tripping Over Any Hurdle as Fatal to Deterrent Effect

A deterrent effect is possible only where all of the prerequisites are satisfied. The absence of any one means there is no deterrent effect whatever. If the potential offender is unaware of the legal rule that is set to influence his conduct, or is aware of the rule but sees no meaningful chance of punishment, or perceives a meaningful chance of punishment but does not see the overall costs as outweighing the overall benefits (because of the high discount of the future punishment or because the present benefit overwhelms because of addiction), or perceives an overall net

---

78 Bureau of Justice Statistics, Drug Use and Crime, *supra* note 30.
79 Nancy Petry, Delay Discounting of Money and Alcohol in Actively Using Alcoholics, Currently Abstinent Alcoholics, and Controls, 154 Psychopharm. 243 (2001).
80 Gregory Madden, Warren Bickel & Eric Jacobs, Discounting of Delayed Rewards in Opium-Dependent Outpatients, 7 Exper. & Clin. Psychopharm. 284 (1999).
81 Nancy Petry & Thomas Casarella, Excessive Discounting of Delayed Rewards in Substance Abusers with Gambling Problems, 56 Drug & Alcohol Dep. 25 (1999).

cost but is unable to bring this information to bear on his conduct choices, then the punishment threat will not deter the person from committing the crime. The point here is that tripping over any one of the prerequisite hurdles is fatal to a deterrent effect.

Different groups of potential offenders can thus fail to be deterred by the possibility of punishment for any one of a number of reasons. Some potential offenders may be too intoxicated or mentally disturbed, or angered or afraid, to contemplate the future consequences of their deeds. A different group may be ignorant of the particular rule adopted under a deterrence rationale to influence their conduct. And so on. The cumulative effect may be that large groups of potential offenders may be unaffected by the deterrent threat for one reason or another.

5. The Cumulative Dissipation Problem

Assume, for the sake of argument, that some potential offenders contemplating some offenses might at least potentially be influenced in their conduct by the deterrence-based rule or policy. That is, assume that not every potential offender is eliminated from a deterrent effect by tripping over one of the prerequisite hurdles. Is the resulting deterrent effect such that it justifies relying upon deterrence analysis in criminal law rule making?

Even if one assumes that the potential offender has some vague sense of what the legal rule or policy might be, that he perceives some modest chance of being punished, and that he is not so drug-addled as to have lost his ability to calculate costs and benefits, it is still the case that any weakness in any prerequisite condition can combine with weaknesses in any other prerequisite to reduce the ultimate deterrent effect to something trivial. This is so because the theoretical character of the function linking the prerequisite conditions into an overall deterrent effect is one of jointly necessary conditions that combine approximately multiplicatively to give the total deterrent effect. Thus, when several of these conditions drop to low values, the resultant weight of deterrence is likely to be negligibly low. To give an example drawing on considerations raised above, consider the case of a set of young males who, because they are jobless, have free time that they spend aimlessly "hanging out." They probably are jobless because of poor skills and impulse control. As they gather, they are likely to engage in alcohol consumption, which induces alcohol myopia, and their joint egging each other to "be bold" is likely to cause them to lose sight of the possibilities of being detected. The weight of deterrence rests very lightly on these young males. The fine debates over which formulation of a criminal law rule will best deter has little meaning for this population and the many others for whom the prerequisites of deterrence are nonexistent or highly dissipated.

B. The Aggregated-Effect Studies

As noted at the start of the chapter, it is not denied that having a criminal justice system that administers punishment can have a deterrent effect. It is even possible that changes in police procedures or allocation of police resources can have an effect on crime rates. But there is reason to be skeptical that the formulation of criminal law rules or sentencing policies or practices can have the deterrent effect that common wisdom assumes it has. Section A has shown how unusual it can be that all of the prerequisites for deterrent effect exist. But some might argue that, although this analysis of criminal law's action path says doctrinal formulation can rarely influence conduct, rule formulation might in fact do so in some mysterious way presently beyond the understanding of human knowledge. One can test this argument by looking at the effect of specific doctrinal formulations on the crime rates they are intended to lower.

The available studies are of what one might call "aggregated effects"—that is, studies that do not concern themselves with how a deterrent effect might come about but look strictly to whether an effect of doctrinal change on crime rate can be found. In the standard form, some change in the criminal law or policy creates the opportunity for examining the resulting change in crime rates. Other aggregated-effect studies examine changes of behavior due to an existing law that by its terms changes over time in its effects on a group, as with an immaturity defense that minimizes punishment amount as long as an offender is below a certain age. Still other studies examine demographically similar jurisdictions that have different criminal law rules.

What aggregation studies share is a reliance on the discovery of differences in crime rates presumably caused by differences in criminal law rules or policies. Given that they aggregate their findings over large data sets, these studies provide powerful possibilities of discovering law-produced deterrent effects. And one must acknowledge that, if aggregated-effect studies show increased deterrence from doctrinal formulation, the arguments against relying on deterrence analysis are accordingly reduced.

But the review of the existing studies suggests these conclusions:

1. Some well-designed studies show no resulting crime reduction even from doctrinal formulations designed toward that end.

2. Some studies purport to reliably show a crime reduction effect from doctrinal formulation, but the observed effect is due (or could as easily be due) to causes other than deterrent effects, such as the increased incapacitative effect that one would expect from increasing prison terms that remove from society those who would repeat offend.

3. The remaining studies really do show a deterrent effect, but the instances in which this occurs only illustrate and buttress the point in Section A that a deterrent effect from doctrinal formulation requires the existence of special conditions that in fact are the exception rather than the rule.

1. Studies That Find No Deterrent Effect from Doctrinal Formulation

The studies that show no deterrent effect include ones that test the effect of a criminal code altering the grade of an offense, or a code's setting different grades for an offense according to variations in a specific offense characteristic, such as punishing "kiting" of checks of greater amounts more severely. In other no-effect studies, conduct was criminalized or decriminalized, with no resulting change in the subsequent frequency of the commission of the offense.

A brutal and much-publicized instance of rape in Philadelphia on Palm Sunday 1966 lead to an increase in rape penalties. However, a study concludes that neither the excitement leading up to the imposition of stronger penalties nor the actual imposition of such penalties affected the rate of rapes in the following months.[82]

In the 1950s, Finland was characterized by a high rate of individuals in prison. And the authorities, concerned about the social consequences of this, decriminalized many offenses and assigned some offenders shorter prison sentences or directed still other offenders to community service, suspended sentences, or heavy fines rather than prison terms. Crime rates

---

82 Barry Schwartz, The Effect in Philadelphia of PA's Increased Penalties for Rape and Attempted Rape, 59 J. Crim. Law, Criminology & Pol. Sci. 509 (1968).

in the following years were not detectably different from those before the reforms and from those of nearby countries.[83]

Zimring conducted an aggregated-effect study using a database from a bank in Nebraska that includes both the number and the dollar amount of bad checks written.[84] The state's criminal law assigns different sentences to checks drawn for over and under $35, a distinction that intuition suggests is not well publicized but might be known among those who regularly write bad checks. The study found little or no differential deterrent effect of the more or less severe sentences for the crime.

Zimring also studied the effects of decriminalizing abortion in Hawaii on estimated rates of the performance of abortions that were illegal in the years just before decriminalization.[85] Several assumptions are needed to estimate the previous rates of abortion, but he concludes that the prior criminalization of abortion did not deter it to a significant extent.

2. Studies That Find Mixed or Conflicting Results

Other studies show mixed success in attempts to deter through doctrinal formulation. Some attempts are characterized by only short-term effects for reasons one may be able to extract. For others, including death penalty studies, the evidence is too conflicting to draw any reliable conclusion.

A well-known study by Ross dealt with crime rate changes when Britain passed a Road Safety Act, which provided higher penalties for offenses such as driving while intoxicated and was coupled with an extensive publicity campaign that implied that the police presence on roads and highways would substantially increase.[86] The deterrent effect of this was initially high, probably due to the public's overestimation of the certainty of apprehension. Over time, however, the police either decreased their enforcement efforts or the public was better able to estimate the real

---

83 Tapio Lappi-Seppala, Regulating the Prison Population, Experience from a Long-Term Policy in Finland, National Research Institute of Legal Policy, Helsinki, at Table F (1998).

84 Frank Zimring, Punishment and Deterrence: Bad Checks in Nebraska: A Study in Complex Threats, in Corrections and Punishment 173 (David Greenberg, ed.,1977).

85 Frank Zimring, Of Doctors, Deterrence, and the Dark Figure of Crime: A Note on Abortion in Hawaii 39 U. Chi. L. Rev. 699 (1972).

86 H. Lawrence Ross, Law, Science, and Accidents, 2 J. Legal Stud. 1 (1973).

frequency of police stops, and the deterrent effect dwindled considerably. In other words, the *criminal law formulation* changes, which created more severe penalties did not increase deterrent effect, absent the considerable increase in likelihood of arrest and conviction produced by police enforcement efforts, which is what the previous analysis would predict.

In several other studies, Ross has pursued the effects of campaigns to affect the rates of drunk driving. These campaigns involve not only increased penalties for drunk driving but also considerable publicity about these increased penalties, publicity that is likely to cause citizens to believe that the rate of surveillance for drunk driving is increased. He uses interrupted-time-series analysis, with the law change as the "interruption," to see if a resulting deterrence effect can be detected. In a study done following the adoption in France in 1978 of a law modeled on the Scandinavian drinking and driving laws, he finds that the law had a notable deterrent effect but that the effect was temporary.[87] Again, *criminal law formulation* in itself was ineffective. If there was to be an increased deterrent effect, it had to come through other changes, such as changing police procedures or reallocating resources.[88]

When considering criminal law changes designed to reduce crime, the death penalty quickly comes to mind in the United States, perhaps because the threat of death is the most frightening penalty within the arsenal of penalties. If a deterrence effect exists at all, it might be argued, it ought to exist for offenses in which this maximal penalty is available. Many reviews have examined the case for deterrent effects of the death penalty.[89] Hood comes to a not atypical conclusion in a major recent review: "In short, the absence of sufficient controls, when taken in

---

87 Laurence H. Ross, Richard McCleary, and Thomas Epperlein, Deterrence of Drinking and Driving and France: An Evaluation of the Law of July 12, 1978, 16 Law & Soc'y Rev. 345 (1982); Laurence H. Ross, Social Control Thought Deterrence: Drinking-and-Driving Laws, 10 Annual Rev. Of Sociology 21 (1984) (concluding drunk driving deterrence efforts have a short-term but not a long-term effect).

88 Andenaes provides an interesting study that confirms the suggestion that increasing the detection rate of drunken driving can lead to its decrease, even when the severity of the penalties for it are decreased! Johannes Andenaes, The Scandinavian Experience, in Social Control of the Drinking Driver 43 (Michael D. Laurence, John R. Snortum & Franklin E. Zimring, eds., 1988). In Finland, prior to 1977, very severe drunken driving sentences were in effect. Post-1977, probably bothered by the large number of prisoners incarcerated in jails, the penalties for drunken driving were reduced to fines and suspended prison sentences for most offenders. However, many more breath tests were given to motorists. The number of instances of driving under the influence was cut in half.

89 *See* Michael L. Radelet & Ronald L. Akers, Deterrence and the Death Penalty: The Views of the Experts, 87 Journal of Criminal Law & Criminology 1 (1996).

conjunction with the other problems already mentioned, should lead any dispassionate analyst to conclude that econometric analyses have not provided evidence from which it would be prudent to infer than capital punishment has any marginally greater deterrent effect than alternative penalties."[90] In any event, the examination of the literature on the deterrent effect of the death penalty tells us less that one would hope about even its efficacy. Because the issue is the deterrent effect of the full range of criminal law rules and penalties on the rates of the crimes and because the death penalty is the penalty for only a few crimes, the issue of its deterrent effect will not be pursued further.

3. Studies That Find a Deterrent Effect from Doctrinal Manipulation

A number of studies have found effects purportedly from doctrinal formulation that they label deterrent effects. In some of these studies, it appears that the "deterrent effect" found is merely an incapacitative effect of the increased prison terms. That is, it is possible that the alteration of crime rate that follows the doctrinal change is a result of locking away for a longer period those repeat criminals who are responsible for a good deal of the crimes committed. This is suggests a clear crime-reduction result, but it is from an incapacitative effect rather than a deterrent effect.[91]

Levitt conducted two studies of the effects of deterrence on aggregate crime statistics that attempt to distinguish the effects of deterrence and incapacitation resulting from changing arrest rates. He does an elegant job in dealing with the problem of measurement error in panel data, which has plagued previous studies on the topic. He uses the assumption that if increased arrest rates have their effects through incapacitation, then an increase in arrest rates for one type of crime will reduce all (or at least all related) crime rates, because criminals who commit burglary, for instance, also commit robberies and being locked away for one crime

---

90 Roger Hood, Capital Punishment, in The Handbook of Crime and Punishment 739, 762 (M. H. Tonry, ed., 1998).

91 Levitt reviews previous studies on the topic, but because they are subject to his criticism of methodological error, they will not be reviewed here. Several of them find evidence that they interpret as supporting a deterrence effect. *See* Steven D. Levitt, Why Do Increased Arrest Rates Appear to Reduce Crime: Deterrence, Incapacitation, or Measurement Error?, 36 Econ. Inq. 353 (1998).

means they also do not commit any other kinds of crimes. But from a deterrence perspective an increase in arrest rates for one crime will lead to a rise in the rates of other crimes as criminals rationally substitute away from committing the now frequently arrested crime to other crimes that have no increase in the frequency of arrest. In doing so, they are responding rationally, being deterred away from the crime for which arrest is likely to other categories of crime for which it is unlikely.

Using this logic, his results "suggest that incapacitation predominates (i.e., is the largest cause in the relationship between arrest rates and drops in crime frequency) for rape, incapacitation, and deterrence are of equal magnitude for robbery and that deterrence effects outweigh incapacitation for aggravated assault and property crimes."[92] Later, he notes that for the crime of murder, error rates make it impossible to conclude that arrest rates affect either deterrence or incapacitation.[93]

The study seems to be the best case that can be made for the operation of deterrence considerations at the aggregate level. Nonetheless, the study offers no challenge to the claim offered here. It demonstrates that increased *arrest rates* through reallocation of police resources can have a deterrent effect;[94] it provides no showing that *criminal law formulation* has a deterrent effect. As has been suggested, many kinds of changes in conditions or procedures—like the number of patrol cars driving by—may effect the behavior of potential offenders. It is producing such effect through the formulation of criminal law rules that is unlikely.[95]

---

92 *Id.* at 354–355.

93 *Id.* at 368.

94 It should also be noted that the police attention needed to increase one crime's arrest rate is likely to generate lower police attention on other crimes, with the predicted increases in crime rates postulated by Levitt himself. Thus, the deterrent effect noted here is not, on policy terms, a ringing endorsement of the practice as a crime-fighting measure.

95 Others share skepticism on this particular point. The United Kingdom Home Office commissioned the Institute of Criminology at Cambridge University to examine studies on deterrence, with a particular focus on whether one can achieve marginal deterrent effects of altering the severity of punishment through changes in sentencing policy. Andrew von Hirsch et al., Criminal Deterence and Sentence Severity: An Analysis of Recent Research (1999). They summarize as follows an influential set of studies conducted by Farrington and his coauthors, with regard to changes in the certainty of punishment—typically requiring changes in police practices—and changes in the severity of punishment—typically achieved through alteration of criminal law rules: "With respect to certainty, the findings are consistent with Farrington and his co-authors' previous studies, of significant negative correlations between most measures of certainty (of arrest and conviction) and crime rates—although these relationships

Levitt's second study, one that does concern a substantive criminal law rule rather than a police practice, is equally methodologically and conceptually sophisticated but is one that again supports the general conclusions offered here.[96] Briefly, he finds that there are sharp drops in the rate of crimes committed as an individual passes out of the jurisdiction of the juvenile court, with its relatively more lenient punishment practices, to the jurisdiction of the adult court, with its associated arsenal of severe punishments.[97]

This is impressive evidence that the transition between court systems has an effect on crime rates, and one obvious interpretation is that the criminal is affected by the differing amount of punishment that he or she anticipates receiving for crimes committed on either side of the jurisdictional divide. Several behind-the-scenes social phenomena can contribute to this. First, the differences in punishment amounts between juvenile and adult courts are one of those general truths that are well known to all. Unfortunately, very few such criminal law rules are so well known. Second, the means of transmission of this knowledge may often be the juvenile gangs in which young potential wrongdoers travel, so it is a result to some extent of the social pressures existing in the gang to take advantage of one's "window of freedom" to offend. The plausibility of this is increased by reports from those who are knowledgeable about the organization of juvenile gangs, who suggest that some of the more violence-prone gang duties, such as carrying weapons and keeping watch for hostile intrusions on ones turf, are delegated to younger gang members specifically because of their ability to avoid the harsher sanctions of the criminal justice system.[98] In other words, the prerequisites to deterrence commonly absent in other instances are present here: first, the legal rule is well known, and, second, the potential offender is highly motivated,

---

are somewhat weaker in the American than the English data. For severity, however, the data mostly do not show significant negative correlations." *Id.* at 26.

96 Levitt quotes the comments of juvenile criminals Glassner and his colleagues interviewed that reveal a sharp awareness of the comparison between the relative easy and shorter time done in a juvenile house of detention as compared with the harder time done in "jail." Barry Glassner, Margaret Ksander, Bruce Berg, & Bruce Johnson, A Note of the Deterrent Effect of Juvenile versus Adult Jurisdiction, 31 Social Problems 219 (1983).

97 *See* Levitt, Juvenile Crime and Punishment, *supra* note 22, at 1159.

98 Terry M. Williams, The Cocaine Kids: The Inside Story of a Teenage Drug Ring 19 (1989).

within himself and by the influence of others on him, to alter his conduct because of the rule.

One final, remarkably interesting study concerns the crime-reducing effects of the felony-murder rule.[99] The felony-murder rule, as is well known, penalizes the felon for any death that takes place during the commission of a crime as if it were an intentional killing, murder. The study and its results are important to the argument because it is one of the few instances to test a doctrine expressly formulated to produce deterrent effects.

The deterrence-based justification for the felony-murder rule is two-fold. First, it is said to induce the criminal to take greater care during the commission of a crime, perhaps to plan against dangerous contingencies such as bank guards unleashing a hail of fire in their general direction and killing some civilian. For example, it might cause the offender to not carry a gun to the scene of the crime. Second, the rule is said to cause the sensible criminal to realize that crime is an inherently chancy, unpredictable, frightening process during which "anything can happen," and many of these anythings are not under the control of the criminal. The sensible criminal, realizing this, will be less inclined to commit the crime in the first place.

The study results are quite surprising and illustrate the complexity of such deterrent effects. As the author remarks, "[T]he felony-murder rule does not simply lower robberies. It lowers robberies that do not result in death, but increases the number of robberies that do result in death. Overall, it increases the rate of deaths during a robbery."[100] As to the effect of the felony-murder rule when the underlying felony is rape, "the estimates suggest that the rule decreases rapes by 0.21 percent, but increases the average number of deaths per rape by 0.37 percent." The overall effect is to increase the total deaths due to rape by 0.15–0.16 percent.[101] One can only speculate about what causes these complex results (i.e., the apparent tendency of those who engage in robbery or rape, when a felony-murder statute is in effect, to be slightly more likely to cause the death of their victim), perhaps those criminals who know of the felony-murder rule

---

99 Anup Malani, Does the Felony Murder Rule Deter? Evidence from the FBI Crime Data (unpublished manuscript).
100 *Id.* at 22.
101 *Id.* at 35.

and nonetheless have undertaken the offense are persons who have already judged that the risk of death-causing conduct is worth taking.

Ultimately, the study seems to suggest that the felony-murder rule does effect conduct. On the other hand, changes in conduct that are fractions of a percent, as reported in the study, are hardly a ringing case for the overall efficacy of basing criminal law formulation on a deterrence analysis. This is particularly true because some of the influence seems to increase the social damage rather than decrease it as the law makers intended. The study's results also illustrate another good reason not to rely upon deterrence analysis in the formulation of criminal law rules: the complexity of the dynamics of deterrence and the lack of information about those factors that are needed to accurately predict an effect. More on this in the next chapter. If anything, the study seems to argue against formulating the felony-murder rule to affect crime rates.

To sum, one does not find that the aggregated-effect studies of deterrence demonstrate a capacity to reduce crime rates as would justify the deterrence orientation that dominates criminal law rule-making. Most studies showing a "deterrent effect" produce it by changes in police practices and attendant publicity that increase the perceived certainty of arrest, not by the formulation of criminal law rules. Where effect on conduct does come from criminal law formulation, it can be both unpredictable in its direction and near trivial in its amount.

C. The Possibilities and Impossibilities of Improving Deterrent Effect

It has been argued thus far that the manipulation of criminal law rules cannot normally materially increase deterrence. But perhaps the existing conditions could be changed so that doctrinal manipulation could enhance deterrence. This section discusses how a deterrent effect might be enhanced and says more about the situations in which doctrinal manipulation might actually have a deterrent effect. The goal here is to give a more realistic view of deterrence as a distributive principle, one that criminal law makers can use as a touchstone before relying upon deterrence analysis. To telegraph the conclusion, it is this: There are indeed reform possibilities to enhance deterrent effect, although many if not most may be unattractive or unconstitutional because of the sacrifices they require. Within the realm of plausible reforms, one could increase the situations in which doctrinal manipulation could have a deterrent effect, but such conditions would remain the exception rather than the rule.

1. Insuring That the Target Audience Knows, Directly or Indirectly, of the Rule Designed to Influence Their Conduct

As Section A notes, most people do not know the law; even career criminals, who have a special incentive to know it, do not; and even when people think they know the law, they frequently are wrong. Potential offenders typically do not read law books and their ability to learn the law even indirectly through hearing or reading of particular cases is limited by the fact that the legal rule—and often there are many rules interacting to produce the case result—is just one of dozens of variables that have play in a case disposition. To divine the operative liability rule, hidden under the effects of all the other variables, would require both a higher number of reported cases than potential offenders are exposed to and a mind for complex calculation beyond that which is reasonable to expect.

But there are some situations in which the criminal law rule can and will be known and ways in which knowledge of it can be increased. First, a bare prohibition itself is the easiest rule to convey, in part because its effects can be dramatic. Either the police think they can arrest for such conduct or they do not, and the police decisions will become known within the target population. The more noteworthy the prohibition, or repeal of a prohibition, the more widely it will be known. If the legislature decriminalizes robbing convenience stores on weekends, the fact would be quickly reported (and would likely quickly increase robberies). Even here, however, for rules as simple as those defining the law's commands, the rule often is not known. Is it criminal to fail to help a stranger in serious danger if one can do so without endangering oneself? Is it a crime for a private person to keep a dead body without burial or cremation? Is it criminal to fail to try to find the owner when you come upon a valuable mislaid item? Most people can only guess (often incorrectly) about these criminal law commands. (The answer in each case is: it depends upon which jurisdiction one is in.)

Some situations exist in which the necessary knowledge for deterrence can be conveyed to the potential offender at the time and place of the potential offense, as where the witness on the stand is reminded of the penalty for perjury, where life-term inmates are informed of their special eligibility for the death penalty, where an offender is told after arrest for seduction that there is a "marriage defense" to the crime, where road signs inform felons of a special duty to register in the jurisdiction, or where a kidnapper is told that he'll get a lesser sentence if he releases the victim alive. But such opportunities for special education are not typically available, and the government often does not take advantage of them when they are.

One could imagine requiring high school seniors to pass a knowledge-of-the-law examination to graduate, much as we give rules-of-the-road examinations before issuing a driver's license. It would be useful for graduates to know the serious penalties associated with domestic violence, the conduct that constitutes criminal harassment, and whether it as a crime to tape-record one's own phone conversation without permission of the other party. (In fact, government tends to rely instead on the maxim "ignorance or mistake of law is no excuse," pushing the full burden of education, unrealistically, on each individual.)

One also could imagine criminal codes written using "plain language drafting" techniques, but the reality is mountains of technical legalese that even lawyers must work to understand. Similarly, one could increase the chances that the legal rule could be known and followed by keeping rules simple. Being able to reduce a rule to a slogan that can be widely advertised might help: "Use a gun, go to jail." By contrast, the standard modern criminal code's complex self-defense rules appear rather silly. It would be unrealistic to think that a person could know and in the pressure of an attack follow those complex rules. But one could distill the rules to embody the basic principles that guided their formulation. The defensive force rule might read simply: "In order to defend yourself against an unlawful attack, you can use only the force that is necessary and that is not disproportionate to the harm threatened."[102]

One might be able to increase the complexity of a rule if it applied primarily to a group of persons who could be specially trained, such as

---

102 See, e.g., Final Report of the Illinois Criminal Code Rewrite and Reform Commission at §416 (2003), *available at* http://www.law.upenn.edu/fac/phrobins/illinois/.

Section 416. Defense of Person

(1) The use of force against an aggressor is justified when and to the extent such conduct is immediately necessary to defend oneself or another person against the aggressor's use of unjustified force.

(2) Definition. "Unjustified" conduct is conduct that satisfies the objective elements of an offense and is not justified by this Article.

the rules governing the conduct of police officers or public officials. Thus, a code might provide detailed rules governing use of force by officers to arrest,[103] or detailed rules limiting a public official's ability to sell political influence,[104] or even detailed rules for doctors governing abortion.[105] This is also the case for any target group that has the ability to, and is on notice of their need to, specially educate themselves, such as rules governing the conduct of corporate officials or special license holders.

One final observation concerns criminal law rules of general application. As noted in Section A, while people rarely know "the law," they generally assume that the criminal law is as they would expect it to be. That is, they use their own intuitions of justice and their own assessments of what is harmful or wrongful as the basis on which to project what they assume the criminal law must provide. This suggests that the criminal law can insure greater knowledge of its commands, with little or no need for special education efforts, if its rules track shared community views. (Conversely, it would be difficult to get compliance with rules that appear to conflict with lay expectations, such as a rule barring force necessary to recapture property from a thief if the thief acts under a mistaken claim of right,[106] barring resistance to an unlawful arrest,[107] or barring use of deadly force necessary for self-defense if one can retreat.[108] Where the law does conflict with lay intuition, a special education drive will be needed.)

2. Insuring That the Target Audience Perceives a Meaningful Net Cost for a Violation

Section A notes the many difficulties in establishing a punishment rate that would be meaningful to potential offenders, in avoiding the delay in imposition of punishment that seriously erodes its deterrent effect and in establishing and modulating the amount of punishment imposed—all

---

103 Model Penal Code §3.07 comment 122 (1985).

104 Model Penal Code §240.7 comment 85 (1980).

105 Model Penal Code §230.3 comment 429 (1980).

106 See Model Penal Code §3.06 comment 74 (1985). See also Paul H. Robinson & John M. Darley, Justice, Liability & Blame: Community Views and Criminal Law 68–69 (1995) (empirical study suggesting a difference between the legal rule and lay intuition concerning the use of force in protection of property).

107 See Model Penal Code §3.04 comment 42–43 (1985); §3.09 comment 148 (1985).

108 See Model Penal Code §3.04 comment 54 (1985). See also Robinson & Darley, Justice, Liability & Blame, supra note 106, at 56–57, 64 (empirical study suggesting a difference between the legal rule and lay intuition concerning the use of deadly force in self-defense).

conditions necessary for effective deterrence. Reforms can improve the system's ability to make and modulate the threat of punishment, although the potential for improvement is at best modest.

a. Probability

The empirical studies seem to agree that increasing the probability of punishment provides a better chance of increasing deterrence than increasing severity.[109] Establishing some base expectation of a meaningful chance of punishment is a necessary condition to any deterrent effect, yet it has previously been noted just how low is the perceived probability of punishment,[110] a result of the very low actual rates, further exacerbated by the human tendency to heavily discount a future event. Sentencing discretion contributes to the uncertainty of punishment, as does the discretion of the many other participants in the criminal justice system whose exercise of discretion can regularly allow offenders to escape punishment or get less than they might. Such uncertainty can in all cases nurture a hope of avoiding punishment.

There appears to be a limit to what can be done to improve the perceived probability of punishment. Increasing punishment certainty would require improving clearance rates (the rate at which an offender is arrested for a given offense) and conviction rates. (The most important may be the first, clearance rates, for these account for the greatest "leakage" of offenders escaping punishment.[111]) Yet such increases would require: a significant increase in the amount spent on law enforcement and criminal justice, an increase in the intrusiveness suffered by citizens from law enforcement, and/or a reduction in the procedural safeguards provided in criminal adjudications. The reality is that most people think they already pay too much in taxes,[112] and limitations on investigative

---

109 Jeffrey Grogger, Certainty v. Severity of Punishment, 24 Econ. Inquiry 297 (1991); Ann Dryden Witte, Estimating the Economic Model of Crime with Individual Data, 94 Q. J. of Econ. 57 (1980).

110 *See supra*, Chapter 3, text accompanying note 42.

111 *See* Paul H. Robinson & John M. Darley, Utility of Desert, 91 Nw. U.L. Rev. Table 1, col. (c) (1997) (only 8.1% of all burglaries, 14.4% of all rapes, and 7.8% of all assaults result in an arrest).

112 Some studies suggest a greater willingness to pay for crime-control measures than had been previously reported. *See* Mark A. Cohen et al., Willingness-to-Pay for Crime Control Programs, 42 Crim. 89 (2004). Of course, these expressions of willingness show a willingness to pay if the expenditures would in fact reduce a particular kind of

intrusiveness and on adjudication procedures commonly are of constitutional base, thus unchangeable by legislative action. No doubt progress could be made around the edges, assuming people were willing to suffer the trade-offs—higher taxes, more governmental intrusion, and few procedural safeguards—but the kind of dramatic changes that would be required to significantly alter our current abysmal clearance rates seem unlikely.

An additional complication in making such reforms, even if people were willing to make the trade-offs required by them, is their effect on the criminal justice system's reputation for procedural fairness, which, like its reputation for moral credibility, has crime-control implications. A system perceived as procedurally unfair will not earn the legitimacy required for the acquiescence and support—by defendants, witnesses, jurors, and officials—that the system needs to operate effectively. For example, we might obtain a higher conviction rate by lowering the standard of proof from the demanding "beyond a reasonable doubt" that we now use. But would criminal conviction retain even its current level of credibility if we did?

Tyler, surveying a large sample of Chicago residents, found that the degree to which respondents felt that they had received fair treatment at the hands of the police predicted those respondents' general confidence in legal authorities, and, importantly, the degree to which they felt obliged to obey the law.[113] Tyler and Huo, reporting on the National Center for State Courts survey, showed that responses to such questions as "the courts are concerned with people's rights" predict respondents' evaluations of the court system and their willingness to obey the laws. To sum, people "were strongly influenced by whether they believed that the police and the courts treated people with respect, dignity, and fairness, and did not harass them or subject them to rude or inappropriate treatment."[114] The point here is that the reputation of the criminal justice system for fair and respectful treatment of people is central to its ability to enlist voluntary compliance from citizens with the law, and the "procedural byproducts" of a criminal justice system that organizes itself to increase arrest rates may bring about highly consequential losses in perceptions of procedural legitimacy.

---

crime. There is little reason to think that such additional funds could actually produce the crime reduction demanded, in which case the willingness to pay would evaporate.

113 Tom Tyler & Yuen Huo, Trust in the Law: Encouraging Public Cooperation with the Police and Courts 179 (2002).

114 *Id.* at 191.

b. Delay

Section A notes that the delay between violation and punishment can dramatically reduce deterrent effect. And, even if the punishment is certain, the more distant it is, the more its weight as a threat will be discounted. Further, when punishment is imposed, the strength of the punishment memory—that is, its recalled punitive "bite" as a perceived threat for a future violation—is dramatically reduced as the length of delay increases. But, as with reforms to increase probability, decreasing delay would require increases in resources or changes in procedural rules, which might be unconstitutional or, if not, would require unpopular trade-offs that could injure the criminal justice system's reputation for fairness and, thereby, its legitimacy.

c. Amount

The greatest difficulties relevant to "amount" of punishment lie not in establishing a punitive bite but rather in manipulating its amount reliably so as to optimize deterrence. It is the element of amount that is the aspect of perceived net cost over which lawmakers assume they have the greatest control. Legislatures (and judges) believe they can manipulate the amount of punishment threatened simply by manipulating the length of the prison term. But as Section A notes, such manipulation of sentence length does not provide the degree of change in punishment amount that lawmakers and judges assume. The forces at work in determining perceived amount of punishment are considerably more complex than has been assumed. Indeed, increasing duration might even have the reverse effect on perceived total bite.

An effective means of increasing total punishment bite may be to increase the intensity of the punishment experience. However, the criminal justice system in the United States, and probably in any liberal democracy, has little ability to increase punishment intensity beyond what it is currently. Earlier times saw attempts to do so in the invention of increasingly excruciating tortures and humiliations ("drawing, hanging, disemboweling, burning, beheading, quartering"[115]). But there would be neither the political will for nor the public acceptance of such torture today, nor

---

115 Fredrick Pollock & Fredrick W. Maitland, 2 The History of English Law Before the Time of Edward I 501 (1898).

of nearly anything much more unpleasant than the current prison experience. Some might tolerate imprisonment at "hard labor," but such a thing would have its details scrutinized for unconstitutional "cruel and unusual punishment."[116] (In one recently reported case, a judge's attempt to bar the use of television as part of a sentence of home detention was challenged by defense attorneys, who persuaded the Second Circuit to temporarily stay the television ban.[117])

Even if more intense punishments were not held unconstitutional, they might well be counterproductive. As Chapter 8 discusses, a criminal justice system that is seen as barbaric or as dispensing disproportionate punishment would likely lose moral authority with the community and, with it, the crime-control power that such moral authority can bring. One practical example relevant here is stigmatization, which can be highly effective in influencing conduct and has none of the financial costs of imprisonment but which depends upon the criminal justice system having earned a reputation for reliability in making criminal liability judgements that accord with the community's shared intuitions of justice. A system would quickly lose its moral credibility if it distributed cruel or disproportionate punishment or liability based upon any number of the factors that deterrence analysis would make central to liability and punishment but which are unrelated to moral blameworthiness.

The best that one may be able to do to increase the threatened punishment bite is to explore ways of inflicting suffering (consistent with human dignity, as the community's moral sense demands) through minor adjustments to prison conditions—that is, more dignified, shorter, but more unpleasant terms—or through nonincarcerative alternatives, which have the advantage of being less expensive. For example, if the unpredictability of prison life contributes to its aversiveness, then it might be possible to intentionally increase its uncertainty and simultaneously shorten the prison term over which it is experienced. For less serious crimes, it has been shown that there are a number of alternatives to prison sentences that people would perceive as having a punitive "bite" comparable

---

116 *See* generally Wayne R. LaFave, Substantive Criminal Law at §3.5, 240–253 (2nd ed. 2003) (reviewing Constitutional limitations on modes of punishment).

117 Benjamin Weiser, Prime Time and Punishment, N.Y. Times March 7, 2002, at A24, col. 1. Whether or not the defendant ultimately prevails says something of the extent of scrutiny of "different" punishments that the Second Circuit would grant the stay.

with that of a short prison term.[118] This means that it is possible to create a sentence of the appropriate severity that would be a mix of these experiences. (For instance, a mix including home confinement, labor-intensive community service, weekends in jail, and a fine.) Again, it might be possible to rotate offenders through various punishment options, which might keep the aversiveness of the experiences fresh. Morally, there is a tightrope to be walked here. One is attempting not to increase the objective negativity of the punishments but to increase the perceived negativity.

One last point on deterrent limitations of sentences, especially imprisonment: Most of what has been said so far focuses on legislative action in setting offense grades and their sentencing consequences. Even if a legislature found the most deterrent-efficient set of punishment rules and enshrined them in the criminal code, such rules would not necessarily produce the intended modulation of punishment amount required by a deterrence-based system. It is judges not legislators who impose sentences, and given the wide sentencing discretion that American judges traditionally have had and continue to have in the vast majority of states, it is judicial discretion not legislative policy that will determine deterrent effectiveness.

No doubt for this reason mandatory minimum sentences have become popular with legislatures in many states.[119] But such legislative sentencing creates the danger—increasingly recognized in public discourse—of increased community perceptions of injustice, which, as before, can undermine the criminal law's moral authority. On the other hand, a common alternative to mandatory minimums, judicial discretion, can produce unjustified disparity in the sentencing of similar cases, which also can produce perceived injustices as noted earlier. The community expectation no doubt is that punishment should depend upon what the offender has done not on the sentencing judge to whom he happens to be assigned.

---

118 George Gescheider, Edgar Catlin & Anne Fontana, Psychophysical Measurement of the Judged Seriousness of Crimes and Severity of Punishments, 19 Bulletin of the Psychonomic Society 275–278 (1982); Robert Harlow, John M. Darley & Paul H. Robinson, The Severity of Intermediate Penal Sanctions: Psychophysical Scaling Approach for Obtaining Community Perceptions, 11 Journal of Quantitative Criminology 71–95 (1995).

119 See, e.g., Gary Lowenthal, Mandatory Sentencing Laws: Undermining the Effectiveness of Determinate Sentencing Reform, 81 Calif. L. Rev. 61, 61–63 (1993).

Judicial discretion is also troublesome because it can produce not only inconsistency among different judges but inconsistency among a single judge's different cases. For example, when a judge picks out one case or another with which to "make an example"—a practice typically justified on deterrence grounds—the sentence is likely to be inconsistent with other cases of similar seriousness. The point of "making an example" of an offender is to give a *higher sentence than what one ordinarily would give in such or similar a case* to boost the deterrent message. But that suggests that each instance of "making an example" risks the criminal justice system's reputation for fairness and uniformity in application.

Further, such a "making an example" can backfire. The open acknowledgment that such offenders have not ordinarily been given such a punishment may tell listeners that the publicized punishment is not the regular punishment, and thus not the punishment that they should expect if they commit the offense, especially given that they will end up being sentenced at a later time and may be sentenced by a different judge. The more newsworthy the "making an example," the more widely it is reported—something deterrent effect normally desires—the more unusual and atypical the sentence may be perceived as being. A more effective deterrent approach would be to advertise how consistent is the sentencing. Yet, that is difficult to do with today's high degree of judicial sentencing discretion.

A common means of compensating for the inconsistency among sentencing judges has been to have the real determination of sentence length made after the public sentencing by a centralized authority such as a state-wide parole commission. But this solution creates its own problems, most importantly the (accurate) perception that the sentence publicly announced after trial does not in fact represent the real punishment. The real sentence in such a system comes to be understood, especially by those familiar with the operation of the system, as much less than the official sentence announced. And the extent of the discount off the announced sentence can be substantial. In some jurisdictions, including the federal system until the Sentencing Reform Act, a sentence of many years imprisonment could mean that the offender in fact is eligible for immediate release.[120] When this truth becomes known, as it generally is in

---

120 In the federal system before the Sentencing Reform Act of 1984, any offender was eligible for immediate release unless the sentencing judge explicitly imposed a term of parole ineligibility, which, even if one was imposed, could never exceed one-third of

an open society, it is no surprise to find that the credibility of the system's punishment threat has been damaged. Further, once burned, the public may wonder, "If the system is misleading us on this issue, on what other issues is it similarly misleading?" This is not a good condition for project- ing a credible punishment threat but rather offers the worst of both worlds: it undercuts the deterrent threat meant to be carried by the pub- licly announced sentences and simultaneously insures inconsistency and injustice that will undermine the system's moral credibility.

Perhaps the best that one can do to improve the credibility to the punishment threat is to institute reforms such as sentencing guidelines that regularize sentences[121] and "truth in sentencing" reforms that require offenders to serve all or most of the sentence imposed.[122]

3. Insuring That the Target Audience Is Capable of and Willing to Bring a Perceived Threat of Punishment to Bear on Their Conduct Decisions

Section A notes the host of conditions—drug or alcohol use, personality types inclined toward impulsiveness and toward discounting conse- quences, and social influences such as the arousal effect of group action and the tendency of group members to identity with group rather than individual interests—that interfere with a potential offender's rational calculation of self-interest. Unfortunately, these conditions are dispro- portionately high among deterrence's target group (those persons for

---

the publicly announced sentence. "[A] court-imposed term of imprisonment in excess of one year frequently has little to do with the amount of time that an offender will spend in prison. The announced term represents only the maximum length of time the offender may spend in prison if he earns no good time credits and if the Parole Commission does not set a release date that falls before the date of expiration of the sentence." Sen. Rpt. 98-255, at 40, 48 (Aug. 4, 1983).

121 "[S]entencing in the Federal courts is characterized by unwarranted disparity and by uncertainty about the length of time offenders will serve in prison. The lack of reason- able consistency in the sentences handed down by the courts is due in large part to the lack of a comprehensive Federal sentencing law. . . . This disparity is fair neither to the offenders nor to the public. *Id.* at 49.

122 The federal system, for example, now requires that an offender serve 85% of the sen- tence imposed. That is, only a 15% reduction is allowed as credit for good behavior in prison. "Under the bill, the sentence imposed by the judge will be the sentence actually served. A sentence that exceeds one year may be adjusted at the end of each year by 36 days for a prisoner's compliance with institutional regulations. . . . The prisoner, the public, and the corrections officials will be certain at all times how long the prison term will be, and of the consequence of causing institutional discipline problems." *Id.* at 56.

whom criminal conduct is not already ruled out by their own internalized norms or by those of family or peers). This bodes ill for effective deterrence because it precludes or at least diminishes a rule's deterrent effect even if the rule is known and is backed up by what is perceived as a meaningful threat of punishment.

Can the rational calculation of self-interest among potential offenders be improved? The present perspective may suggest an interesting twist on the modern skepticism about the effectiveness of treatment and rehabilitation programs. Though thinking that criminals can be "rehabilitated" into good citizens may not be realistic, it is somewhat more realistic to think that the behavioral sciences could find a way to make potential offenders *more able to exercise rational self-interest in response to a perceived threat of punishment.* And though current treatment techniques may not be able to make potential offenders good people, perhaps they could increase their susceptibility to being deterred!

There remain serious limitations on the effectiveness of many if not most such treatment programs. Kleiman has suggested the conditions under which a monitoring program is likely to be successful in inhibiting drug or alcohol consumption.[123] But it might be that the shift in focus proposed here—toward improving a person's ability for rational self-interest calculation—in both the selection of programs to use and the selection of offenders to which they are to apply—could better utilize what effectiveness there is in such programs.

One suggestion for increasing the effectiveness of treatment programs consists of increasing the level of surveillance until detection of lapses is nearly certain. Daily breathanalyzer tests for those who drink and drive or daily urine tests for those who use drugs will at least sort out those who lack the "willpower" to restrain themselves from lapsing when the penalties for lapsing are nearly certain. Those who continue to lapse under these detection conditions may require more incarcerative treatments to keep them from committing crimes while under the influence of alcohol or drugs. One can imagine that these sorts of high-frequency surveillance programs can be costly. But those costs need to be compared with the costs expended on keeping the offenders in prison. Further, costs can be reduced by enlisting in the task recent developments in computational power and electronic surveillance. Breathanalyzers now can be

---

123 Mark Kleiman, Coerced Abstinence: A Neopaternalist Drug Policy Initiative, in The New Paternalism: Supervisory Approaches to Poverty 182 (Lawrence Mead, ed., 1997).

coupled to car ignitions that will keep people from driving if they have taken alcohol. Drug abusers can now be randomly beeped, for instance, to give a blood test that could be electronically tested for illicit drugs. And if these methods fail, then electronically enforced daily periods of "house arrest" could leave an offender able to continue employment while being restricted from other activities. These efforts are remarkably intrusive, even Orwellian, procedures to contemplate using, but they perhaps violate the person's autonomy and dignity less than the alternative, which is generally prison.

One final point on clearing the rational-choice hurdle. The absence of rational decision making seems greater for offenses that do not require sustained planning efforts. This is true both because persons who can plan are also likely to be able to calculate self-interest, and because the longer the planning stage, the greater the opportunity for self-interest to intervene to override impulsiveness or other forces toward irrationality. This suggests that, if rehabilitating programs are to be revised to enhance a potential offender's self-interest calculation, the primary population for such treatment is not the white-collar criminal who may have been the primary client of rehabilitation programs in the past but rather is the more dysfunctional, perhaps impulsive offender.

4. Summary and Conclusion

It has been argued that the standard practice of formulating criminal law liability and punishment rules to optimize deterrent effect is indefensible given the rarity with which such rule formulation is likely to have the intended effect on crime decisions. Potential offenders commonly do not know the legal rules, either directly or indirectly, even those rules that have been explicitly formulated to produce a behavioral effect. If they know the legal rules, potential offenders commonly cannot or will not bring such knowledge to bear to guide their conduct in their own best interests, such failure stemming from a variety of social, situational, or chemical influences. And even if they know the rules and are able to bring that information to bear on their conduct decision, the cost-benefit conclusions that potential offenders reach commonly lead to a conclusion suggesting violation rather than compliance, either because the perceived likelihood of punishment is so small, or because it is so distant as to be highly discounted, or for a variety of other or a combination of reasons.

Thus, even if the punishment to be imposed had real bite, it nonetheless would have that bite heavily discounted because it would occur so far in the future. Even if the discounted bite were still seen as painful, it would have no deterrent effect if the chance of suffering it is perceived as de minimis. (The pickpockets working the crowd at the pickpocket's hanging illustrate the point.[124])

In the absence of any one of these prerequisites to deterrence—knowing the legal rule, being willing and able to bring such information to bear on one's conduct decision, and perceiving the threat of punishment to exceed the benefit of the offense—can be fatal to a deterrent effect. A well-known rule carrying a credible threat of punishment that exceeds the benefit of the offense nonetheless will be ineffective in deterring a person caught up in rage or the social pressures of group or drug effects. A rational calculator who fears any form of punishment even if the likelihood of it is slight, nonetheless will not be deterred by a rule of which he does not know. And a rule known by a rational calculator and perceived to carry a meaningful penalty nonetheless will not deter if the chance of getting caught is seen as trivial. Even if no one of these three hurdles is fatal to law's behavioral influence, their cumulative effect commonly is.

Reforms can indeed enhance deterrent effect, although many if not most may be unattractive or unconstitutional because of the sacrifices they require. Within the realm of plausible reforms, one could increase the situations in which doctrinal manipulation could have a deterrent effect, but such conditions would remain the exception rather than the rule.

Given the rarity of situations in which the prerequisites of deterrence are present and of nonnegligible effect, the standard use of deterrence analysis to formulate criminal law doctrine seems wildly misguided. At the very least, deterrence analysis ought to be considered in criminal law debate only after a showing that the deterrence-prerequisite conditions might actually exist.

The next chapter suggests that there may be good reasons for not relying upon a deterrence distributive principle even if the prerequisite conditions for deterrent effect do exist.

---

124 *See* V.A.C. Gatrell, The Hanging Tree 59–60 (1994).

CHAPTER 4

Deterrence as a Distributive Principle

C hapter 3 concludes that there is reason to be skeptical about criminal law's deterrent effect—that is, skepticism about the ability to deter crime through the manipulation of criminal law rules and penalties. What does this mean for the fundamental question, to which this chapter returns: Should deterrence be used as a distributive principle for criminal liability and punishment? One may conclude, somewhat obviously, that deterrence ought not be used as a distributive principle except in those situations where there is reason to think that the three prerequisites to deterrent effect in fact exist. Yet, as Section A below makes clear, deterrence is a standard, if not *the* standard, method of modern analysis in formulating criminal law rules. Rules typically have been set to optimize deterrence on the assumption that they *always* will have effect.

Even if one concludes that the analysis of the previous chapter is unpersuasive, good reasons for serious concern remain. Section B offers arguments for being skeptical about using deterrence as a distributive principle even if the three prerequisites for deterrent effect were commonly met.[125]

---

125 Much of this chapter is taken from Paul H. Robinson & John M. Darley, The Role of Deterrence in the Formulation of Criminal Law Rules: At Its Worst When Doing Its Best, 91 Georgetown Law Journal 949 (2003).

First, a disabling problem for deterrence as a distributive principle is its need for information that is not available and not likely to be available any time in the foreseeable future. Formulating criminal law rules according to a deterrence analysis can produce erroneous results if based upon missing or unreliable data. In fact, inadequately informed analyses can produce criminal law rules that reduce rather than increase the possibility of deterrence. In such an informational void, it makes sense to follow a distributive principle that at the very least can achieve its objectives.

Further, even if full and perfect information were available, the dynamics of deterrence are dramatically more complex than has been supposed. The deterrence process involves complex interactions, like substitution effects, that make deterrence predictions enormously difficult. And the deterrence process is a dynamic rather than a static one. Even if a criminal law rule manipulation increases deterrent effect as hoped, that effect itself can change the existing conditions and thereby change the deterrence calculations.

Second, *any* distributive principle for criminal liability and punishment will produce some deterrent effect (if any is to be had). A deterrence-based distribution makes sense only if it can provide *meaningfully greater* efficient deterrent effect than that already inherent in competing distributions that advance other useful goals, such as doing justice. This means that deterrence can do better than another distribution—such as a desert distribution—only where it deviates from it. That is, a deterrence-based distribution can deter better than a justice-based distribution only where it deviates from a just result.

However, it is just these instances of deviation from desert in which getting a deterrent effect is most difficult. People assume the law is as they think it should be, which is according to their own collective notions of justice. (And, as will be discussed in Chapter 7, the empirical research suggests that people's intuitions of justice are based upon their assessment of desert not some other principle.) Thus, the deterrence prerequisite of making the deterrence-based rule known becomes a difficult task: deterrence can only do better than desert by deviating from it; however, when it does deviate, the deterrence-based rule is not likely to be known. Further, it is these deviation-from-desert cases in which the system's deterrence-based rules are least likely to be followed. Because people intuitively assess criminal liability and punishment in terms of justice rather than deterrence, the exercise of police, prosecutorial, and judicial discretion, as well as jury nullification can subvert application of deterrence-based deviation rules, thus subverting the deterrence program and confusing the deterrence message.

Finally, even if one assumes for the sake of argument that a deterrence-based distribution produces a greater deterrent effect than a desert-based distribution despite its special deviation problems, there is reason to be concerned that the deterrence-based distribution simultaneously produces crime because its deviation from the community's shared intuitions of justice can undercut the criminal law's moral credibility, lessening its crime-control power as a moral authority, a dynamic that may have significant crimogenic effect, as Chapter 8 suggests. Thus, even if a deterrence-based distribution did successfully produce a greater deterrent effect than a justice-based distribution, that greater deterrent effect might be offset by its greater crimogenic effect in undercutting the moral authority of the criminal law.

A. The Traditional Assumption That the Formulation of Criminal Law Doctrine Will Influence Conduct

Chapter 3's view of a limited deterrent effect stands in stark contrast to the view of criminal law makers of the past four decades who have relied heavily, almost primarily, on deterrence analysis in formulating criminal law rules on the assumption that deterrence always works and is relevant to nearly every aspect of criminal law doctrine. Deterrence is said by some commentators to be the criminal law's "primary purpose"[126] or its "core purpose."[127] The Model Penal Code drafters, for example, see incapacitation and desert as merely "subsidiary themes."[128] As illustrated below, criminal code commentaries, court opinions, legislative histories, and sentencing hearing transcripts are full of the language of deterrence in justifying every manner of criminal law rule and practice.

---

126 Glanville Williams, Criminal Law: The General Part §191 at 601 (2nd ed., 1961); Wayne R. LaFave & Austin W. Scott, Jr., Substantive Criminal Law §2.1 n.88 (1986).

127 Warren v. U.S. Parole Commission, 659 F.2d 183, 188 (D.C. Cir. 1981).

128 Model Penal Code §1.02 comment 14 (1985) states: "Subsidiary themes are to subject those who are disposed to commit crimes to public control [and] to prevent the condemnation of conduct that is without fault."

1.   Doctrinal Formulations Calculated to Deter

a. Prohibitions[129]

The most common use of deterrence rationales is in shaping the criminal law's prohibitions. They have been used in formulating liability doctrines determining who should be held criminally liable: in support of the use of corporate/enterprise liability, in opposition to the use of corporate/enterprise liability, in support of limiting liability of corporate officials to the board of directors or high management, in support of the use of vicarious liability, in opposition to the use of vicarious liability, and in support of *Pinkerton* and "common design" rules in complicity.

Deterrence also is used as the guiding rationale in formulating inchoate liability rules: in support of the proximity test for attempt, in support of a "substantial step" test for attempt, in support of limiting the renunciation defense to cases where the offender is successful in avoiding the offense, and in opposition to an impossibility defense for inchoate liability. A useful example of deterrence-based analysis, which nicely illustrates how drafters really do imagine that the rule they adopt will translate into influence over decision on the street, is seen in the Model Penal Code drafters' justification of a renunciation defense to attempt:

> [The defense] provide[s] actors *with a motive for desisting from their criminal designs*, thereby diminishing the risk that the substantive crime will be committed. While under the proposed subsection *such encouragement* is held out at all stages of the criminal effort, its significance becomes greatest as the actor nears his criminal objective and the risk that the crime will be completed is correspondingly high. . . . [B]ecause of the importance *of encouraging desistance* in the final stages of the attempt, the defense is allowed even when the last proximate act has occurred but the criminal result can be avoided, as for example when the fuse has been lit but can still be stamped out. If, however, the actor has put in motion forces that he is powerless to stop, then the attempt has been completed and cannot be abandoned.[130]

---

129 For specific authorities, *see* Role of Deterrence, *supra* note 125, at 957–958.
130 Model Penal Code §5.01 comment 359–360 (1985) (emphasis added).

Similar kinds of behavioral control reasoning is found in justifying liability rules for solicitation and conspiracy.[131]

A deterrence rationale also is relied upon in justifying decisions *not* to criminalize certain conduct, often on the view that a sanction would be ineffective or unnecessary as a deterrent. A deterrence rationale has been offered to explain, for example, the decriminalization of suicide, assisting a suicide, failing to pay a valid debt, self-abortion and the preparation of home-made abortifacients, and for limiting the "joyriding" offense to the person who actually operates or aids in the operation of the vehicle (thus, excluding willing passengers).

b. Culpability Requirements, Mitigations, and Defenses

Lawmakers' view that doctrinal manipulation can enhance or maintain deterrent effect appears as well in the formulation of culpability requirements, mitigations, and excuse defenses. For example, in *United States v. Park*,[132] the president of Acme Markets, Inc., a national retail food chain with approximately 36,000 employees, 874 retail outlets, 12 general warehouses, and 4 special warehouses, was held criminally liable for violations of the Federal Food, Drug, and Cosmetic Act when a company warehouse in Baltimore, Maryland, held food in a building that could be exposed to contamination by rodents, even though there was no indication that Park was negligent as to the violation.[133] Such strict liability is defended on deterrence grounds:

> [A] person engaged in a certain kind of activity *would be more careful* precisely because he knew that this kind of activity was governed by a strict liability statute.... [T]he knowledge that certain criminal sanctions will be imposed if certain consequences

---

131 Model Penal Code §5.02 comment 366 (1985); Model Penal Code §5.03 comment 458 (1985).

132 421 U.S. 658 (1975).

133 It could be argued that Park was blameworthy for his failure to take sufficient remedial steps after being informed of the violation—he ordered a cleanup but gave this order to the same people who had allowed the problem to occur. But, while one might argue that the government could have shown Park's negligence—it is unclear whether they could have—the point is that the *Park* opinion allows statutes that do not require such a showing and, thus, allow criminal liability even if it is clear that no such showing can be made, the defendant acted entirely reasonably. *See* Norm Abrams, Criminal Liability of Corporate Officers for Strict Liability Offenses—A Comment on *Dotterweich* and *Park*, 28 U.C.L.A. L. Rev. 463, 476–477 (1981).

ensue might *induce a person to engage in that activity with much greater caution* than would be the case if some lesser standard prevailed.[134]

Another useful example is found in the well-known case of *Regina v. Dudley and Stephens*,[135] in which the defendants, adrift in an open boat at sea and soon to die from starvation, killed and drank the blood of a near-death cabin boy, an act that kept them alive long enough to be rescued. They were convicted of murder and sentenced to death. The court denied their claim of a necessity defense in large part because the court feared that recognition of such a defense would undercut criminal law's prohibitions at a time when its deterrent threat must be at its strongest.

> We are often compelled to set up standards we cannot reach ourselves, and to lay down rules which we could not ourselves satisfy. But a man has no right to declare temptation to be an excuse, though he might himself have yielded to it, nor allow compassion for the criminal *to change or weaken in any manner the legal definition of the crime.* It is therefore our duty to declare that the prisoners' act in this case was wilful murder.[136]

The influence of a deterrence rationale is also apparent in the formulations of the test for negligence. Many jurisdictions continue to use a purely objective standard against which to judge whether a person's failure to be aware of a prohibited risk is culpable. They refuse to take account of the particular capacities of the person at hand—of whether the person had the capacity to have met the reasonable person standard—for fear that any individualization would undercut the force of the law's prohibitions.

---

134 Richard A. Wasserstrom, Strict Liability in the Criminal Law, 12 Stan. L. Rev. 731, 736 (1960) (emphasis added). He also notes that the deterrent effect may be in deterring people from engaging in the strict Liability activity at all if they were concerned that they might not be able to avoid the prohibited harm. "[T]he presence of strict liability offenses might have the added effect of keeping a relatively large class of persons from engaging in certain kinds of activity." *Id.* at 737.

135 14 Q.B.D. 273 (1884). For more details on the case, *see* Paul H. Robinson, Criminal Law Case Studies 14 (2nd ed. 2002); Brian Simpson, Cannibalism and the Common Law: The Story of the Tragic Last Voyage of the Mignonette and the Strange Leading Proceeding to Which it Gave Rise (1984).

136 14 Q.B.D. at 288 (emphasis added). The Crown afterwards commuted the defendant's sentence to six months' imprisonment. *Id.*

Thus, in *State v. Williams*,[137] loving parents with little education and limited intelligence were held to have failed to meet the reasonable person standard in failing to get needed medical care for their seventeen-month-old child, who died of complications from what began as a toothache. The court ruled that it was sufficient negligence to support liability for manslaughter if "the conduct of a defendant, regardless of his ignorance, good intentions and good faith, fails to measure up to the conduct required of a man of reasonable prudence."[138] Reliance upon a purely objective (unindividualized) standard of negligence is justified in much the same way as the result in *Dudley and Stephens*: as necessary to maintain a clear standard of conduct. As Holmes concludes, the reason for adopting deterrence is the criminal law's "immediate object and task to establish a general standard . . . of conduct for the community, in the interest of the safety of all."[139]

To give just a few of many examples, deterrence arguments are used: in support of strict liability offenses, in opposition to strict liability offenses, in opposition to liability based upon negligence, in support of liability for negligent homicide and negligent assault with a deadly weapon, in support of an objective (unindividualized) standard of recklessness, in support of a purely objective (unindividualized) standard for the provocation mitigation to murder, in opposition to the individualized extreme emotional disturbance mitigation, in support of the partial responsibility mitigation in murder, in support of recognizing an insanity defense, an immaturity defense, a duress defense, in support of a reasonableness requirement for a mistake as to a justification defense, an involuntary act defense, a statute of limitation, and an entrapment defense, and in opposition to recognizing a general reasonable mistake of law excuse and a duress defense. Deterrence arguments also have been used to support particular formulations of excuse defenses, including in support of a formulation of the insanity defense that recognized only a

---

137 4 Wn. App. 908, 484 P.2d 1167 (Wash. App. 1971).

138 *Id.* at 913. Similarly, in Edgmon v. State, 702 P.2d 643, 645 (Alaska App. 1985), the court holds that the "peculiarities of a given individual—his or her intelligence, experience, and physical capabilities—are irrelevant in determining criminal negligence . . . since the standard is one of a reasonably prudent person."

139 Commonwealth v. Pierce, 138 Mass. 165, 176 (1884). *See also* Richard Singer, The Resurgence of Mens Rea: II—Honest But Unreasonable Mistake of Fact In Self Defense, 28 B.C.L. Rev. 459, 489 (1987).

cognitive dysfunction and in support of one that also recognized a control dysfunction.[140]

c. Grading Judgments[141]

An assumption that doctrinal formulations control deterrent effect also is reflected in the rationales offered in setting offense grades. An example is found in the popular felony-murder rule, which treats even a purely accidental killing during all or certain felonies as murder. The rule's traditional rationale sees the deterrent threat of murder's severe sanctions as making felons more careful to avoid accidental injury.

> [I]f experience shows, or is deemed by the law-maker to show, that somehow or other deaths which the evidence makes accidental happen disproportionately often in connection with other felonies, or with resistance to officers, or if on any other ground of policy *it is deemed desirable to make special efforts for the prevention of such deaths,* the law-maker may consistently treat acts which, under the known circumstances, are felonious . . . as having a sufficiently dangerous tendency to be put under a special ban. The law may, therefore, throw on the actor the peril, not only of the consequences foreseen by him, but also of consequences which, although not predicted by common experience, the legislator apprehends.[142]

The rule is thought to have the useful collateral effect of providing an additional deterrent to felonies generally, especially to dangerous felonies.[143]

Another example of adjusting grade to enhance deterrence is found in the "three strikes" and other habitual offender statutes. Part of their justification no doubt is the incapacitation of dangerous offenders, future dangerousness being shown by the repeated past offenses. But such provisions also are sought to be justified on deterrence grounds. As the

---

140 For specific authorities, *see* Role of Deterrence, *supra* note 125, at 961–963.
141 For specific authorities, *see* Role of Deterrence, *supra* note 125, at 964.
142 Oliver W. Holmes, The Common Law 49 (1881) (emphasis added).
143 "[The] rational function of the felony-murder rule is to furnish added deterrent to the perpetration of felonies which, by their nature or by the attendant circumstances, create a foreseeable risk of death." State v. Goodseal, 220 Kan. 487, 492, 553 P.2d 279, 285 (1976).

federal sentencing guidelines explain, "General deterrence of criminal conduct dictates that a clear message be sent to society that repeated criminal behavior will aggravate the need for punishment with each recurrence."[144] Indeed, it is in this context—habitual offender statutes— that it has been argued that "deterrence is the surest ground for punishment."[145]

Rummel v. Estelle[146] illustrates such deterrence reliance. Thirty-year-old Rummel frequently engaged in petty larceny or petty fraud. On a hot summer day, Rummel offered to fix a bar's broken air conditioner for $129.75, with no intention of doing so. He was caught and convicted of theft, a felony under then-existing state law. After the state presented evidence of two prior felonies, a "three-strikes" recidivist statute required that Rummel receive a sentence of life in prison without parole. The United States Supreme Court denied his appeal, concluding that the statute did not violate the Eighth Amendment's prohibition against cruel and unusual punishment.[147] Rummel's crime, a minor fraud, hardly seems to deserve life imprisonment without parole. Indeed, the cumulative effect of his entire criminal career—whether or not he had been formally sanctioned and punished for his earlier crimes—does not seem to merit such severe liability, at least on desert grounds. Yet three-strikes laws are willing to tolerate this deviation from justice in part in the name of general deterrence. This same use of grading determinations to optimize deterrent effect has been offered in support of a variety of offense grade aggravations, such as grading according to type of victim (old, young,

---

144 U.S.S.G. ch.4, pt. A, intro. comment.

145 "[S]ince retributive norms are so unsettled and since incapacitation may, by removing one offender from the pool of offenders, simply make a career in crime more attractive to someone else, who is balanced on the razor's edge between criminal and legitimate activity and who now faces reduced competition in the crime 'market.'" U.S. v Jackson, 835 F.2d 1195, 1197 (1987) (Posner, Circuit Judge, concurring, citing Ehrlich, On the Usefulness of Controlling Individuals: An Economic Analysis of Rehabilitation, Incapacitation, and Deterrence, 71 Am. Econ. Rev. 307 (1981)).

146 For a more detailed account of the Rummel case, *see* Rummel v. Estelle, 498 F. Supp. 793 (W.D. Tex. 1980); Tom Nelson, Rummel Ordered Released for Appeal, San Antonio Express, Oct. 4, 1980, at 11C; S.A. Man Gets Life, San Antonio Express, Apr. 13, 1973; Appeals Court Upholds Life Sentence for San Antonian, San Antonio Express, Jan. 13, 1979; S.A. Man Finally Free After 8-Year Ordeal, San Antonio Express, Nov. 15, 1980; Courts to Review Tough Texas Law: Billy Sol Bilks Companies Out of Millions; Rummel's Fraud Totals $229.11. Estes Serving 10 Years—Rummel Gets Life, San Antonio Express, Sept. 9, 1979, at 14A.

147 *See* Rummel v. Estelle, 445 U.S. 263 (1980).

or police officer) or location (school), along with countless other grading decisions that elevate punishment to "send a message."[148]

d. Sentencing Decisions

Sentencing judges and sentencing guideline drafters share the apparent assumption of code drafters and appellate judges that their decisions will influence the extent of deterrent effect. Consider the case of DeSean McCarty, a young African American from a crime-ridden South Chicago neighborhood.[149] McCarty accepted an offer from one Griffin to "rent" Griffin's fiancée's car if McCarty, a drug user, would give Griffin some drugs. The exchange was made, but McCarty did not return the car at the agreed time. A few days later, McCarty was sitting in the car when a police cruiser drove by. Not wanting to get caught in the stolen car with drugs, he sped off, then abandoned the car and fled on foot. A police vehicle, in giving chase, ran down and killed an officer pursuing on foot. McCarty

---

148 Deterrence arguments have been used in support of a separate offense of robbery (rather than relying upon offenses of theft and assault); in support of grading a vehicular killing while intoxicated as manslaughter even without a showing of negligence or causation; in opposition to application of the felony-murder rule to killings by nonfelons during the felony; in support of the premeditation aggravation for first degree murder; in rejecting a mere grade reduction for renunciation (preferring a complete defense); in support of grading inchoate liability less than that for the substantive offense, and, where it is graded the same as the substantive offense in support of making an exception to this rule for first degree felonies; in support of grading theft of livestock more than other thefts of equal or greater value because the former are particularly easy to commit and difficult to detect; in support of a lower grade for intercourse upon invalid consent (by mistake or trick) than by force; in support of grading theft by amount stolen; in support of reduced grading for "joyriding" (in comparison to theft); in support of grading credit card fraud of even a trivial amount as at least a misdemeanor; in support of grading incest no higher than a class three felony, even if extreme moral indignation of the community would call for a higher grade; in support of a grading reduction for a kidnapper who "voluntarily releases the victim alive and in a safe place prior to trial"; and in support of relatively low grading of perjury. For specific authorities, see Role of Deterrence, supra note 125, at 965–967.

149 For a more detailed account of the McCarty case, see Telephone Interview by C. Todd Inniss, Eve Brensike, & Colette Routel with Frank Rago, Public Defender, Markham Public Defender's Office (Feb. 1999) (notes on file with authors); Sarah Karp, Mother Copes with Cop's Death; Markham Officer Struck by Harvey Police Car, Daily Southtown, Sept. 22, 1997; Karen Mellen, Reckless Abandon; Families Want Driver Charged with Murder, Chicago Tribune, Oct. 7, 1998; T. Shawn Taylor, Cops Arrest Teen Linked to Officer's Fatal Chase; Police Want Subject Held Accountable, Chicago Tribune, Sept. 23, 1997; T. Shawn Taylor, Markham Cop's Death Becomes Murder Case; Bond Hearing Set in Fatal Police Chase, Chicago Tribune, Sept. 24, 1997; Paul H. Robinson, Criminal Law Case Studies 1–5 (2nd ed. 2002).

was convicted for the death of the officer under the Illinois felony-murder rule, which punishes as first-degree murder any causing of death in the course of a felony.[150] As has already been noted, the felony-murder rule itself has strong deterrent backing. The sentencing judge in *McCarty* also thought to advance deterrence through the exercise of his sentencing discretion. Though he could have mitigated the harshness of the rule, instead he imposed a sentence of forty years in prison, explaining that he needed to "send a message" and that "a sentence does need to be imposed that would deter others from committing such a crime, a high speed chase with the police."[151] Such a deterrence rationale is common in the formulation of a wide range of sentencing rules and policies.[152]

2.   "Deterrence Speak" versus Deviations from Justice

a. "Deterrence Speak"

It is possible to give too much meaning to the ubiquitous use of deterrence rationales, for much of the use of deterrence as a justification may be just a form of thoughtless expression, the standard vocabulary that modern criminal law theorists and lawmakers have come to use to express themselves. Instead of saying that "conduct X is harmful or evil" and, therefore, should be criminalized, it may have become common to say "conduct X should be deterred." (And instead of saying that "the conduct was involuntary" and, therefore, should be exculpated, one might refer to it as "nondeterrable.") One may speculate about the reasons for such

---

150 Illinois continues to read the felony-murder rule broadly where it applies, although the rule's application has been limited to "forcible" felonies. Ill. Comp. Stat. §5/9-1(a)(3); *see*, e.g., People v. Lowery, 687 N.E.2d 973 (Ill. 1997) (upholding felony-murder conviction for robber where victim shot at fleeing robber with gun robber had dropped, killing bystander).

151 People v. McCarty, Circuit Court of Cook County, No. 97 CR 27339, Sentencing Transcript 00392:11–13 (Sept. 15, 1998).

152 This includes, for example, arguments in support of the death penalty, in opposition to the death penalty, in support of automatic imposition of the death penalty on life-imprisonment prisoners who kill, in support of jail time for drunk driving, in support of a statutory maximum for fines of double the pecuniary gain, in support of applying a mandatory penalty enhancement for a subsequent offense to a second offense on a simultaneous conviction, in support of higher fines for corporate offenders, in support of a judicially imposed minimum term of imprisonment, in support of fines for offenses of pecuniary gain, and in guidelines for the exercise of judicial discretion in setting the length of a prison sentence and the amount of a fine. For specific authorities, *see* Role of Deterrence, *supra* note 125, at 968.

reliance upon "deterrence speak." Kahan argues that, "Citizens conventionally defend their positions in deterrence terms only because the alternative is a highly contentious expressive idiom, which social norms, strategic calculation, and liberal morality all condemn."[153]

"Deterrence speak" is common in a variety of contexts in which the end result is to suggest a rule that makes sense under nearly any distributive principle, including that of doing justice. It is used, for example, as the explanation for criminalizing: intercourse with young children, tampering with private records, incest, corruption in sporting events, retaliation against participants in official proceedings, witness tampering, bail jumping, obstruction of a public passageway, public indecency, and in support of greater punishment for armed robbery than for unarmed robbery.[154]

These criminalization decisions are hardly startling conclusions. One could as easily say in each instance that such conduct ought to be criminalized because "it is condemnable conduct." In other words, a deterrence explanation for the rule does not necessarily mean that the writer is in reality relying upon a deterrence cost-benefit analysis and has concluded that the deterrent benefits outweigh the deterrent costs. That deterrence language may have simply become the common mode of expression in modern criminal law analysis is supported by the fact that it commonly is offered both in support of and in opposition to the same position, as seen in many instances in the above lists of positions justified with deterrence rationales.

Indeed, some deterrence explanations for a conclusion are sufficiently frivolous as to suggest that no actual deterrence analysis has gone on, for any such analysis would surely suggest a different or at least a more nuanced conclusion. For example, as noted above, some writers offer a deterrence explanation for providing excuse defenses, such as insanity, immaturity, or duress. They reason that a general deterrent purpose

> would not be served by conviction and punishment of the insane, for "the examples are likely to deter only if the person who is *not* involved in the criminal process regards the lessons as applicable to him," which he is likely to do "only if he identifies with the offender and with the offending situation." It is unlikely that the sane person . . . will identify with the insane defendant, and thus

---

153 Dan M. Kahan, The Secret Ambition of Deterrence, 113 Harv. L. Rev. 413, 414 (1999).

154 For specific authorities, *see* Role of Deterrence, *supra* note 125, at 971–972.

the insane cannot be effectively used as a deterrent example to others.[155]

One may speculate that the conclusion—in favor of recognizing an insanity defense—came first to the writer, and that the "analysis" is simply a best effort at giving the obligatory deterrence argument in support of the desired conclusion. Clearly, a true general deterrence analysis might as easily suggest the opposite conclusion or at least would reveal conflicting deterrent interests. Though the insane defendant at hand might not be deterrable, and though he will be seen by third parties as different from themselves, there is reason to think that (if general deterrence works at all) it would be advanced by sanctioning the insane offender. The insane offender provides a useful opportunity for the law to make clear just how serious it is about punishing the violation. "If the law sanctions even an insane offender," it might be understood as saying, "make no mistake that it will sanction you if you commit this offense." Indeed, punishing the insane offender may be the only means by which the law can dissuade those potential offenders who assume that, if caught, they can escape the threatened sanction by false claims of excuse.[156]

Whatever the reasons for the use of "deterrence speak," the practice highlights just how pervasive is the deterrence orientation of modern criminal law. Deterrence may have become not only the standard analytic form but also the standard expressive form, shaping how we are to think and talk about problems of criminal law theory. This analytic and linguistic domination is bizarre indeed if criminal law formulations rarely have deterrent effect.

b. Deterrence Rationales That Do Real Work: Deviations from Justice

Not all use of deterrence arguments is habitual "deterrence speak" or fabricated arguments to give a deterrence justification for a formulation

---

155 LaFave & Scott, *supra* note 116, at §7.1, 520–521 (emphasis in original), quoting Abraham Goldstein, The Insanity Defense 13 (1967).

156 Further, there is a deterrence argument for imposing greater liability in all cases of excuse in which either internal or external forces press an actor toward a violation. As Stephen notes in arguing against a duress defense, for example, "it is at the moment when temptation to crime is strongest that the law should speak most clearly and emphatically to the contrary." James Fitzjames Stephen, 2 A History of Criminal Law in England 107 (Lenox Hill Publishing, 1973) (1883).

based, in truth, on other considerations. Deterrence analysis often does generate results that conflict with other distributive principles, such as desert, and is followed nonetheless.

Some examples from discussions above illustrate the point. Recall the felony-murder rule, as seen applied in the *McCarty* case, which authorizes (and a deterrence-focused sentencing judge imposes) a forty-year sentence for fleeing from police. In *Dudley and Stephens*, the need to keep clear the deterrent threat against killing and cannibalism demands the death penalty, even though the court essentially concedes it is imposing a standard of conduct that it might not be able to meet itself. In *Park*, the president of Acme Markets, Inc., a national retail food chain with approximately 36,000 employees, 874 retail outlets, 12 general warehouses, and 4 special warehouses, is held criminally liable for a health violation in one of the company warehouses, even though Park knew nothing of and was not negligent as to the violation. In *Rummel*, the defendant is given a life sentence for a $129.75 air conditioner repair fraud because of his prior felony convictions of a similar nature. In *Williams*, loving parents of limited intelligence and education are held for criminally negligent homicide when their failure to get medical care for their baby leads to its death, despite their likely inability to meet the purely objective standard of care the court insists upon. In each case, the lawmakers and courts use deterrence explanations to help justify liability rules and the exercise of discretion that produces a disposition in conflict with desert.

How do these five cases fare in light of the deterrence-skeptical conclusions summarized in Chapter 3? One or more of the deterrence-prerequisite hurdles is likely to trip up a deterrent effect for many if not most of these cases. McCarty, who gets felony-murder liability and a forty-year sentence for fleeing from police, probably knew nothing of the felony-murder rule or its application to him when he chose to flee, nor are others like him likely to apply the intended lesson in their drug-addled brains when the next police car appears. For Dudley, and others like him, for whom a painful death from starvation looms, little, if anything, will deter. People like Rummel might stop their petty frauds if they knew they would result in life imprisonment, but few are likely to perceive a meaningful chance of suffering such a sentence for such a fraud—and they would be right: they have a greater chance of being struck by lightning. Most of such potential offenders probably don't even know that such a life imprisonment rule is applicable to them. (Do you know the terms of your state's habitual offender statute, or even if it has one?) Park, as the executive of a large and respectable corporation, no doubt would be appalled at the thought of a criminal conviction, but he also is not likely to know about the rodent droppings in Baltimore or, even if he did, that they create a risk of criminal conviction for him. (If executives did believe that they would be strictly *criminally* accountable for such instances—rat feces in a warehouse in Baltimore—we would have few volunteers for Park's vacant position.) The Williamses, and other parents like them, will know little of the criminal law's liability rules or the nuances of the alternative negligence standards and, in any case, they will have no reason to think that such rules are applicable to them because, in their view, their baby only has a tooth ache. Yet these dubious contributions to the law's deterrent threat are purchased at some considerable expense, in both the injustices they do and the reputational damage they cause to a criminal justice system that is seen as indifferent to doing injustice. More on this in Section B.4. below and in Chapter 8.

B. Difficulties of Deterrence as a Distributive Principle

There are a number of reasons that one might decide against distributing criminal liability and punishment to optimize deterrence. The most obvious reason comes from Chapter 3's conclusion that doctrinal manipulation to optimize deterrence will rarely achieve its desired effect. That is, deterrence may be a good reason for *having a criminal justice system* that punishes violators, but it is at best ineffective as a guide for *distributing liability and punishment* within that system. Deterrence may be a sound justificatory purpose for the *institution* of punishment but a poor principle for its *distribution*.

Assume for the sake of argument, however, that some deterrent effect exists. Indeed, it is conceded that some doctrinal manipulation can have a deterrent effect. The new leaders in Aliabad introduced a policy that worked to reduce what they regarded as lawlessness: the bullet-ridden robbers' bodies were hung from a tank barrel outside the village for two days.[157] But even less draconian rules can work. In specific situations the rules may be publicly known, the target actors may be dispositionally rational and in circumstances that allow for rational calculation, the rate

---

157 C. J. Chivers, New Leaders Send a Signal By Hanging Bandit's Body, N.Y. Times, Dec 3, 2001, at B4, col. 6.

of detection may be high and a reasonable certainty of punishment may exist. But even in such situations, there remain good reasons to be skeptical of relying upon deterrence analysis in formulating criminal liability and punishment rules.

1. The Information and Complexity Problems

Building a deterrence-based liability and punishment system requires an enormous amount of information, most of which we do not have and are not likely to have in the foreseeable future. The dynamics of the deterrence effect, where it does exist, can be enormously complex and can have interactive effects that we do not yet understand. In the absence of adequate information and of an understanding of the complexities of the dynamics of deterrence, reliance upon deterrence analysis to formulate criminal law doctrine seems reckless. Such uninformed analysis can as easily lead to formulations that reduce deterrence as increase it.

Consider the wide-range of factors that Chapter 3 shows to be important to a deterrence calculation. For example, what does a potential offender: perceive as the chance of getting caught, convicted, and punished? predict to be the amount of punishment associated with each of the possible conviction outcomes? perceive to be the degree of painfulness associated with each possible punishment outcome? (i.e., how painful does he consider, say, a $10,000 fine, two weeks in jail, a three-year prison sentence, solitary confinement for life?) perceive to be the likely delay in any anticipated punishment? perceive to be the attractiveness of the anticipated benefit of the contemplated offense?

Further, deterrence calculations require a sense of the equation by which the target audience gives relevant weights to each of these factors. For example, it was noted previously that, if the probability of punishment is high—that is, that a potential offender is likely to get caught for drunk driving or running a red light—even moderately painful punishments seem sufficient to deter the conduct, but there no doubt is a break point of punishment probability below which the extent of punishment threatened becomes irrelevant to the target. Where is that break point? Does it vary with the offense and the situation? The animal data similarly hints that, as the likelihood of punishment declines, the deterrent effect soon becomes greatly reduced or even negligible. Does that suggest that the probability of punishment might best be weighted more highly in the deterrence equation than should the intensity of the punishment? What weight should be given to the delay in punishment (which the animal studies also suggest can be a powerful variable)? A reliable deterrence calculation would need to sort out just how much more weight should be given to probability of punishment than to its intensity or to its timing or to other factors.

Consider as well the difficulty in obtaining a reliable measure of the relevant information. We not only need "objective" measures of those factors but also "psychophysical" measures that translate, for instance, the objective measure of the average prison sentence for robbery, of say five years, into the quantum of Benthamite pain corresponding to five years of prison in the mind of the person contemplating the crime. As the adaptation and duration-neglect discussions in Chapter 3 illustrate, this calculation can be enormously complex and counterintuitive.

Still further, one cannot underestimate the ability of erroneous data on one factor to distort the calculation. Part of the point here is that deterrence calculations are not intuitive. The results will depend upon the numbers, not on a general principle that by itself may make sense. For example, one aspect of deterrence analysis would want to impose a greater punishment on a more serious offense—murder more than assault or burglary—if for no other reason than to deter a person who has committed the lesser offense from going further to commit the greater offense—for example, to keep the burglar who is discovered by the home owner from killing the home owner to avoid being identified as a burglar. However, imagine a situation where the punishment rate is high for the more serious offense and low for a less serious offense. (In fact, the punishment rate for murder is approximately thirty times that for burglary.[158]) The deterrence calculations might actually suggest that the less serious offense should be punished more severely. Recall that the probability of punishment is an important determinant of the total punishment cost. Thus, a deterrence analysis may increase punishment on a low capture-rate offense in order to maintain a sufficiently serious deterrent threat. Therefore, *depending on exactly how the punishment weight calculations come out*, a deterrence optimizing theorist might conclude that one should have a greater penalty for the less serious offense! The point is not a hypothetical one. Recall, for example, the drug laws driven by the logic of deterrence set prison terms for possession of relatively small amounts

---

158 *See* Paul H. Robinson & John M. Darley, Does Criminal Law Deter?, *supra* note 17, at 173, Table 1, col. (d).

of cocaine as considerably higher than those given for various crimes of violence.[159]

Even if one had good information on the basic conditions that may influence deterrent effect, the calculations are all the more complex because of potential dynamics that one's proposed rule itself may trigger. That is, one rule might make sense given the conditions that presently exist, but the introduction of that rule might quickly change the conditions. For example, Katyal points out that substitution effects are important to consider.[160] One might be inclined to increase the threatened punishment in order to deter an offense of moderate harm, but before doing so, one must consider whether the potential offender will substitute an offense of more serious harm. There are drug addicts who steal to obtain money for their addictive habits. If we increase the punishment for burglaries of empty houses, will we cause the addicts to turn to assaults of citizens to gain the money to support their habits?

Consider another example. Bar-Gill and Harel suggest that, while we normally think of the crime rate as *a product of* the factors that effect deterrence—such as the probability and amount of the expected sanction—in fact the crime rate can be *a determinant of* these factors.[161] For example, a higher crime rate makes fewer resources available per crime and reduces the probability of detection; a lower crime rate may have a reverse effect. An increased rate of crime also may delay the imposition of punishment due to congested courts, for example, which causes the future punishment discount to be incrementally higher, thus reducing the perceived punishment "cost"; a decrease in crime rate might have the reverse effect.[162]

---

159 *See*, e.g., Mark Osler, Indirect Harms and Proportionality: The Upside-down World of Federal Sentencing, 74 Miss. L.J. 1, 1–2 (2004) ("Under [Federal Sentencing] Guidelines, a woman who holds just six grams of crack for her own use is assigned a higher offense level (twenty-six) than someone who commits criminal sexual abuse of a minor (offense level twenty-four), a man who commits negligent homicide by recklessly shaking a baby to death (offense level eighteen), a woman caught stealing six million dollars of public money (offense level twenty-four), or the executive who orders employees to dump a truckload of toxic waste knowing that people may die as a result (twenty-four). The crack possessor, in fact, receives the same offense level as that applicable to those who finance terrorist organizations (offense level twenty-six). That's right—possessing crack is treated the same as funding al-Qaeda." (footnotes omitted)

160 Neil Kumar Katyal, Deterrence's Difficulty, 95 Mich. L. Rev. 2385 (1997).

161 *See* Oren Bar-Gill & Alon Harel, Crime Rates and Expected Sanctions: The Economics of Deterrence Revisited, 30 J. Legal Stud. 485, 485–486 (2001).

162 *Id.*

Thus, one might set rules based on present conditions but then, as soon as one's rules begin to have effect, it would cause those conditions to change—and thereby change the calculations that justified the rules! In other words, not only does reliable deterrence analysis require information that is not now available and an understanding of the interrelation among the relevant factors that we do not now have, but it also requires a constant updating of the analysis because the relevant factors themselves are constantly in motion. These are not the circumstances under which it one can have much confidence in setting criminal law doctrine according to attempts at deterrence analysis.

2. The Problem of Comparative Deterrent Effect: The Deterrent Effect Inherent in Other Distributive Principles

All distributions of punishment will have some kind of deterrent effect. The claim of a deterrent distribution is that it can have a greater (efficient) deterrent effect than any other distribution. If one chooses instead to focus on factors that advance another distributive principle, such as those that would optimize rehabilitation or incapacitation of the dangerous, one might well increase the effectiveness of those other crime-control mechanisms but at the expense of the deterrence mechanism. Thus, when deciding between deterrence and incapacitative criterion, for example, one would want to look at their relative crime-control benefit through both deterrence and incapacitation.

A deterrence distribution will have some incapacitative effect, just as an incapacitation distribution will have some deterrent effect. Presumably, the deterrence distribution will produce greater deterrence than the incapacitation distribution, but its actual deterrence advantage is not measured by its total deterrent effect but rather by the extent of its greater deterrent effect over that inherent in the incapacitation distribution. (By the same token, the incapacitation value of an incapacitation distribution as compared to deterrence distribution is not its full incapacitative effect, but only its incapacitative effect beyond the incapacitative effect inherent in a deterrent distribution.)

This comparative point has special implications for deterrence when compared to a desert distribution. Most people see value in having a criminal justice system that does justice, either for instrumentalist or deontological reasons, or both.[163] More on this in Chapters 7 and 8. The point of advocates for a deterrence-based distribution is not that doing justice has no value but that crime reduction through precisely adjusted deterrent punishments has a greater value. Deterrent advocates would concede, presumably, that a desert distribution of punishment would have some deterrent effect. To prefer a deterrence distribution to other distributions, such as a deserts-based distribution, it must be shown that the deterrence distribution provides *greater* efficient deterrence than that inherent in a desert distribution.

But to provide greater deterrence than a desert distribution, the deterrence distribution obviously must deviate from desert. That is, it can only do better than desert where it does something different from desert. However, there is reason to suspect that whenever deterrence deviates from desert, in order to establish a reason to prefer it over desert, it faces special difficulties in producing a net crime-control benefit, both because it is just these deviation-from-desert cases that a deterrence distribution is at its weakest and because the deviation from desert itself can be crimogenic. These are the subjects of Subsections B.3. and B.4. below.

3. The Problem of Deviating from Desert: Deterrence at Its Worst When Doing Its Best

The special difficulties in producing a deterrent effect when deviating from desert arise from several sources. First, citizens are quite unlikely to know the content of the law if the law deviates from their own notions of justice. Several studies have shown that people assume the law is as they think it should be, which is according to their own collective notions of justice. One study examined people's knowledge of criminal law rules that different states formulated differently. Each state in the study took the minority view on at least one of the rules. The study found that citizens in all of the states had generally the same belief as to the existing legal rule, thus were generally ignorant of their state's position on the law. Interestingly, they did not always think the rule was that of the majority view. Their belief in the rule was better predicted by their view about

---

163 *See* Paul H. Robinson & Michael T. Cahill, Law Without Justice: How and Why Criminal Law Deliberately Sacrifices Justice 16 (Oxford 2003).

what the rule should be than by the actual content of the law.[164] Other studies have come to a similar conclusion.[165]

As this makes painfully clear, just making the desert-deviation rule known to those whose behavior it is designed to control becomes a special task for those who seek to manipulate behavior by deterrence-driven changes in the laws. Because people assume the law is as they think it should be, according to their perceptions of shared intuitions of justice, it is in the deviation cases that criminal law has its greatest difficulty in conveying its rule, for it is in the deviation cases where the legal system must affirmatively change the community's existing contrary assumption about what the law provides. Yet it is rare that the law makes the needed special effort to bring the law's nonintuitive rule into the community consciousness.

Further, it is the deviation-from-desert cases in which the system's deterrence-based rules are least likely to be honored during criminal justice adjudication. This is so because those who take the various discretionary roles within the criminal justice system are likely to have the same intuitions about justice as the other members of the community and are likely to commonly allow those intuitions to influence their decisions. Thus, the exercise of discretion by police, prosecutors, judges, and juries, including the operation of jury nullification, will commonly subvert the deviation rule, thus confounding the deterrence program and confusing the deterrent message. Juries may refuse to convict a person, even if the legal rules would seem to call for it, if the jurors believe it would be unjust to do so.[166] Prosecutors may similarly exercise discretion in subversion of rules that produce what they see as an unjust result. Judges, by exercising

---

164 Darley, Carlsmith & Robinson, The Ex Ante Function of the Criminal Law, supra note 18, at 701.

165 In another study, in a survey of New Jersey citizens, it was found that they perceived that the morally appropriate penalty for attempts at crimes was an increasing prison sentence the nearer the perpetrator came to committing the crime. But even an attempt that came in "dangerous proximity" to the completed crime was penalized less that the completed crime. And when asked about the laws of the state in which they lived, they reported that those laws essentially matched their moral intuitions. But they were badly wrong. New Jersey is a Model Penal Code state that grades an attempt at a crime that goes past a substantial step toward its completion as heavily as it grades the completion of the crime. John Darley, Catherine Sanderson & Peter LaMantia, Community Standards for Defining Attempt: Inconsistencies With the Model Penal Code, 39 American Behavioral Scientist 405 (1996).

166 Irwin A. Horowitz, The Effect of Jury Nullification Instructions on Verdicts and Jury Functioning in Criminal Trials, 9 Law and Human Behavior 25 (1985).

sentencing discretion or approving of lenient plea bargains, also may subvert the deterrence-based system's rule, moving in the direction of justice considerations. So if it is these adjudication decisions that the deterrence theorist is counting on to perform the needed deterrence-rule re-education task, the hope seems a vain one. Decision makers are often likely to follow their own intuitions of justice and ignore the law's contrary rule or at least look for ways to minimize the rule's effect. And this kind of distortion in application means that case dispositions often obfuscate rather than clarify the deterrence-based legal rule sought to be conveyed.

It might be thought that desert advocates should applaud these processes that move the system toward desert. The problem is, however, that the exercise of this sort of subversion is likely to be uneven. Some sentencing judges will be influenced by justice considerations and may subvert the unjust rule. Yet, recall, for example, the *McCarty* case cited earlier, in which the judge, specifically to deter others from fleeing police, gave a strikingly high sentence to a person entangled in one of the more far-reaching construals of the felony-murder rule.

To generalize this, juries, prosecutors, and judges may deal more leniently with offenders who are more attractive,[167] racially matched to the jurors,[168] more capable of mustering legal resources to defend themselves or who are otherwise advantaged in public opinion. And, on the other side of the coin, it is also possible for the justice system to accuse and convict those who are regarded as deviants within the community for crimes for which others would not be prosecuted. So one problem with the "under the table" intrusions of justice into a deterrence-based legal system is the unevenness with which it may occur, with the disparity in application creating its own form of injustice.

Another difficulty for the deterrence program in deviating from desert is this: To the extent that the threat of official punishment stems from a legal rule that people perceive as unjust, the offender may discount the threat of punishment in the belief that, no matter what the law on the books says, the lawyers, judges, and jurors in the system would not

---

167 John Clark, The Social Psychology of Jury Nullification, 24 Law and Psychology Review 39 (2000).

168 Erick L. Hill & Jeffrey E. Pfeifer, Nullification Instructions and Juror Guilt Ratings: An Examination of Modern Racism, 16 Contemporary Social Psychology 6 (1992).

in fact be so unjust as to actually enforce the rule as written.[169] They may assume that the system will "slip" to some extent, thus the formal threat must be accordingly discounted.

A final problem with deterrence in deviation cases is that its workings often need to be disguised. If the judge is applying justice considerations in cases in which the deterrence-based legal rules dictate another outcome, then the judge's case dispositions and written explanations are likely to be exercises in obfuscation rather than clarity. This is likely to not only muddle the deterrence message but to also generate contempt for legal rulings, which can have a long-term crimogenic effect. (More on this below and in Chapter 8.)

4. The Problem of Offsetting Crimogenic Effect: The Utility of Desert

The difficulty for deterrence is not only that it will have a difficult time getting a deterrent effect in the cases of deviation from desert—the only cases by which it can show greater deterrent effect than that inherent in a desert distribution—but also that, even if it can produce a greater deterrent effect, its deviation from desert may produce crime-control costs that outweigh the crime-control benefits of its added deterrent effect. The bulk of the discussion of this point must wait until Chapter 8, which, together with Chapter 7, looks closely at desert as a distributive principle. However, to show how these points can be relevant to the assessment of deterrence as a distributive principle, a thumbnail sketch of those arguments are included here. The central point offered is this: by intentionally and regularly doing injustice and failing to do justice in the community's view, a deterrence principle can reduce the system's crime-control effectiveness. Those crime-control costs arise from a variety of sources.

---

169 *See*, e.g., Irwin A. Horowitz, Jury Nullification: The Impact of Judicial Instructions, Arguments, and Challenges on Jury Decision Making, 12 Law & Hum. Behav. 439 (1988) (finding that juries that are informed of the possibility of nullification are more likely to acquit a sympathetic defendant); Michael Kades, Exercising Discretion: A Case Study of Prosecutorial Discretion in the Wisconsin Department of Justice, 25 Am. J. Crim. L. 115 (1997); Robert A. Weninger, Factors Affecting the Prosecution of Rape: A Case Study of Travis County, Texas, 64 Va. L. Rev. 357 (1978); Donna M. Bishop & Charles E. Frazier, Transfer of Juveniles to Criminal Court: A Case Study and Analysis of Prosecutorial Waiver, 5 Notre Dame J.L. Ethics & Pub. Pol'y 281 (1991).

Deviating from a community's intuitions of justice can inspire resistance and subversion among participants—juries, judges, prosecutors, and offenders—where effective criminal justice depends upon acquiescence and cooperation (a broader form of the argument in Section B.3. above). Relatedly, some of the system's power to control conduct derives from its potential to stigmatize violators. With some persons this is a more powerful, yet essentially cost-free mechanism, than the system's official sanction. Yet the system's ability to stigmatize depends upon it having moral credibility with the community; for a violation to trigger stigmatization, the law must have earned a reputation for accurately assessing what violations do and do not deserve condemnation. Liability and punishment rules that deviate from a community's shared intuitions of justice undermine that reputation.

The system's intentional and regular deviations from desert also undermine efficient crime control because they limit law's access to one of the most powerful forces for gaining compliance: social influence. The greatest power to gain compliance with society's rules of prescribed conduct may lie not in the threat of official criminal sanction but rather in the influence of the intertwined forces of social and individual moral control. The networks of interpersonal relationships in which people find themselves, the social norms and prohibitions shared among those relationships and transmitted through those social networks, and the internalization by individuals of those norms and moral precepts.

The law is not irrelevant to these social and personal forces. Criminal law, in particular, plays a central role in creating and maintaining the social consensus necessary for sustaining moral norms. In fact, in a society as diverse as ours, the criminal law may be the only society-wide mechanism that transcends cultural and ethnic differences. Thus, the criminal law's most important real-world effect may be its ability to assist in the building, shaping, and maintaining of these norms and moral principles. It can contribute to and harness the compliance-producing power of interpersonal relationships and personal morality. Nevertheless, a criminal justice system that intentionally and regularly does injustice and fails to do justice diminishes its moral credibility with the community and thereby its ability to influence conduct by shaping these powerful norms.

The criminal law also can effect gaining compliance with its commands through another mechanism. If it earns a reputation as a reliable statement of what the community perceives as condemnable, people are more likely to defer to its commands as morally authoritative in those borderline cases in which the propriety of certain conduct is unsettled or ambiguous in the mind of the actor. The importance of this role should not be underestimated. In a society with the complex interdependencies characteristic of ours, an apparently harmless action can have destructive consequences. When the action is criminalized by the legal system, one would want the citizen to "respect the law" in such an instance even though he or she does not immediately intuit why that action is banned. Such deference will be facilitated if citizens are disposed to believe that the law is an accurate guide to appropriate prudential and moral behavior.

The extent of the criminal law's effectiveness in all these respects—in avoiding resistance and subversion of an unjust system; in bringing the power of stigmatization to bear; in facilitating, communicating, and maintaining societal consensus on what is and is not condemnable; and in gaining compliance in borderline cases through deference to its moral authority—depends to a great extent on the degree to which the criminal law has earned moral credibility with the citizens governed by it. Thus, the criminal law's moral credibility is essential to effective crime control and is enhanced if the distribution of criminal liability is perceived as "doing justice," that is, if it assigns liability and punishment in ways that the community perceives as consistent with their shared intuitions of justice. Conversely, the system's moral credibility, and therefore its crime control effectiveness, is undermined by a distribution of liability that deviates from community perceptions of just desert.

To summarize, a deterrence-based distribution potentially can forfeit any crime-control gains when that distribution undermines the system's moral credibility with the community it governs. That is, even if one assumes for the sake of argument that there would be some greater deterrent effect of a deterrence-based distribution of punishment over a desert-based distribution of punishment, one would still question whether this marginal benefit exceeds the loses that the use of a deterrence-based system would incur. When combined with the problems of unavailable information and complexity discussed above, one might conclude that there is too much danger and too little payoff in a deterrence distributive principle to justify its adoption.

CHAPTER 5

Rehabilitation

Would rehabilitation make a good distributive principle for liability and punishment? Like special deterrence, it operates upon the offender at hand (rather than the population at large, as general deterrence does), to reduce the future inclination to commit an offense. However, it seeks to alter that choice not through the deterrent threat of punishment but by altering the person's nature, capacities, or inclinations such that the person will be uninclined, or at least less inclined, to want to commit the offense. Rehabilitation also is different from deterrence in that some people believe it to have a value beyond its crime-control utility. It can allow an offender to live a more meaningful and fulfilling life, thereby providing not only a societal but also a personal benefit.

As with deterrence, there is some question about the effectiveness of rehabilitation, at least under currently available programs. The success rate of rehabilitation programs is typically quite modest and commonly limited to a narrow range of offenders and offenses.[170] Section A looks

---

170 *See* generally Steve Aos, Marna Miller & Elizabeth Drake, Washington State Institute for Public Policy, Evidence-Based Public Policy Options to Reduce Future Prison Construction, Criminal Justice Costs, and Crime Rates 9 (2007); D. A. Andrews et al., Does Correctional Treatment Work? A Clinically Relevant and a Psychologically Informed Meta-analysis, 28 Criminology 369 (1990).

more carefully at when rehabilitation works and when it does not. With this background, Section B considers the question of whether rehabilitation would make an attractive distributive principle for criminal liability and punishment.

A. Does Rehabilitation Work?

Claims that "nothing works" overstate the case. Some rehabilitation programs have had some success. Where successful, the programs typically have achieved modest reductions in recidivism.

1. Programs for a General Prison Population

Three main areas have experienced some success on general prisoner populations: educational programs, vocational and work programs, and therapy. In addition, drug rehabilitation has been effective in certain instances for rehabilitating incarcerated offenders whose criminal behavior stems from addiction.[171]

Prison education programs have been an integral part of American prisons since the late nineteenth century. By 2000, more than 80 percent of private prisons, 90 percent of state prisons, and 92 percent of federal prisons offered some form of education program. In addition to almost ubiquitous basic education programs, generally focusing on literacy, the vast majority of prisons now offer secondary education, geared toward prisoners receiving the General Education Development (GED) certificate.[172] Inmates who receive their GED may be more employable upon leaving prison.

Education programs have remained staples in part because they are effective. Prisoners who take advantage of educational opportunities, particularly secondary and college level programs have lower rates of recidivism.[173] (Indeed, not having a high-school diploma or equivalent is a risk factor for incarceration. A survey of state and federal prisons

---

171 Elizabeth Drake, Washington State Institute for Public Policy, Washington's Drug Offender Sentencing Alternative: An Update on Recidivism Findings (2006).

172 James J. Stephan & Jennifer C. Karberg, Bureau of Justice Statistics, Census of State and Federal Adult Correctional Facilities 10 (2000).

173 Doris Layton MacKenzie, What Works in Corrections: Reducing the Criminal Activities of Offenders and Delinquents 83–84 (2006).

in 1997 found that 41 percent of inmates had not completed high school or its equivalent, compared with 18 percent of the general adult population.[174])

How effective education is in reducing recidivism is somewhat unclear. As educational programs are available to all prisoners, little research has been done using control groups. Instead, comparisons are generally made between prisoners who choose to participate against those who choose not to. Thus, the resulting difference in recidivism between the two groups may reflect a difference in the prisoners making the choice to participate rather than reflecting an effect of the educational program itself.

Vocational programs, correctional industries, and work-release also have been an important part of correctional offerings. Vocational programs involve teaching in a classroom setting the skills needed for particular jobs. Correctional industries are not classes but rather allow inmates to work while in prison, during which they may acquire job skills. Work-release programs integrate the soon-to-be released offender into a job as a transition back into the community. In lieu of general educational attainment, these programs focus on giving prisoners the opportunity to acquire and improve marketable skills. In addition, the prisoners' work can create valuable goods for the government and offset prison costs.[175] Like educational programs, these opportunities are routinely found in both state and federal prisons, with around 91 percent of all correctional facilities having some such program.[176]

Part of the appeal of such vocational training and work programs is to give prisoners an alternative to illegal means of obtaining money. This can be particularly useful for offenders who have not previously held gainful, regular employment. For prisoners who make rational calculations about engaging in legal versus illegal activities for their economic survival, these programs may change the calculus by creating more appealing lawful options. It is unclear, however, what percentage of inmates actually makes such rational calculations.

Vocational training may reduce recidivism, but the evidence is unclear. At the state level, vocational and work programs have shown

174 Catherine Wolf Harlow, Bureau of Justice Statistics, Special Report: Education and Correctional Populations 1 (Revised April 2003).
175 Timothy J. Flanagan, Prison Labor and Industry, in The American Prison (Lynne I. Goodstein & Doris L. MacKenzie, eds. 1989).
176 Stephan & Karberg, Census, *supra* note 172, at 10.

either no differences in recidivism or only modest differences.[177] In the federal system, prison work programs correlate with reduced recidivism by 24 percent and increased employment after release by 14 percent.[178] However, reliable data is somewhat lacking, again because the available studies tend to lack a control group. Where vocational programs exist, they typically are open to all qualifying inmates, leaving most studies to compare the self-selecting groups of inmates who choose to participate against those who chose not to participate. The programs may aid individual prisoners, but this success may not be widespread.

A third avenue that can create successful rehabilitation outcomes is the employment of psychological services for inmates. This approach builds on research indicating that criminal conduct often is at least in part the result of psychological or psychiatric conditions. Offenders as a population show greater than average incidence of a host of disorders.[179] These can contribute to the inability of the offender to conform his actions to the requirements of the law. By addressing these issues, offenders may be better equipped to reintegrate into society and avoid future criminality.

On the psychology side, the cognitive-behavioral therapy (CBT) approach, in particular, has been shown to reduce recidivism in certain circumstances.[180] CBT is a widely accepted and commonly employed method of psychotherapy that generally focuses on the interaction among cognition, emotion, and action to achieve behavioral modification.[181] Research indicates that CBT can be particularly successful at reducing re-offending when employed as a bridge between the end of imprisonment and reintegration into society.[182] However, even when this program is successful, it does not necessarily prevent all future criminality; it may instead lead to a reduction of criminal behavior as offenders change behavior and then attempt, not always successfully, to maintain the

---

177 MacKenzie, What Works, *supra* note 173, at 107.

178 UNICOR Federal Prison Industries, Inc., The Annual Report: 2002 9 (2002), *available at* http://www.unicor.gov/information/publications/pdfs/corporate/CATAR2002.pdf.

179 Committee on Community Supervision and Desistance from Crime, National Research Council, Parole, Desistance from Crime, and Community Integration 4–14 (Prepublication copy, 2007).

180 *Id.* at 4-6-4-7.

181 *See* generally, Richard F. Farmer & Alexander L. Chapman, Behavioral Interventions in Cognitive Behavior Therapy: Practical Guidance for Putting Theory Into Action (2007).

182 National Research Council, *supra* note 179, at ES-2, 4–7.

behavior change. Where the criminal behavior is motivated in whole or in part by a psychiatric disorder, CBT may not be effective. Finally, as is often the case with rehabilitation programs, a deficit of methodologically sound research on the actual effect of CBT is found.

There may be reason to believe that combining education, training, and therapy would be the most productive means of reducing recidivism, but yet again, research is lacking. Though various rehabilitation strategies may function to reduce future criminality, it remains true that each strategy rehabilitates only a fraction of offenders. For a wide variety of offenders, no programs exist that can be relied upon to reduce recidivism in even modest terms.

2. Programs Targeting Specific Offenders, In and Out of Prison: Drug Users and Sexual Offenders

The previous subsection describes the classic rehabilitation efforts for prisoners generally. Of course, programs commonly are available to non-incarcerated offenders as well. In dealing with this larger population, however, the available programs typically target specific offender groups, in particular drug users and sexual offenders. Below is sketched the current practice in dealing with these two groups of offenders, both in and out of prison.

a. Drug Users

Prisoners incarcerated for drug offenses represent a large portion of all inmates. In 2003, 55 percent of federal prisoners and an estimated 20 percent of state prisoners were incarcerated for drug offenses.[183] The vast majority of these offenders are drug users. Drug use is also linked to the commission of violent crimes, property crimes, and public disorder offenses. State prisoners report drug use at the time of committing their offense in over a quarter of violent and public disorder crimes and nearly 40 percent of property crimes.[184] For all crimes, more than half of both state and federal prisoners report drug use in the prior month, and more

---

183 Bureau of Justice Statistics, Bulletin: Prisoners in 2005 9–10 (November 2006).
184 Christopher Mumola & Jennifer Karberg, Bureau of Justice Statistics, Drug Use and Dependence: State and Federal Prisoners, 2004 5 (Revised 2007).

than 17 percent committed their crime to pay for narcotics.[185] Perhaps most strikingly, 53.4 percent of state prisoners and 45.5 percent of federal prisoners suffer from drug dependence, abuse, or both.[186] Further, 84 percent of state and 75 percent of federal prisoners with drug use or dependency have prior criminal records; slightly over one-quarter had between three and five prior convictions.[187] Given the implications of drug use and dependency, successful drug rehabilitation programs could offer the hope of significantly reducing recidivism (and, if extended to potential offenders, might avoid the original offending).

Programs for persons coping with addiction include among others: drug courts, pharmacological treatment, outpatient drug treatment, residential drug treatment, and prison-based therapeutic community treatment.

Drug courts provide a specialized alternative to the traditional criminal justice system for drug offenders and offenders with drug dependency, providing mandated treatment in lieu of traditional penal sanctions. There are nearly 1,700 such courts in the United States. They vary in the composition and type of treatment offered. While rigorous data on the effectiveness of drug courts is limited,[188] evidence suggests that such courts can reduce recidivism for graduates, particularly when combined with postrelease treatment.[189] One meta-analysis found a 26 percent reduction in recidivism across all drug court studies, although only a 14 percent reduction in the two most methodologically rigorous studies.[190]

Pharmacological programs are generally used for opiate addicts. Methadone treatment uses a synthetic opiate to stabilize patients by blocking the effects of illicit opiates while reducing withdrawal symptoms and opiate cravings. Another treatment is the use of naltrexone, an antagonist that rather than providing a substitution for the opiate removes the euphoria associated with it. This treatment is only effective for individuals who have ceased using any opiate and is generally considered effective only for individuals who are highly motivated to

---

185 *Id.* at 2, 6.
186 Mumola & Karberg, Drug Use and Dependence, *supra* note 184, at 1.
187 *Id.* at 7.
188 David B. Wilson, Ojmarrh Mitchell & Doris L. McKenzie, A Systematic Review of Drug Court Effects on Recidivism, 2 J. Experimental Crim. 459, 471–475 (2006).
189 National Institute of Justice, Drug Courts: The Second Decade 2–3 (2006).
190 *See* Wilson, Mitchell & McKenzie, Systematic Review, *supra* note 188, at 479.

overcome their addiction.[191] A therapy program generally accompanies these treatments.

Perhaps the most promising response to ending drug use and related criminality is the therapeutic community approach. This model functions by establishing a "community" to help individuals overcome substance abuse. Treatment generally occurs in stages at a drug-free residential facility, with an emphasis on both the use of group therapy and individual self-help. The principle is to use the peer-reinforcement power of the community of individuals in recovery as well as that of staff to facilitate the learning and assimilation of substance-free social norms.[192] In the prison setting, the therapeutic community approach begins with removing participants from the general prison population to undergo intensive addiction therapy. Ideally, the in-prison treatment is followed by therapy coupled with work release in the transitional, pre-release phase, and then monitoring and therapy in the post-release aftercare phase.[193] A best-practice model established in Delaware found significant improvements in both the likelihood of being drug free and re-arrest free after five years for those who completed a therapeutic community program. In perhaps a measure of effectiveness of the different components, those who completed the program and participated in aftercare were more likely to remain drug and arrest free than those who completed the in-prison component only, while those who completed the in-prison program had better outcomes in both categories than program dropouts, who, in turn, fared better than those who did not participate at all.[194] Even with the positive outcomes, however, nearly 50 percent of the aftercare group would be expected to be rearrested within five years, but this is compared with nearly 75 percent of those receiving no treatment.[195] Thus, while reductions in recidivism can be achieved, the recidivism rates for such offenders remain high.

---

191 Betty Tai & Jack Blaine, Naltrexone: An Antagonist Therapy for Heroin Addiction, National Institute on Drug Abuse, National Institutes of Health (1997), *available at* http://www.nida.nih.gov/MeetSum/naltrexone.html.
192 National Institute on Drug Abuse, Research Report Series, Therapeutic Community 1 (2002).
193 James A. Inciardi, Steven S. MartIn & Clifford A. ButzIn, Five-Year Outcomes of Therapeutic Community Treatment of Drug-Involved Offenders after Release from Prison, 50 Crime & Delinquency 88, 91–92 (2004).
194 *Id.* at 101.
195 *Id.*

b. Sexual Offenders

Treatment for sexual offenders similarly can be effective for targeted populations. Like drug offenders, this group is not homogenous. Not every sex offender has a sexual disorder, thus treatment is not always a viable option.[196] For offenders whose criminality is the result at least in part of a sexual disorder, some may benefit from therapy or treatment.

On the treatment side, chemical or medical castration can be employed to incapacitate the offender or potential-offender from the commission of sex crimes. This approach, used exclusively for male offenders, reduces testosterone levels, either through pharmacological agents or by removing the testes. This leads to a reduction or removal of the sexual gratification gained from the offense, thus removing the root of the offense. While surgical castration has the most pronounced effect on recidivism, it is controversial and only used in the United States with the offender's consent and, therefore, has limited application. Chemical castration is also effective, reducing recidivism to an estimated 12 percent,[197] without the same degree of ethical and constitutional issues faced by surgical castration.

Also effective for some sex offenders with sexual disorders are therapeutic approaches. CBT and relapse prevention have been estimated to reduce recidivism to around 9 percent.[198] It is difficult to compare these recidivism rates with the hormonal therapy noted, however, because the hormonal approach is generally offered outside the correctional context and only for treatment of specific sexual disorders (generally pedophilia and exhibitionism), while therapeutic responses have mostly been studied in prison settings with violent sexual offenders also included.[199] What is shown, nevertheless, is that both responses may effect reductions in offense rates for potential sex offenders and re-offenders.

c. Conclusion

Despite the existence of particular rehabilitation programs that can benefit individual offenders or groups of offenders, even the most successful

---

196 *See* MacKenzie, What Works, *supra* note 173, at 140.
197 *Id.* at 162.
198 *Id.*
199 *Id.*

programs demonstrate only modest success rates, typically reducing the likelihood of reoffending by less than 10 or 15 percent.[200] Of course, even such a modest success rate can be significant if one considers the societal cost of recidivism. Every offense avoided saves not only the costs associated with the harm of the offense but also the costs associated with punishment, which can be more than $30,000 per year for an incarcerated offender.[201] In other words, it might well be cost-efficient to run rehabilitation programs even if their success rates are quite modest.

Unfortunately, there has been little systematic evaluation of the success of different rehabilitation programs.[202] Much of what we think we know about the effectiveness of programs is based upon data gleaned from studies lacking the methodological rigor that would lead to reliable conclusions. Further, the absence of truly effective rehabilitation programs may be because the programs typically are not sufficiently tailored to the individual rehabilitation needs of each individual within a diverse population. If this is the case, for a rehabilitation regime to be broadly successful, it may have to be individually tailored and therefore may be significantly more costly than current programs.

B. Rehabilitation as a Distributive Principle

Perhaps because of skepticism about its effectiveness, there often is little support for the use of rehabilitation as a distributive principle. Few existing American codes give significant deference to it. Indeed, some explicitly reject it as a distributive principle,[203] while others do so implicitly. The Model Penal Code, for example, omits rehabilitation from its list of the "general purposes of the provisions governing the definition of offenses."[204]

---

200 *See* Aos, Miller & Drake, Evidence-Based Public Policy Options, *supra* note 170, at 9. *See* generally, MacKenzie, What Works, *supra* note 173.
201 *See* James J. Stephan, Bureau of Justice Statistics, State Prison Expenditures, 2001 3 (2004).
202 *See* generally MacKenzie, What Works, *supra* note 173.
203 The Federal Sentencing Reform Act of 1984, for example, in giving instructions for the creation of the U.S. Sentencing Guidelines, directs that "The Commission shall insure that the guidelines reflect the inappropriateness of imposing a sentence to a term of imprisonment for the purpose of rehabilitating the defendant." 28 U.S.C. §994(k) (Supp. III 1985).
204 *See* Model Penal Code §1.02(1) (1985). *See also* California Uniform Sentencing Act, Cal. Penal Code §1170(a)(1) (West 1985 & Supp. 1987) ("The legislature finds and declares that the purpose of imprisonment for crime is punishment.").

Commentators also have suggested that rehabilitation should not be considered in distributing sanctions because of its potential immorality and its tendency to invite abusive punishment in the guise of therapy.[205]

But even if one assumes for the sake of argument that rehabilitation programs are effective and cost-efficient, it does not follow that rehabilitation would be a desirable distributive principle for liability and punishment. For example, rehabilitation as the distributive principle would give no justification for maintaining control over an offender for whom rehabilitation is not possible. On the other hand, releasing all offenders who cannot be rehabilitated would seem to be an obviously intolerable arrangement, for it would frustrate both crime control and deontological desert goals to no beneficial effect.

Perhaps rehabilitation is difficult to justify as a distributive principle on its own but might have some useful role when combined with another distributive principle. For example, one might combine rehabilitation with incapacitation to serve as a hybrid distributive principle. That is, where rehabilitation is not possible, one could shift to an incapacitation principle, taking jurisdiction over the offender for as long as he was dangerous. Of course, the success of such a system would depend upon our ability to identify if and when an offender is rehabilitated, an ability that current behavioral science may not yet have attained. With our current limited abilities, such a distributive hybrid might end up being primarily a distributive principle of incapacitation rather than rehabilitation. More on this in Chapters 10 and 11.

Another argument against using rehabilitation as a distributive principle is found in the fact that one need not use it as such to rehabilitate offenders. Punishment distributed according to any other principle nonetheless would provide an opportunity to rehabilitate an offender, if such is possible. One might attempt adopt a correctional policy of rehabilitating offenders whenever possible, without using rehabilitation to determine how long the period of criminal justice control would be. That is, one might promote rehabilitation as much by setting it as the *correctional system's primary operating policy* than as adopting it as the *criminal justice system's distributive principle*.

---

205 *See*, e.g., Francis A. Allen, The Borderland of Criminal Justice 25–41 (1964); Norval Morris, The Future of Imprisonment: Towards a Punitive Philosophy, 72 Mich. L. Rev. 1161, 1174 (1974).

CHAPTER 6

Incapacitation of the Dangerous

Incapacitation as a distributive principle does not suffer the concerns about ineffectiveness that dog both deterrence and rehabilitation. It clearly is possible to prevent future crimes by incapacitating potential offenders, commonly by incarceration, although nonincarcerative measures also can be effective. Concerns about incapacitation as a distributive principle are of a different sort. Because the current system does so poorly in predicting future dangerousness, it detains many nondangerous persons and fails to detain many dangerous. It thus can be criticized for both (1) being unfair and wasteful in detaining those who would not commit crimes and (2) failing to provide effective protection for society in its failure to detain those who would commit crimes. Both of these difficulties are exacerbated by the current practice of obscuring the nature of preventive detention efforts by dressing them up as if they were the imposition of punishment for past offense, that is, by cloaking preventive detention as if it were criminal justice. Using the criminal justice system as the preventive detention mechanism—where the criminal justice system is popularly conceived of as punishing offenders for what they have done—creates the felt need to make the preventive detention look like deserved punishment. The disguise efforts, however, tend to exaggerate the ineffectiveness and inaccuracies of the preventive detention program.

Section A discusses how and why the current system's preventive detention measures are cloaked as criminal justice. Section B shows the justice problems that arise from this. These justice problems obviously cause unfairness to the individual defendant but the intentional and regular injustice also undermine the system's moral credibility with the community and thereby undermine its crime-control effectiveness. Such cloaking also produces preventive detention problems, illustrated in Section C. Section D explores the advantages that might be available if the preventive detention and criminal justice functions were segregated. This would mean barring incapacitation as a distributive principle *for the criminal justice system* in favor of establishing an open and explicit civil preventive detention system.[206]

A. Cloaking Preventive Detention as Criminal Justice

Laypersons have traditionally thought of the criminal justice system as being in the business of doing justice: punishing offenders for the crimes they commit.[207] Yet during the past several decades, much of the justice system's focus has shifted from punishing past crimes to preventing future violations through the incarceration and control of dangerous offenders. Habitual-offender statutes, such as "three-strikes" laws, authorize life sentences for repeat offenders.[208] Jurisdictional reforms have

---

206 Much of this chapter is derived from Paul H. Robinson, Punishing Dangerousness: Cloaking Preventative Detention as Criminal Justice, 114 Harv. L. Rev. 1429 (2001) [Hereinafter Robinson, Dangerousness].

207 Modern academics have become comfortable with using nondesert crime-control principles, such as deterrence and the incapacitation of dangerous people, to govern the distribution of criminal punishment. Laypersons, however, generally do not share this perspective. *See*, e.g., John M. Darley, Kevin M. Carlsmith & Paul H. Robinson, Incapacitation and Just Deserts as Motives for Punishment, 24 Law & Hum. Behav. 659, 659 (2000).

208 *See*, e.g., 18 U.S.C. §3559 (1994) (requiring life imprisonment on a third serious violent felony conviction); Mont. Code Ann. §46-18-219 (1999) (requiring life imprisonment without the possibility of release after a second or third felony conviction, depending on the felonies committed); *see* generally John Clark, James Austin & D. Alan Henry, "Three Strikes and You're Out": A Review of State Legislation 9–10 (Nat'l Inst. of Justice: Research in Brief, NJC 165369, 1997) (noting that many states have expanded preexisting repeat-offender statutes); Nat'l Conference of State Legislators, "Three Strikes" Sentencing Laws 24 (1999) (noting that between 1993 and 1999, twenty-four states and the federal government enacted "three-strikes" laws and that nearly all states have some type of sentence enhancement applicable to habitual offenders).

decreased the age at which juveniles may be tried as adults.[209] Gang membership and recruitment are now punished.[210] "Megan's Law" statutes

---

The protective rationale for these laws is evident in the legislative history of the federal three-strikes statute. After citing the "problem [of] a significant percentage of crimes . . . committed by people who previously have committed crimes" and concluding that, to date, "the response of the criminal justice system to both violent crime and recidivism has been inadequate," the Report of the House of Representatives states that the purpose of the legislation is "to take the Nation's most dangerous recidivist criminals off the streets and imprison them for life." H.R. Rep. No. 103-463, reprinted in H.R. 3981, 103d Cong., at 3–4 (codified at 18 U.S.C. §3559 (1994)). Senate Majority Leader Trent Lott explained the need for the federal legislation by noting that "there is no doubt that a small hardened group of criminals commit most of the violent crimes in this country" and that "many of the people involved in these crimes are released again and again because of the 'revolving door' of the prison system." 139 Cong. Rec. 27,822–823 (1993).

209 Legislative histories provide evidence of the protective rationale underlying these reforms. The report for the 1994 California legislation, for example, explains the need for lowering the age of criminal prosecution from sixteen to fourteen by noting that "the public is legitimately concerned that crimes of violence committed by juveniles are increasing in number and in terms of the level of violence," and concluding that the legislation "is a rational response to the legitimate public desire to address what is a serious problem." A.B. 560, 1993-1994 Leg., Reg. Sess. (Cal. 1994) (enacted). The Congressional Research Service similarly summarizes the rationale for such state legislation: "locking up dangerous kids so that they will not commit further crimes." Cong. Research Serv., Pub. No. 95-1152, Juveniles in the Adult Criminal Justice System: An Overview 5 (1995). Federal legislation that the House passed and that is pending in the Senate would reduce the age of presumptive adult prosecution to fourteen and would allow prosecution at thirteen for violent offenses and drug offenses. The "Background and Need for the Legislation" section of the bill indicates that "in America today no population poses a larger threat to public safety than juvenile criminals." H.R. Rep. No. 105-86, at 14 (1997).

210 See, e.g., Nev. Rev. Stat. 193.168 (1999) (enhancing criminal penalties for felonies committed to promote criminal gang activities); Okla. Stat. Ann. tit. 21, §§856(D)-(F) (West Supp. 2000) (creating a crime encompassing gang recruitment activities); Cal. Penal Code §186.22(a) (West Supp. 2001) (providing special penalties for facilitating gang crime); see generally Bart H. Rubin, Note, Hail, Hail, The Gangs Are All Here: Why New York Should Adopt a Comprehensive Anti-Gang Statute, 66 Fordham L. Rev. 2033 (1998) (discussing the attributes of anti-gang statutes). The California statute is part of the state's Street Terrorism and Enforcement Prevention Act, which was a response to "a state of crisis which has been caused by violent street gangs whose members threaten, terrorize, and commit a multitude of crimes against the peaceful citizens of their neighborhoods." Cal. Penal Code 186.21 (West Supp. 1998).

This list of recent reforms focusing on dangerousness is not exhaustive. Many death penalty provisions also use dangerousness explicitly as a ground for imposing the death penalty rather than life imprisonment. See, e.g., Va. Code Ann. §19.2-264.2 (Michie 2000); Wash. Rev. Code Ann. §10.95.070(8) (West Supp. 1999); Wyo. Stat. Ann. §6-2-102(h)(xi) (Michie 1999). Sometimes lack of dangerousness is a mitigating factor in death penalty cases. See, e.g., Md. Code Ann., Crimes and Punishments §413(g)(7) (1996). Occasionally criminal history is considered in sentencing instead of dangerousness. See, e.g., Ark. Code Ann. §5-4-604(31) (Michie 1997); Okla. Stat. tit. 21, §701.12(1) (1991); Cal. Penal Code §190.3(c) (West 1999); see also

require community notification of convicted sex offenders.[211] "Sexual predator" statutes provide for the detention of sexual offenders who remain dangerous at the conclusion of their criminal commitment.[212] And sentencing guidelines commonly dramatically increase the sentence of offenders with criminal histories because such offenders are seen as the most likely to commit future crimes.[213] These reforms boast as their common denominator greater official control over dangerous persons, a rationale readily apparent from each reform's legislative history.[214]

Although the individual legislative histories may be open about the preventive rationale that has motivated each of the reforms, the system's general shift from punishment toward prevention has not been

---

People v. Hawkins, 897 P.2d 574, 597 (1995) (finding that it was not error for a prosecutor to argue that the future dangerousness of the defendant was a factor weighing in favor of the death penalty). Correctional officers are sometimes required to exclude allegedly dangerous offenders from certain release programs. N.Y. Legis. Exec. Order 5.1 (1996). Some shaming penalties are designed to "prevent future dangerous acts, rather than punish past action." Art Hubacher, Every Picture Tells a Story: Is Kansas City's "John TV" Constitutional?, 46 U. Kan. L. Rev. 551, 587 (1998) (internal quotation marks omitted).

211 Federal legislation creates financial incentives for states to enact such sexual offender registration statutes. 42 U.S.C. §§14071(g), (i). Most states have done so. See, e.g., Nat'l Inst. of Justice, Sex Offender Community Notification I (Feb. 1997).

212 Washington was the first state to pass such a law. See Wash. Rev. Code §71.09 (1992). Other states have since enacted similar laws. See, e.g., Iowa Code §901A.1 et seq.; Kan. Stat. Ann. §59-29a01 (1994); Minn. Stat. §§253B.18,.185 (1994); Wis. Stat. Ann. §980 (West 1998). The constitutionality of the Kansas statute was challenged in December 1996. See Kansas v. Hendricks, 521 U.S. 346, 350 (1997) (sustaining the act). At that time, 6 states had such statutes—the other 5 being Arizona, California, Minnesota, Washington, and Wisconsin— and 38 states, including New Jersey and New York, filed amicus briefs successfully urging the Justices to uphold the law. Id. at 371.

The promulgation of the Kansas statute was based on a finding that "sexually violent predators generally have anti-social personality features which are unamenable to existing mental illness treatment modalities[,] and those features render them likely to engage in sexually violent behavior[,] and that sexually violent predator' likelihood of engaging in repeat acts of predatory sexual violence is high." Kan. Stat. Ann. §59-29a01 (1994).

213 See, e.g., U.S. Sentencing Guidelines Manual ch. 4, pt. A (1998–99); id. at ch. 5, pt. A (providing guideline sentences as a function of "Offense Level" and "Criminal History Category"); Ariz. Rev. Stat. §16-90-801(b)(1) (1995); Del. Code Ann. tit. II, §6580(c)(1) (1995); Wash. Rev. Code Ann. §9.94A.010(1) (West 1985).

The rationale for heavy reliance upon criminal history in sentencing guidelines is its effectiveness in incapacitating dangerous offenders. As the Guidelines Manual of the United States Sentencing Commission explains, "the specific factors included in [the calculation of the Criminal History Category] are consistent with the extant empirical research assessing correlates of recidivism and patterns of career criminal behavior." U.S. Sentencing Guidelines Manual 289 (1999).

214 See supra notes 208–213.

accompanied by a corresponding shift in how the system presents itself. The system still alleges that it is doing criminal "justice" and imposing "punishment." Yet it is logically impossible to "punish dangerousness," at least within the normal meaning of those terms. To "punish" is "to cause (a person) to undergo pain, loss, or suffering for a crime or wrongdoing"[215]—therefore, punishment can only exist in relation to a past wrong. "Dangerous" means "likely to cause injury, pain, etc."[216]—that is, dangerousness describes a threat of future harm. One can "restrain," "detain," or "incapacitate" a dangerous person, but one cannot logically "punish" dangerousness.

1. The Practical Value to Reformers of Creating Desert-Dangerousness Ambiguity

Why obscure the shift to preventive detention? Why the wish to keep the old criminal "punishment" facade? If reformers want to detain dangerous offenders, why not adopt a system that is open about its preventive detention nature? Most jurisdictions allow civil commitment of persons who are dangerous because of mental illness, drug dependency, or contagious disease.[217] Why is there reluctance to similarly preventively detain offenders who are dangerous for other reasons or who remain dangerous at the conclusion of their deserved criminal terms of imprisonment?

The intense controversy surrounding the preventive detention legislation of the 1960s may help to explain the reluctance.[218] Critics denounced the legislation as "Clockwork Orange"[219] and "'Alice in Wonderland' justice"

---

215 Webster's New World College Dictionary 1180 (2nd ed. 1959) (emphasis added).

216 *Id.* at 372.

217 *See* Paul H. Robinson, Foreword: The Criminal-Civil Distinction and Dangerous Blameless Offenders, 83 J. Crim. L. & Criminology 693, 711–714 & notes 57–68 (1993).

218 For a chronological list of preventive detention enactments, *see* Barbara Gottlieb, The Pretrial Processing of "Dangerous" Defendants: A Comparative Analysis of State Laws (Nat'l Inst. of Justice Study, 1984), reprinted in Report on Bail Reform Act of 1984, H.R. Rep. No. 98-121, app. A, at 90. The first statutes appeared in Alaska and Delaware in 1967, Maryland and South Carolina in 1969, Vermont in 1967 and 1969, and the District of Columbia in 1970. Despite the constitutional approval of pretrial preventive detention, United States v. Edwards, 430 A.2d 1321, 1343 (D.C. 1981), cert. denied, 455 U.S. 1022 (1982), many jurisdictions have refused to enact such a system. The 24 states authorizing pretrial detention are listed in Gottlieb, *supra* note 218, at 76.

219 Glen Elsasser, U.S. Defends Pretrial Jailings of Suspects Seen as Dangerous, Chi. Trib., Jan. 22, 1987, 1, at 16 (quoting critics).

in which the punishment precedes the offense and as introducing a "police state" and "fostering tyranny." Opponents described it as "intellectually dishonest," characterized it as "one of the most tragic mistakes we as a society could make," and feared that it "would change the complexion of American justice." Preventive detention was "simply not the American way."[220]

A large part of the perceived problem with the 1960s preventive detention legislation was that it provided pretrial preventive detention. In contrast, most current reforms provide preventive detention only after trial and conviction, an important difference. Yet the primary criticism of pretrial preventive detention—that the sentence precedes the trial—can also be applied to the postconviction preventive detention reforms. Detention for longer than the deserved term of imprisonment is justified as preventing predicted future crimes. Such detention not only punishes an offense for which the detainee has not yet been convicted but indeed punishes for an offense that he has not yet committed.

But the ability to "punish" the uncommitted crime, and thereby prevent it, is the political genius of the current system's cloaking of preventive detention as criminal justice. By obscuring the preventive nature of the liability and sentence, by making it appear not so entirely different from a criminal justice system of deserved punishment, the preventive detention controversy can be avoided.

The practical advantage of such cloaking lies in the opportunity it provides to bypass the logical restrictions on preventive detention. First, if the justification for detention is dangerousness, then logically the government ought to be required periodically to prove the detainee's continuing dangerousness. If the dangerousness disappears, so does the justification for detention. However, if the detention is characterized as deserved punishment for a past offense, there is little reason once a sentence is imposed to revisit the justification for the detention. The factors relevant to determining deserved punishment may be weighed at the time of sentencing: the offender's conduct, state of mind, and capacities at the time of the offense, and the resulting harm or evil. Characterizing preventive detention as deserved punishment obscures the need for periodic review.

---

220 For authorities, *see* Robinson, Dangerousness, *supra* note 206, at 1444–1445.

Second, if a person is detained for society's benefit rather than as deserved punishment, the conditions of detention ought not be punitive. The preventive detainee is not being punished but rather is suffering an intrusion of liberty for the benefit of society. The mentally ill, drug-dependent, or contagious disease detainee logically ought to and often does enjoy better conditions than the person suffering punishment. In contrast, if confinement serves to impose deserved punishment, the offender has little justification for complaining about punitive conditions. One of the points of imprisonment is, within the bounds of human dignity, to induce suffering. By cloaking preventive detention as deserved punishment, the system avoids having to justify its failure to provide nonpunitive conditions of preventive detention.

Third, prevention-justified restraint should logically be limited to the minimum required to ensure the community's safety. If house arrest, an ankle bracelet, drug therapy, or other alternatives to incarceration provide adequate protection, then greater levels of restraint cannot be justified. No such minimum-restraint principle applies to deserved punishment. Indeed, Dan Kahan and others argue that imprisonment may be a preferred form of punishment because of its expressive power of condemnation.[221] Cloaking preventive detention as criminal justice, then, permits authorities to avoid demonstrating that detention method used is the least intrusive that will provide adequate protection.

Finally, consistent with the preventive detention principle of minimum restraint, a detainee should be entitled to treatment if such can reduce the length or intrusiveness of the restraint. No similar claim to treatment is available if the justification for incarceration is retributive. The person incarcerated as deserved punishment has no greater claim to government-provided treatment than any other citizen.

Thus, reformers benefit from all of these practical implications by cloaking preventive detention as criminal justice. By continuing to

---

221 *See*, e.g., Dan M. Kahan, Social Influence, Social Meaning, and Deterrence, 83 Va. L. Rev. 349, 362–363, 384 (1997) (suggesting that the form of punishment conveys a social meaning: "Imprisonment is an extraordinarily potent gesture of moral disapproval; because of the symbolic importance of individual liberty in American culture, there is never a doubt that society means to condemn someone when it takes that person's freedom away."); Dan M. Kahan, What Do Alternative Sanctions Mean?, 63 U. Chi. L. Rev. 591, 594–605 (1996) (discussing the "expressive dimension" of punishment and the significance of imprisonment for moral condemnation). Of course, the more incarceration is used for preventive detention rather than deserved punishment for a past offense, the less clearly imprisonment will convey condemnation of a past wrong.

present itself as "doing justice"—by obscuring the preventive nature of reforms with ambiguity as to their purpose—the system can provide preventive detention without the constraints that logically would attend an explicit preventive detention system.

2. The Start to Modern Cloaking: The Model Penal Code's Surreptitiously Discounting the Significance of Resulting Harm

Diverting the criminal justice system from upholding justice to advancing preventive detention is not an entirely new phenomenon. The seeds of this shift from desert to dangerousness were planted at least as early as the 1950s with the rehabilitation and incapacitation movement. For example, the Model Penal Code, promulgated in 1962, generally grades inchoate offenses the same as substantive ones.[222] Attempted rape has the same grade as rape, attempted arson the same as arson. The judgment implicit in such grading conflicts with the strongly held lay belief that resulting harm aggravates an offender's blameworthiness and calls for greater punishment.[223] However, the Code's grading approach makes sense if the goal is to maximize societal control over dangerous people. The offender who fails to cause harm because police are able to interrupt him may be as dangerous as the offender who completes the offense. The two are thus equal candidates for rehabilitation and incapacitation. This approach is consistent with the Model Sentencing Act, which minimizes the significance of offense seriousness.[224]

---

222 Model Penal Code 5.05(1) (1962). The drafters explain: "The theory of this grading system may be stated simply. To the extent that sentencing depends upon the antisocial disposition of the actor and the demonstrated need for a corrective sanction, there is likely to be little difference in the gravity of the required measures depending on the consummation or the failure of the plan." Model Penal Code §5.05(1) cmt. at 490 (1985). The drafters exempt inchoate offenses to commit a first-degree felony because of the overriding deterrent purpose. *Id.* at 489–490.

223 *See* Paul H. Robinson & John M. Darley, Justice, Liability & Blame: Community Views and the Criminal Law 14–28, 33–42 (1995).

224 The Report of Model Sentencing Act proudly points out: "The [Act] diminishes [differences in] sentencing according to the particular offense. Under [the Act] the dangerous offender may be committed to a lengthy term; the nondangerous defendant may not. It makes available, for the first time, a plan that allows the sentence to be determined by the defendant's make-up, his potential threat in the future, and other similar factors, with a minimum of variation according to the offense." *See* Robinson, Dangerousness, *supra* note 206, at 1441.

This approach—discounting the significance of resulting harm and offense seriousness in assessing punishment—became somewhat less attractive in the mid-1970s, when the limited ability of social and medical science to rehabilitate offenders became clear.[225] Crime and the consequent need for criminal justice would not disappear through the power of clinical advances, as had been hoped. But an important step had been taken: the disconnect between criminal punishment and desert had been formally legitimized.

Reformers soon realized that even if rehabilitation was unrealistic, at the very least incapacitation could prevent future crimes, and soon followed the modern preventive detention reform ideas—three strikes, lowering the age of eligibility for prosecution as an adult, and others. If desert does not constrain the criminal justice system, then liability and punishment can be distributed in any way that the crime-control calculus suggests may reduce crime.

Rather than openly recharacterize the system to reveal its nature as preventive detention, the reformers, then as now, appeared anxious to maintain the false image of a system of deserved criminal punishment. If the drafters believed that resulting harm should be irrelevant to grading, they could have simply eliminated all result elements from the Model Penal Code's offense definitions and defined all offenses in terms of conduct and accompanying mental state: "Engaging in conduct by which one intends to" burn a building, falsify an official document, or injure another. In fact, the Code retains the result elements in offense definitions, implying that the Code considers resulting harm significant, only to then negate the effect of the result elements by grading inchoate conduct the same as the completed offense. Why take this peculiar approach? One might speculate that the drafters saw value in maintaining the appearance, if not the spirit, of a criminal punishment system.[226]

3. The Inevitable Conflict Between Desert and Dangerousness as Distributive Criteria

The natural conflict between pursuing justice and incapacitating dangerous persons is noted in Chapter 2. Dangerousness and desert have

---

225 *See* Chapter 5.A.
226 *See*, e.g., Paul H. Robinson, The Role of Harm and Evil in Criminal Law: A Study in Legislative Deception?, 5 Journal of Contemporary Legal Issues 299–322 (1994).

distinct criteria that commonly diverge. Desert arises from a past wrong, whereas dangerousness arises from the prediction of a future wrong. A person may be dangerous but not blameworthy, or vice versa. Consider, for example, a dangerous mentally ill offender. A desert distributive principle may acquit the dysfunctional person of all criminal liability because the person is not to blame for the offense; he deserves no punishment. But an incapacitation principle would impose liability and require incapacitation because the offender is dangerous.

In a reverse set of cases, an incapacitation principle does not call for punishment of an offender even though the desert principle does. The recently discovered, elderly former Nazi concentration camp official is not dangerous but deserves punishment, as is true of the practitioner of "voodoo" who attempts to kill another by placing a spell or by sticking needles into a doll. Because the person's conduct is harmless and the person is not otherwise dangerous, an incapacitation principle suggests that imposing criminal sanctions is a waste of resources. The desert principle, in contrast, takes the person's attempt to kill as evidence of blameworthiness deserving punishment.

The inherent conflict between incapacitation and desert has practical implications, as in the difference in the kinds of factors that would be taken into account in assessing liability and determining sentences. If incapacitation of the dangerous alone determined the distribution of criminal sanctions, prison terms would be set according to those factors that best predicted future crime. The higher the likelihood of recidivism, the stronger the case for imprisonment and, often, the longer the sentence. One of the best predictors of future criminality is employment history.[227] Thus, unemployment for the two years preceding the crime could aggravate the grade of an offense or increase the imposed sentence. An offender's age and family situation are also good predictors of future criminality[228] and thus could also determine the offender's liability and

---

227 *See*, e.g., Don M. Gottfredson, Leslie T. Wilkins & Peter B. Hoffman, Guidelines for Parole and Sentencing 41–67 (1978) (including employment history in a list of nine factors best predicting future criminality); Peter W. Greenwood with Allan Abrahamse, Selective Incapacitation 105–106 (1982) (noting that employment history "is somewhat associated with . . . offense rates").

228 Researchers have found age to be an effective predictor of future violence. *See*, e.g., Joseph J. Cocozza & Henry J. Steadman, Some Refinements in the Measurement and Prediction of Dangerous Behavior, 131 Am. J. Psychiatry 1012 (1974). Various aspects of an offender's family situation are also of predictive value. *See*, e.g., Alfred Blumstein, David P. Farrington & Soumyo Moitra, Delinquency Careers: Innocents, Desisters,

sentence: younger offenders and offenders without fathers in the home would receive longer prison terms. Indeed, if incapacitation of the dangerous were the only distributive principle, there would be little reason to wait until an offense were committed to impose criminal liability and sanctions; it would be more effective to screen the general population and "convict" those found dangerous and in need of incapacitation.[229]

Yet openly relying on the factors relevant to an incapacitative principle would be offensive to a system of just punishment. A person does not deserve more punishment for an offense because he has a poor employment history, is young, or has no father in his household. And certainly, no person deserves punishment before committing an offense. The incapacitative principle not only focuses on different criteria than the desert principle but also wholly neglects factors central to the desert principle. Even the nature of the crime committed may be of little relevance if the goal is future prevention. The point is that the traditional principles of incapacitation and desert conflict; they inevitably distribute liability and punishment differently. To advance one, the system commonly must sacrifice the other.

4. Denying the Conflict

One of the most troublesome aspects of the conflict between incapacitation and desert is the denials that such a conflict exists. People commonly claim that incapacitation and desert somehow can combine or reconcile in a way that allows both to achieve their objectives. Chapter 2 has already noted that the Model Penal Code, for example, lists all of the traditional purposes of sentencing, including incapacitation and desert, and then directs judges to fashion sentences that most effectively further all of the purposes.[230] The Code's commentary explains that if the alterative

---

and Persisters, in 6 Crime and Justice: An Annual Review of Research 187, 198 (Michael Tonry & Norval Morris eds., 1985).

229 One study suggests that rapists may be distinguished from nonrapists based on their penile erection response to certain stimuli. Gene G. Abel, David H. Barlow, Edward B. Blanchard & Donald Guild, The Components of Rapist's Sexual Arousal, 34 Archives Gen. Psychiatry 895, 895 (1977). If the predictive technique were sufficiently refined, a pure incapacitation distributive principle might find it an appropriate basis for distributing criminal liability. See generally Sanford H. Kadish, The Decline of Innocence, 26 Cambridge L.J. 273 (1968).

230 Model Penal Code 1.02(2) (1962).

purposes should be "justly harmonized."[231] But how can this be done? When incapacitation and desert conflict, the principles suggest different sentences, and a judge or sentencing commission must choose between purposes. Furthering one aim necessitates sacrificing the other. If a judge simply averages the sentences advocated by the two conflicting purposes, the resulting sentence may serve neither function effectively.[232]

Norval Morris and others offer another argument to deny the existence of the conflict—a system may set sentences according to dangerousness without violating desert principles simply by avoiding any extreme disparity between levels of punishment and blameworthiness.[233] This view conceives of desert as having only vague requirements, which operate at the extremes of disproportionality. Under this view, desert requires no particular sentence; it merely sets the outer limits of a range of just punishments.

But as Chapter 7 discusses in greater detail, the demands of desert are not so vague or flexible. Von Hirsch, for example, notes that the principle of desert necessitates an ordinal ranking of cases[234]—justice requires that offenders of lesser blameworthiness receive less punishment than offenders of greater blameworthiness. Given the finite range over which the amount of punishment can vary and the large number of distinctions commonly recognized between degrees of blameworthiness, the punishment deserved in a particular case falls into a narrow range. The range is determined not by some special connection between that degree of blameworthiness and that amount of punishment but by the need to distinguish a given case from the large number of other cases of distinguishable blameworthiness. Empirical research supports this view.[235] Small differences in facts often create a significant shift in shared lay perceptions of the punishment deserved.

---

231 Model Penal Code 1.02 cmt. at 2 (Tentative Draft No. 2, 1954).

232 *See* generally Paul H. Robinson, Hybrid Principles for the Distribution of Criminal Sanctions, 82 Nw. U. L. Rev. 19 (1987); Paul H. Robinson, Why Does the Criminal Law Care What the Lay Person Thinks Is Just? Coercive Versus Normative Crime Control, 86 Va. L. Rev. 1939 (2000).

233 *See* Morris, The Future of Imprisonment, *supra* note 205, at 73–76; Norval Morris & Marc Miller, Predictions of Dangerousness, 6 Crime and Justice: An Annual Review of Research 1, 35 (1985).

234 *See* Andrew von Hirsch, Past or Future Crimes: Deservedness and Dangerousness in the Sentencing of Criminals 40 (1985) [hereinafter von Hirsch, Past or Future Crimes].

235 *See,* e.g., Robinson & Darley, Justice, Liability, and Blame, *supra* note 223, at 229–271, 273.

B. The Justice Problems

The cloaking of preventive detention as criminal justice is problematic in part because it undermines justice. For example, lowering the age for adult prosecution, with its longer terms of imprisonment, may well increase societal protection; juveniles are committing an increasing number of serious crimes.[236] But decreasing the age at which a juvenile can be prosecuted as an adult increases the number of cases in which a young offender lacking the capacity for moral choice is nonetheless held criminally liable.

It is beyond dispute that many young offenders, especially those below the age of fifteen, lack the cognitive and control capacities of normal adults. Some may not appreciate the enormity of the consequences of their acts and others may lack normal behavior control mechanisms.[237] If an adult offender is similarly dysfunctional due to mental illness or involuntary intoxication for example, an excuse defense is readily available.[238] Yet a young offender impaired in a similar way by immaturity has no defense or mitigation because adult courts traditionally have not recognized an immaturity excuse.[239] Courts had no need for to such an excuse in the past because juvenile courts dealt with cases involving youthful offenders. The recent trend toward trying youths in adult courts has created the need for such an excuse defense, but none has been

---

236 Juveniles as a group are more dangerous persons today than a decade ago. For example, in 1976, juveniles between the ages of 14 and 17 accounted for 10.6 offenders per 100,000 in terms of murders and nonnegligent homicides; by 1995, the figure had more than doubled to 23.0 offenders per 100,000. Bureau of Justice Statistics, Sourcebook of Criminal Justice Statistics—1995, at 340 Tbl.3.132 (1996).

237 *See*, e.g., Arthur T. Jersild, Charles W. Telford & Jane M. Sawrey, Child Psychology 157 (7th ed. 1975); Williams, Criminal Law, *supra* note 126 at 818 ("It is only in a special sense that the child member of a delinquent gang can be said to know shoplifting or receiving stolen goods to be 'wrong.' He knows that such conduct is frowned upon by the police, and perhaps by his parents; but he does not himself feel it to be wrong.").

238 Insanity, involuntary intoxication, and duress excuse a violator who has caused the harm or evil prohibited by an offense but who lacks the capacity to appreciate the wrongfulness of her conduct or to conform her conduct to the requirements of law. *See*, e.g., Model Penal Code 2.08(4), 2.09(1), 4.01(1) (1962). Because a person's lack of maturity can cause these same excusing conditions, an immaturity defense logically should be part of the criminal law's system of excuses. For a general discussion of the conceptual analogy among excuses, *see* Paul H. Robinson, Criminal Law 477–494 (1997).

239 Instead, states provide for the transfer of jurisdiction to juvenile court for all defendants below a given age. *See* generally 2 Paul H. Robinson, Criminal Law Defenses 175 (1984 & Supp. 1998).

developed, perhaps because the defense would interfere with the goal of gaining control over dangerous offenders.

A more common and more damaging distortion of justice derives from the use of "three strikes" and other habitual-offender statutes, and the use of prevention-oriented sentencing guidelines that multiply the length of sentences for offenders with prior criminal records. Shocking cases of long-term imprisonment for minor offenses are well known. In *Rummel v. Estelle*,[240] for example, discussed in Chapter 4, the defendant took $129.75 from a bar owner to fix the bar's air conditioner with no intention of actually doing so. His conviction for fraud was his third, qualifying him for a term of life imprisonment without the possibility of parole under an early "three-strikes" statute.[241] But problems are inherent not only in the shocking cases but in every case in which a habitual-offender statute or prior-record-based sentencing guideline applies. In these cases, the sentence imposed exceeds the deserved punishment, albeit to a less dramatic extent than life imprisonment for minor check fraud.

The imposition of that excess punishment is, of course, the motivating goal of such statutes: they significantly increase the sentence beyond the level deserved for the crime because a prior record commonly predicts future criminality. But the effect of such a policy is that the criminal justice system regularly imposes sentences that exceed the punishment deserved. Sentencing guidelines that give great weight to prior criminal records and "three strikes" and related habitual-offender provisions commonly double, triple, or quadruple the punishment imposed on repeat offenders.[242] An initial portion of the sentence may well be deserved, but

---

240 445 U.S. 263 (1980). The three prior fraud convictions that qualified Rummel for a life term involved a total of $ 229.11. *Id.* at 265–266.

241 *Id.* at 284–285.

242 Under three-strikes statutes, e.g., the criminal history often quadruples the sentence that would be imposed for the identical offense by the identical offender with no criminal history. A 25-year-old offender committing a felony that normally carries a 10-year sentence, for which less than 10 years ordinarily would be served, can get mandatory life imprisonment without the possibility of parole, which may mean a sentence of 45 years or more. *See* Clark, Austin & Henry, *supra* note 208, at 7–9, exhibit 9; *see also*, e.g., Del. Code Ann. tit. 11, 4214 (1995) (stating that a third felony conviction carries a life sentence for violations including kidnapping and aggravated robbery); 720 Ill. Comp. Stat. Ann. 5/33B-1 (West Supp. 1998) (stating that a third felony conviction carries a life sentence for violations including Class X felonies and criminal sexual assault). Sentencing guidelines that tie a sentence in part to an offender's criminal history provide for a similar increase in punishment for dangerousness. Under the Federal Guidelines, for example, an individual who commits a

what follows is a purely preventive detention portion that cannot be justified as deserved punishment.

One can construct a theory that makes a prior criminal record relevant to deserved punishment, as Andrew von Hirsch has done.[243] By committing an offense after a previous conviction, an offender might be seen as "thumbing his nose" at the justice system. Such disregard may justify some incremental increase in deserved punishment over that deserved by a first-time offender, but it seems difficult to justify the doubling, tripling, or quadrupling of punishment because of nose thumbing. The recidivist nature of a second robbery is only one of many characteristics that determine blameworthiness for it.[244] The "nose thumbing" inherent in a second robbery may make it more condemnable than the first, but it can hardly make it more condemnable than the second robbery itself (a conclusion needed to double the deserved punishment) and certainly not twice as condemnable as the second robbery itself (a conclusion needed to triple the deserved punishment).[245] But although nose thumbing may justify only a minor portion of the dramatic increases imposed for a prior record, the theory allows proponents of preventive detention to implement their program while obscuring its deviation from a system of criminal punishment.

Further, if such "nose thumbing" really provided the justification for repeat offender statues, the aggravation of blameworthiness and increased punishment would apply to all repeat offenses, not just a select few. That is, if "nose thumbing" is itself condemnable, then it ought to be condemnable in every context, not just in selected contexts. The "nose thumbing" inherent in a second violent offense might somehow be more condemnable

---

level 10 offense receives a sentence of 6 to 12 months if he has no criminal record but receives a sentence of 24 to 30 months if he has a significant record; an individual who commits a level 19 offense receives a sentence of 30 to 37 months if he has no criminal record but receives a sentence of 63 to 78 months if he has a significant record; and an individual who commits a level 37 offense receives a sentence of 210 to 262 months if he has no criminal record but receives a sentence of 360 to life imprisonment if he has a significant record. See U.S. Sentencing Guidelines Manual ch. 5, pt. A, sentencing tbl. (1997).

243 Andrew von Hirsch, Doing Justice: The Choice of Punishments 85 (1976). But von Hirsch later withdrew much of his support for such a theory and relied instead on a different theory suggesting that a discount in punishment may be appropriate for first-time offenders. See von Hirsch, Past or Future Crimes, supra note 234, at 78–85.

244 Von Hirsch agrees with this conclusion. See von Hirsch, Past or Future Crimes, supra note 243, at 131–136.

245 Cf. Robinson & Darley, Justice, Liability & Blame, supra note 223, at study 18 (1995) (demonstrating community views relating to multiple offenses).

than the "nose-thumbing" inherent in a second theft offense, but the nose thumbing inherent in the second theft offense would hardly be irrelevant. Yet the three strikes provisions typically apply only to a limited class of offenses—commonly violent offenses[246]—and typically account for only certain kinds of criminal history—again, commonly a history of violent offenses.[247] It seems difficult to construct a desert theory of "nose-thumbing" disrespect that allows for such selective increases in punishment. Note, however, that applying habitual-offender schemes only to violent offenses does make sense under a prevention rationale because these offenses most demand prevention.

The criminal justice system's focus on dangerousness also causes, albeit less frequently, distortions of the reverse sort: failures of justice in which a person fails to receive the punishment deserved. This kind of error can occur both in the assignment of liability and in the assessment of the proper amount of punishment. For example, the Model Penal Code provides a defense to inchoate liability if a person "presents [no] public danger" and the person's attempt was "inherently unlikely" to succeed.[248] Such a defense may make sense for a system designed to incapacitate the dangerous person because incarcerating the nondangerous attempter is a waste of preventive resources. But if the person believes his conduct will cause a criminal harm, the person deserves punishment whether or not the chosen method is likely to succeed. For example, the HIV-positive offender who attempts to kill under the mistaken belief that he can do so by spitting on the victim,[249] can escape liability under the Code's defense if the killing method is impossible and he is not otherwise dangerous. But if the intention to kill is real and he has shown a willingness to carry out the intention fully, his blameworthiness for the attempt is clear.

Such failures of justice are more common in sentencing, at least in the discretionary systems that abounded two decades ago and that still exist in many jurisdictions. The judge who focuses on prevention instead

---

246 *See* Clark, Austin & Henry, *supra* note 208, at 7–9, exhibit 9 (providing a table that lists the various offenses that states include in habitual-offender sentencing schemes).

247 *See*, e.g., Wash. Rev. Code §§9.94A.030(23), 9.94A.030(27), 9.94.120(4) (1985); Md. Ann. Code art. 27, §643B (1996).

248 Model Penal Code 5.05(2) (1962).

249 For examples of such HIV-mistaken-effect attacks, *see* State v. Smith, 621 A.2d 493 (N.J. Super. Ct. App. Div. 1993).

of desert[250] will give a minor sentence for a serious offense if the offender is no longer dangerous. Thus, the recently discovered, elderly former Nazi concentration camp official can escape the punishment he deserves.

The justice problems resulting from the conflict between incapacitation and desert are significant not only because doing justice is an important value in its own right—the nonconsequentialist, retributivist view—but also because doing justice can have important crime-prevention effects—a consequentialist, utilitarian argument. As Chapter 4 has noted and as Chapter 8 will examine in greater detail, the moral credibility of the criminal law, built on community perceptions that the criminal justice system distributes liability and punishment justly, gives the criminal law crime-control power. If the criminal law has moral authority, it can avoid resistance and subversion by participants—police, witnesses, prosecutors, judges, and jurors—that can undermine a system seen as unjust. In a similar vein, the criminal law's moral credibility can help avoid vigilantism that can be inspired when the law is seen as failing in its perceived obligation to do justice. A criminal law with moral credibility can stigmatize offenders and thereby induce compliance. More importantly, moral authority gives the criminal law persuasive power to label as morally condemnable conduct that was not previously seen as such. That is, it can facilitate the internalization of norms that counsel against prohibited conduct. It is this internalization of norms by individuals and their family and acquaintances that has the greatest effect in controlling conduct, more than threats of official liability and punishment. Finally, a criminal law with moral authority can influence conduct by giving criminal law a role in shaping community norms.

The strength of these crime-control powers of criminal law is a function of the criminal law's moral credibility. A criminal justice system in the business of preventive detention, rather than doing justice, can expect no more moral authority than that afforded doctors who determine whether a mentally ill person is sufficiently dangerous to be civilly committed. Requiring the criminal justice system to distribute punishment according to predictions of future dangerousness rather than blameworthiness for past crimes can only undermine the system's moral credibility.

---

250 In a 1981 study, 45% of judges did not think that "just deserts" was important. *See* S. Rep. No. 98-225, at 41 n.18 (1983) (citing INSLAW/Yankelovich, Skelly & White, Inc., Federal Sentencing III-4 (1981)); *see also* Anthony Partridge & William B. Eldridge, Federal Judicial Center, The Second Circuit Sentencing Study: A Report to the Judges of the Second Circuit (1974).

Citizens initially pleased by the added protection that preventive detention reforms provide, nonetheless may accurately perceive that the system is no longer in the business of doing justice. As criminal liability is increasingly disconnected from moral blameworthiness, the criminal law will have less authority to shape norms, to promote the internalization of norms, to stigmatize violators, or to avoid vigilantism, resistence, or subversion. In the long run, then, using the criminal justice system as a mechanism for preventive detention can undermine the goal of crime prevention, the very goal offered to justify such use.

C. The Preventive Detention Problems

Section A has shown a variety of ways in which the current criminal justice system surreptitiously provides preventive detention at the expense of just punishment. Ironically, such cloaked preventive detention also seriously impedes the system's preventive detention effectiveness.

For example, instead of examining each offender to determine the person's actual present dangerousness, the current system uses prior criminal record as a proxy for dangerousness. Prior record has some correlation with dangerousness but is only a rough approximation, and its use in preventive detention guarantees errors of both inclusion and exclusion. A behavioral scientist's ability to predict future criminality using all available data is poor;[251] using the proxy of prior criminal history as the basis for prediction is even less accurate. It is often true that a person who has committed an offense will do so again. But it is also frequently false—many offenders do not commit another offense.[252] An explicit assessment of dangerousness would reveal this (that many second-time offenders are no longer dangerous), yet these offenders can receive long

---

251 For a review of the available studies, *see* Stephen J. Morse, Blame and Danger: An Essay on Preventive Detention, 76 B.U. L. Rev. 113, 126 n.39 (1996). Morse concludes that "the ability of mental health professionals to predict future violence among mental patients may be better than chance, but it is still highly inaccurate, especially if these professionals are attempting to use clinical methods to predict serious violence." *Id.* at 126.

252 *See* Office of the Legislative Auditor, State of Minnesota, Recidivism of Adult Felons, *available at* http://www.auditor.leg.state.mn.us/ped/1997/pe9701.htm (reporting that 55% of all felony offenders in the study were not convicted of a subsequent offense during three years following their initial arrest and finding that homicide offenders had one of the lowest recidivism rates); *see* also Bureau of Justice Statistics Special Report, Recidivism of Prisoners Released in 1983 (1989).

preventive terms under three-strikes statutes and criminal-history-based guidelines. At the same time, a direct and explicit reliance upon danger-ousness, rather than its proxy of criminal record, would reveal that many first-time offenders are dangerous; yet these offenders are not preven-tively detained under three-strikes statutes and criminal-history-based guidelines.[253]

Indeed, this particular cloaking device stands good prevention on its head. Evidence suggests that criminality is highly age related.[254] Whether due to changes in testosterone levels or something else, the offending rate drops off steadily for individuals beyond their twenties. The prior-record cloak leads us to ignore younger offenders' coming crimes when they are running wild and leads us to begin long-term imprisonment, often life imprisonment under "three strikes," just when the natural forces of aging would often rein in the offenders. Offenders with their criminal careers before them are not detained because they have not yet compiled their criminal resumes, whereas offenders with their criminal careers behind them are detained because they have the requisite criminal records. Such a scheme produces a costly and wasteful prevention system of prisons full of geriatric life-termers. Simultaneously, the scheme leads to ineffective

---

253 The chronic spouse abuser who turns to obsessive violence when the battered spouse leaves may have no criminal history—battering spouses are often able to persuade their victims not to press criminal charges—yet the abuser may present a clear and immediate danger. Similarly, a stalking and threat offense, depending on its circum-stances, may suggest a high risk of serious danger. See, e.g., John Douglas & Mark Olshaker, Obsession 266 (1998). Yet most such offenses would not trigger the danger-ousness add-on provisions that are components of recent reforms. That is, even if the circumstances and nature of the offense suggest a life-threatening level of violence, a system that looks to criminal history rather than to dangerousness will have no grounds to detain the perpetrator.

254 E.g., only 15% of those arrested for crime in 1994 were in their forties or older, although that age group made up 40% of the U.S. population. Bureau of Justice Statistics, *supra* note 236, at 397 tbl.4.4 In contrast, persons in their thirties made up 25.3% of arrests but accounted for only 16.9% of the population. *Id.* Persons between the ages 19 and 29 made up 37.1% of arrests but only 15.9% of the population. *Id.* Homicide arrest rates suggest an even greater drop-off in criminality with age in 1993: 11.9 of 100,000 males in the 35 to 44 age bracket were arrested for homicide. *Id.* at 423 tbl.4.18. Of those aged 25 to 29, the rate was more than two and a half times higher, 30.0 per 100,000. *Id.* For those between 21 and 24, the rate was almost 5 times higher, 56.8. *Id.* Of those between 18 and 20, the rate was almost 8 times higher, 91.3. The trend of the last several decades has been toward even less criminality by middle-aged persons. In 1970, the homicide arrest rate for males between 35 and 44 was two-thirds higher than it was in 1993—19.5 per 100,000 versus 11.9 per 100,000. *Id.* Yet the current reforms will detain a greater number of middle-aged offenders for a longer period of time.

prevention because the system does little or nothing during that period in a criminal's life when the need for preventive detention is greatest. A rational and cost-effective preventive detention system would more readily detain young offenders during their crime-prone years and release them for their crime-free older years. Yet the need to cloak preventive detention with deserved punishment prompts the use of prior record as a substitute for actual dangerousness.

An equally counterproductive aspect of the cloaked system is its mandating of fixed ("determinate") sentences soon after a guilty verdict or plea. In determining the length of a deserved sentence, all of the relevant information is known at the time of sentencing—the nature of the offense and the personal culpability and capacities of the offender. Thus, sentencing judges determining deserved punishment have little reason to impose any sentence other than a fully determinate one (i.e., one that sets the actual release date) soon after trial. A system that instead allows a subsequent reduction of sentence, as by a parole board, undercuts deserved punishment. Citizens become cynical that a just sentence will be undermined by early release. It is this cynicism that gives rise to the demands for "truth in sentencing" and the legislative response of establishing determinate terms and abolishing early release on parole.[255]

To maintain its justice cloak, the cloaked preventive detention system must follow this practice of imposing determinate sentences soon after trial. But this practice is highly inappropriate for effective prevention detention. It is difficult enough to determine a person's present dangerousness—whether he would commit an offense if released today. It is all the more difficult to predict now an offender's future dangerousness—whether he would commit an offense if released at some future date, such as at the end of the deserved punishment term. It is still more difficult, if not impossible, to predict today precisely how long the future preventive detention will need to last. Yet that is what determinate sentencing demands: the imposition now of a fixed term that predicts preventive detention needs far in the future.

---

255 One of the prime motivations for the federal Sentencing Reform Act of 1984, which among other things abolished the United States Parole Commission, was an attempt to reestablish credibility with an emphasis on "truth in sentencing" that determinate sentences bring. *See*, e.g., U.S. Sentencing Comm'n, Sentencing Guidelines and Policy Statements 1.2 (1987) (stating that "Congress first sought honesty in sentencing . . . to avoid the confusion and implicit deception" arising out of the then-extant indeterminate sentencing system).

A sentencing judge or guideline drafter is left to the grossest sort of speculation, inevitably doomed to setting either a term too long—thus unfairly detaining a nondangerous offender and wasting preventive resources—or a term too short—thus failing to provide adequate prevention. In deciding between these two bad choices, decision makers commonly opt for errors of the first sort rather than the second, resulting in the recent increases in the terms of imprisonment.

A rational preventive detention system would do what current civil commitment systems do: make a determination of present dangerousness in setting detention for a limited period, commonly six months, and then periodically revisit the decision to determine whether the need for detention continues.[256]

Other inefficiencies resulting from the use of the cloak are found in the method of restraint. A rational preventive detention system would follow a principle of minimum intrusion: a detainee would be held at the minimum level of restraint necessary for community safety. If house arrest or regular medication would provide the same level of community safety as imprisonment, then the former choices would be preferred as less intrusive to the offender and less costly to society. Implementing deserved punishment, in contrast, may often require a prison term to reaffirm the community's strong condemnation of the offense. House arrest or regular medication may be unacceptable substitutes if they are perceived as trivializing the offense. If preventive detention must operate under the cloak of criminal justice, it too often must follow the punishment preference for imprisonment even in situations in which prevention would be satisfied with less intrusive restraint.

The preventive detention system hidden behind the cloak of criminal justice not only fails to protect the community efficiently but also fails to deal fairly with those being preventively detained. As noted above, the inaccuracies created by the use of prior record as a substitute for actual dangerousness result in the unnecessary detention of a greater number of nondangerous offenders. The inaccuracies created by the use

---

256 See, e.g., Idaho Code 66-337(a) (Michie 2000) (requiring department directors to examine a patient's need for commitment at the end of the first ninety days and every one hundred twenty days thereafter); R.I. Gen. Laws 40.1-5.3-4(f) (1997) (permitting courts to commit dangerous persons, but requiring courts to review such orders every six months); S.D. Codified Laws Ann. 27A-10-14 (Michie 2000) (requiring a board to review a patient who has been committed for mental illness at least once every 6 months for the first year and at least once every 12 months thereafter).

of determinate sentences can have the same effect. In cases in which a nonincarcerative sentence would provide adequate protection, the use of a prison term provides one more example of needless restraint.

The irrationalities of the cloak of criminal justice extend to other aspects of the preventive detention system, such as the conditions of detention. As noted above, punitive conditions are entirely consistent with a punishment rationale for the incarceration. But if an offender has served the portion of his sentence justified by deserved punishment and continues to be detained for entirely preventive reasons, punitive conditions become inappropriate. Similarly, an offender being preventively detained should logically have a right to treatment, especially if such treatment can reduce the length or intrusiveness of the preventive detention—a specialized application of the principle of minimum restraint. If treatment can reduce the necessary individual sacrifice,[257] the offender ought to receive it.

D. Segregating Doing Justice and Preventive Detention

Real world problems commonly present conflicting interests that cannot be reconciled but can only be compromised. The natural conflict between fair trials and a free press, for example, cannot be resolved; we can at best strike a balance in how much of each that we sacrifice. Similarly, society's interest in effective investigation of crime competes with individuals' interest in privacy, and Fourth Amendment analysis, the standard mechanism for resolving this competition, strikes a complex balance between the two.

Fortunately, however, there is no need to compromise either justice or preventive detention to advance the other, for the conflict between justice and preventive detention can be avoided by simply segregating the two functions into two systems. The first would be a criminal justice system that focuses exclusively on imposing the punishment deserved for the past offense, and the second would be a postsentence civil commitment system that considers only the protection of society from future offenses by a dangerous offender. An explicit system of postcriminal

---

257 E.g., a number of encouraging studies have recently suggested that comprehensive treatment of pedophilia has a 90% or better success rate. *See* Robert E. Freeman-Longo, Reducing Sexual Abuse in America: Legislating Tougher Laws or Public Education and Prevention, 23 New Eng. J. on Crim. & Civ. Confinement 303, 323 (1997).

commitment would better serve both the community and potential detainees.

To summarize the arguments above that make the point, under a segregated system, the community would be better off because such a system offers both more justice and increased protection from dangerous offenders. Giving the criminal justice system a better chance of doing justice is valuable for its own sake. It also creates greater moral credibility for the system and thus greater long-term crime-control power. An explicit preventive detention system offers better protection because it can directly consider a person's present dangerousness and more accurately predict who is dangerous. Such a system also enhances accuracy by allowing for periodic re-evaluations, in comparison with the present system's need to make a single prediction of dangerousness years in advance. Greater accuracy leads to more detention of the dangerous, thus better protection, and less detention of the nondangerous, thus saving resources.

A segregated system also benefits the potential detainees for many of the same reasons. Better accuracy in prediction means less detention of nondangerous offenders. Periodic re-evaluation leads to detention limited to periods of actual dangerousness. Acknowledging the preventive nature of the detention also logically suggests a right to treatment, a right to nonpunitive conditions, and the application of the principle of minimum restraint, meaning greater freedom among those who are detained.

The sticking point in this proposal is not in having a criminal justice system that is guided only by justice. Most laypersons assume that the criminal justice system has always sought this goal. The difficulty comes, instead, with the open acknowledgment of a system of preventive detention.

There is some precedent for preventive detention. As noted previously, all states have some form of civil commitment operating to protect society.[258] Even more direct precedent exists in states that currently have postcriminal-incarceration civil commitment of some criminal offenders, typically "sexual predators."[259] Under these civil commitment systems, the government can attempt to detain an offender at the

---

258 *See* Robinson, Dangerousness *supra* note 206, at 1444.
259 *See Id.* at 1431.

conclusion of his criminal term if the government can show continuing dangerousness.[260]

Despite the precedent, concerns about creating a broader system of explicit preventive detention are understandable:[261] the Gulag Archipelago potential for governmental abuse is real. But if the alternative is the present system of cloaked preventive detention, the risk is worth taking. An open system of preventive detention ought to be preferred precisely because it is open rather than cloaked. No one can guarantee that a legislature or court will not attempt to abuse its power. But an open system makes abuse harder, not easier. The openly preventive nature of the system invites closer scrutiny, which the present cloaked system escapes. Instead of the current debates—which typically reduce to disagreements about, for example, whether "three-strikes" sentences are "too long"—the debate would shift to the many aspects of preventive detention that cry out for debate: What is the reliability of the predictions of dangerousness? Is the threatened danger sufficient to justify the extent of intrusion on personal liberty? Are there less expensive or less intrusive measures that would as effectively protect the community? Under the current cloaked system, these issues never arise because the system is said to be doing justice not preventive detention.

Imagine a legislature considering an explicit preventive detention statute that would provide life preventive detention on a third conviction for a minor fraud offense, the disposition provided by the statute in *Rummel*. Such legislation would be difficult to defend and would be unlikely to find support in any political quarter. Indeed, imagine the Supreme Court's review of *Rummel* if Rummel were being preventively detained. Life terms without the possibility of parole may be common and acceptable in a criminal justice system in which horrible crimes

---

260 Unlike the proposal made here, there is no indication that the current "sexual predator" legislation excludes reliance on dangerousness in setting the criminal commitment. It is less a segregated system than a cloaked system followed by a preventive detention system.

261 The postsentence civil commitment proposal might be held unconstitutional. Although the permissible scope of civil commitment has recently been expanded slightly, it still appears to require not only a finding of dangerousness but also some additional factor, such as mental abnormality. Kansas v. Hendricks, 521 U.S. 346, 358 (1997) (citing Heller v. Doe, 509 U.S. 312, 314-15 (1993); Allen v. Illinois, 478 U.S. 364, 366 (1986)). But this would be an odd result: barring the civil commitment with periodic review of dangerousness of a dangerous murderer, but permitting, as the Court did in Rummel, the life imprisonment without parole of a petty fraud offender.

deserve severe punishment. But life commitment with no further dangerousness review for a property offense would be preposterous on its face in a civil preventive detention system.

Some people will argue that it is simply not politically feasible in the United States today to create an explicit system of preventive detention, even one limited to dangerous felons about to be released from prison. Less feasible, however, is political inaction in the face of recurring serious offenses that are preventable. The inevitable pressure for protection will express itself in one form or another. If the only choices are an open preventive detention system and a cloaked one, both the community and potential detainees ought to prefer the open system. If there is a danger of governmental abuse of preventive detention, that danger is greatest when preventive detention is cloaked as criminal justice.

CHAPTER 7

Competing Conceptions of Desert: Vengeful, Deontological, and Empirical

Should desert be the distributive principle for criminal liability and punishment? The role desert should play, if any, has been the subject of long and turbulent debate. There is some indication that desert—referred to variously as deserved punishment, just punishment, retributive punishment, or simply "doing justice"—may be in ascendance, both in academic debate and in real world institutions.[262] A number of modern sentencing guidelines have adopted it as their distributive principle. Desert is increasingly given deference in the "purposes" section of state criminal codes, where it can be the guiding principle in the interpretation and application of the code's provisions. Indeed, the American Law Institute recently adopted a change to the Model Penal Code (the first since the Code's promulgation in 1962) that sets desert as the official dominant principle for sentencing. And courts have identified desert as

---

262 *See* authorities collected at Paul H. Robinson, Competing Conceptions of Modern Desert: Vengeful, Deontological, and Empirical, 67 Cambridge Law Journal 145, 145–146 (2008).

the guiding principle in a variety of contexts, as with the Supreme Court's enthroning retributivism as the "primary justification for the death penalty."

But a good deal of controversy over the reliance upon desert remains. Some strenuously argue that desert is inappropriate as a distributive principle because it is mean spirited and harsh, because it has an unhealthy preference for prison, because it is based upon only vague notions that at most mark punishment extremes to be avoided, because people are in hopeless disagreement about what it requires, because it fails to avoid avoidable crime, because it is immoral, and because it is impractical to implement.

Many of these objections are valid, at least when applied to some conceptions of desert, but at least three distinct conceptions of desert are to be found in the current debates, typically without distinction being made among them. The three include what might be called vengeful desert, deontological desert, and empirical desert. Each of the offered criticisms of desert is a fair objection to one of these conceptions of desert but an unfair objection to another. Thus, an accurate assessment of desert as a distributive principle requires that these three conceptions of desert be distinguished from one another and that the strengths and weaknesses of each conception be judged on its own.

A. Competing Conceptions of Desert

Consider the three conceptions of desert are evident in the present debates over the propriety of desert as a distributive principle.

1. Vengeful Desert

A conception of desert used by many writers that might be termed "vengeful desert" is captured in the often-quoted biblical phrase: "eye for eye, tooth for tooth, hand for hand, foot for foot, burning for burning, wound for wound, stripe for stripe."[263] It urges punishing an offender in a way that mirrors the harm or suffering he has caused, typically identified as lex talionis: "the principle or law of retaliation that a punishment

---

263 Exodus 21:24–25.

inflicted should correspond in degree and in kind to the offense of the wrongdoer."[264] In Kant's words: "For the only time a criminal cannot complain that a wrong is done to him [by punishment] is when he brings his evil deed back upon himself, and what is done to him in accordance with penal law is what he has perpetrated on others."[265]

Some writers argue that lex talionis does not require inflicting the exact harm on the offender that the offender inflicted on his victim but only requires the imposition of a relevantly similar deprivation.[266] This variation, then, offers a less demanding form requiring only that the punishment be *proportionate* to the harm caused, sometimes captured by the suggestion that "the punishment should fit the crime."[267] But even in this diluted form, the primary focus of vengeful desert remains the extent of the harm of the offense.[268]

Because of this focus on the harm done, the vengeful conception of desert commonly is associated with the victim's perspective. Retributive justice "consists in seeking equality between offender and victim by subjecting the offender to punishment and communicating to the victim a concern for his or her antecedent suffering."[269] "[I]n willing the crime, he

---

264 The Random House Dictionary of the English Language, 825 (1966). *See* also Black's Law Dictionary 913 (6th ed. 1990) ("Lex talionis" is defined as "the law of retaliation, which requires the infliction upon a wrongdoer of the same injury which he has caused to another . . . as expressed in the Mosaic law by the formula, 'an eye for an eye; a tooth for a tooth.'").

265 Immanuel Kant, The Metaphysics of Morals 169 (Mary Gregor trans., Cambridge University Press 1991) (1797). Other writers express a similar view. *See*, e.g., George P. Fletcher, Punishment and Responsibility, in A Companion to Philosophy of Law and Legal Theory 517 (Dennis Patterson, ed., 1996) ("The justification of punishment . . . requires that the criminal's maxim be universalized and applied to him."); G.W.F. Hegel, Elements of the Philosophy of Right 129 (Allen W. Wood, ed., H. B. Nisbet trans., 1991) (1821) (punishment is "the crime turned round against itself"); Erik Luna, Punishment Theory, Holism, and the Procedural Conception of Restorative Justice, 2003 Utah L. Rev. 205, 220 (explaining a "'see-saw' vision of justice [where] that violence imposed on the offender balances his violence against the victim").

266 *See* Jeremy Waldron, Lex Talionis, 34 Ariz. L. Rev. 25, 25–27 (1992).

267 This is a common phrase used by writers describing desert as a distributive principle. *See*, e.g., J. C. Oleson, Comment: The Punitive Coma, 90 Calif. L. Rev. 829, note 59 (2002) ("One of the governing principles of retribution ("just deserts" theory) is proportionality, making sure that the punishment fits the crime."); Russell L. Christopher, The Prosecutor's Dilemma: Bargains and Punishments, 72 Fordham L. Rev. 93, 127 (2003) ("Retributivism 'insists that the punishment must fit the crime.'").

268 *See* authorities collected at Robinson, Competing Conceptions, *supra* note 262, at 147.

269 George P. Fletcher, The Place of Victims in the Theory of Retribution, 3 Buff. Crim. L. Rev. 51, 58 (1999).

willed that he himself should suffer in the same degree as his victim."[270] And the association with the victim's suffering, in turn, associates vengeful desert with the feelings of revenge and hatred that we commonly see in victims. Thus, punishment under this conception of desert is sometimes seen as essentially an institutionalization of victim revenge; it is "injury inflicted on a wrongdoer that satisfies the retributive hatred felt by that wrongdoer's victim and that is justified because of that satisfaction."[271]

2. Deontological Desert

A second conception of desert found in the literature, what might be termed "deontological desert," focuses not on the harm of the offense but on the blameworthiness of the offender and is drawn primarily from the arguments and analyses of moral philosophy. "It is morally fitting that a person who does wrong should suffer in proportion to his wrongdoing. That a criminal should be punished follows from his guilt, and the severity of the appropriate punishment depends on the depravity of his act."[272]

Thus, the criterion for assessing punishment is broader and richer than that for vengeful desert: Anything that affects an offender's moral blameworthiness is taken into account in judging the punishment she deserves. The extent of the harm caused or the seriousness of the evil done will be part of that calculation but so too will be a wide variety of other factors, such as the offender's culpable state of mind or lack thereof and the existing conditions at the time of the offense, including those that might give rise to claims of justification, excuse, or mitigation. A typical expression of this conception might be: "The offender deserves a particular punishment not simply for an act which causes harm but according to his personal responsibility for committing the act. This evaluation necessarily includes a review of the broad array of forces operating upon the individual to ascertain the extent of the individual's responsibility."[273]

---

270 Joel Feinberg & Hyman Gross, Philosophy of Law 541 (1980).

271 Philosophy of Law 793 (Joel Feinberg & Jules Coleman, eds., 6th ed. 2000).

272 John Rawls, Two Concepts of Rules, 64 Phil. Rev. 3, 5 (1955). Central here are the writings of Immanuel Kant. See The Metaphysics of Morals, in Immanuel Kant: Political Writings 131, 156 (Hans Reiss, ed. & H. B. Nisbet trans., 1991).

273 Samuel Pillsbury, Emotional Justice: Moralizing the Passions of Criminal Punishment, 74 Cornell L. Rev. 655, 663 (1989).

A key aspect of the deontological conception of desert, which distinguishes it from empirical desert, discussed immediately below, is that it transcends the particular people and situation at hand and embodies a set of principles derived from fundamental values, principles of right and good, and thus will produce justice without regard to the political, social, or other peculiarities of the situation at hand. As Henry Sidgwick famously put it, moral judgments are made "from the point of view of the universe."[274]

3. Empirical Desert

Like deontological desert, empirical desert focuses on the blameworthiness of the offender. But in determining the principles by which punishment is to be assessed, it looks not to philosophical analyses but rather to the community's intuitions of justice. The primary source of empirical desert principles, then, is not moral philosophy but empirical research into the factors that drive people's intuitions of blameworthiness.[275] The existing studies suggest that the variety of factors at work are as rich and varied as those at work in determining deontological desert.[276] The extent of the harm or evil plays an important role but is only one of a wide variety of factors, including many related to the offender's situation and personal capacities.

It is not the community's view of deserved punishment in a particular case that is relevant here. This conception of justice, like deontological desert, envisions a set of liability and punishment rules to be applied identically to all defendants, not ad hoc case dispositions. Further, in collecting data to construct the rules, real cases (especially publicly known cases) typically are not a useful source. People's views on such cases are commonly biased by political or social context or by other factors, such as race or class, that all would agree have no proper role in setting

---

274 Henry Sidgwick, The Methods of Ethics 420–421 (7th ed.).

275 For a general discussion of the concept, *see* Robinson & Darley, Utility of Desert, *supra* note 111, at 453, 456–458 ("The desert-based liability system that we advocate is one that normally assigns liability and punishment according to the principles of justice that the community intuitively uses to assign liability and blame").

276 *See,* e.g., Robinson & Darley, Justice, Liability & Blame, *supra* note 223, at 203–208 (reviewing a wide variety of factors that reported studies have shown influence laypersons' judgments about the amount of liability and punishment deserved).

principles of justice.[277] Instead, empirical desert derives from the community's intuitions of justice as revealed by controlled social science studies that determine the factors that influence people's assessment of a violator's blameworthiness. These studies do not ask people about abstract factors but rather have them "sentence" a variety of carefully constructed cases to see what factors in fact influence people's punishment judgments.[278] In other words, the studies seek to reveal people's shared views about justice, which commonly are not the product reasoning but the result of intuition.[279] The principles drawn from such studies are then used to construct liability and punishment rules that apply in a like manner to all defendants.

It is obvious why one might support a deontological desert distribution: to do justice. But why would one support an empirical desert distribution? Why should one care about the community's intuitions of justice? Just because the community's intuitions see some punishment as justice, it does not make it so, even if there is a strong agreement on those intuitions.

The reasons offered in support of an empirical desert distribution, which are examined in Chapter 8, lie not in its moral implications but in its practical consequences. If the criminal law tracks the community's intuitions of justice in assigning liability and punishment, it is argued, the law gains access to the power and efficiency of stigmatization, it avoids the resistance and subversion inspired by an unjust system, it gains compliance by prompting people to defer to it as a moral authority in new or grey areas (such as insider trading), and it earns the ability to help shape powerful societal norms.

4. Vengeful versus Other Conceptions of Desert

Vengeful desert differs from deontological and empirical desert in several ways that ultimately have important implications.

---

277 Paul H. Robinson & Robert Kurzban, Concordance & Conflict in Intuitions of Justice, 91 Minn. L. Rev. 1829, 1867–1890 (2007).

278 For a discussion of the common methodology and the reasons for the methodology, see Robinson & Darley, Justice, Liability & Blame, *supra* note 223, at 7–11, 217–228.

279 *See* Paul H. Robinson & John M. Darley, Intuitions of Justice: Implications for Criminal Law and Justice Policy, 81 S. Cal. L. Rev. 1 (2007).

a. The Role of Punishment Amount: Ordinal Ranking of Cases versus Punishment Continuum Endpoint

The most important difference between vengeful desert and the other two conceptions of desert is the importance the former gives to the absolute amount of punishment to be imposed. For vengeful desert, this absolute amount is its central focus: It must be equal in amount, if not also in means, to the suffering caused by the offense conduct. But for deontological and empirical desert, the absolute amount of punishment is of limited interest. Their central concern is the relative amount of punishment among cases of differing degrees of moral blameworthiness. These latter conceptions of justice focus primarily on ensuring that the offender is given not a particular amount of punishment but rather is given that amount of punishment that puts him in his proper ordinal rank among all cases of differing degrees of blameworthiness.[280]

Once a society has committed itself to a particular endpoint for its punishment continuum, which all societies must do—be it the death penalty, life imprisonment, fifteen years imprisonment, or something less—the ordinal rank of any given case necessarily converts to a specific amount of punishment: that amount of punishment that sets the offender at his appropriate ordinal rank. But for deontological and empirical desert, the amount of punishment has little other significance. If the endpoint of the punishment continuum changes, the amount of punishment that an offender deserves under these two conceptions of justice also changes, to that amount of punishment necessary to keep its proper ordinal rank.

Thus, while the absolute severity of punishment is central to vengeful desert—it ought to approximate the suffering of the offense—it is of limited relevance to deontological and empirical desert. Those latter conceptions of desert may play some role in a society's setting its punishment continuum endpoint, but in performing this role these conceptions of desert operate differently than they do when performing their core function of establishing the proper ordinal rank of each case. In setting the punishment continuum endpoint, these conceptions of desert typically can offer only general guidance as to extremes that should be avoided, rather than to give guidance as the specific endpoint to pick.

---

280 Andrew von Hirsch, Past or Future Crimes, *supra* note 243, at 39-46 (with regard to deontological desert, von Hirsch explains, "Desert should be treated as a determining principle in deciding *ordinal* magnitudes.").

b. The Role of Punishment Method: Punishment Method versus
   Amount

Another characteristic that deontological and empirical desert share,
which vengeful desert does not share, is the role given punishment
method. Only the latter cares about the method of punishment: Ideally, it
matches the punishment to the means by which the victim was made to
suffer. Failing this, punishment should be imposed in a way that is at least
relevant to the nature of the offense, if that is possible. Thus, for example,
the vengeful conception of desert is thought to support the use of the
death penalty in cases of murder.

In contrast, deontological and empirical conceptions of desert have
no such interest in the method of punishment. Their focus is on the
amount of punishment—an amount that will put the offender in his
proper ordinal rank according to his blameworthiness. As long as the
total punitive "bite" of the punishment achieves this ranking, these conceptions of desert have little reason to care about the method by which
that amount of punitive "bite" is imposed.

Where a variety of different sanctioning methods are used, the
offender should get punishment "credit" for each in proportion to the
punitive "bite" of that method. This requires, then, establishment of ratios
between the different punishment methods that reflect the differences in
their punitive "bite." If the "bite" of one week in jail is equivalent to that
of a month of weekends in jail or is equivalent to that of eighty hours of
community service, these conceptions of desert would be satisfied with
any of these sentences, so long as that amount of punishment was the
amount deserved given the offender's blameworthiness. The ideal equivalency table would be one that generates alternative sanctions about which
an offender and a community are indifferent as to which is imposed.

5. *Deontological versus Empirical Desert*

The discussions above suggest that deontological desert and empirical
desert have many similarities. Most importantly, they both focus upon
the blameworthiness of the offender. However, there also are important
differences between the two, as is one might expect, given that the notions
of blameworthiness upon which the two are based are quite different.
The deontological conception of desert is based upon reasoned analysis
from principles of right and good, which produces a transcendent notion

of justice independent of the intuitions of justice of the community. The empirical conception of desert has no such independent basis. It does not look to true moral blameworthiness in any transcendent sense; it looks only to people's shared intuitions about assigning blameworthiness.

These differences in underlying criterion can produce important differences in the distribution of liability and punishment. For example, moral philosophers disagree about the significance of resulting harm and each side of the debate has plausible arguments to make.[281] In contrast, all available data suggest a nearly universal and deeply held view among the community that resulting harm does matter, that it increases an offender's blameworthiness and deserved punishment.[282] This is only one of a host of issues on which moral philosophy's analytic conclusions are likely to vary from the empirical data on laypersons' intuitions of justice.[283]

Perhaps even more important than such differences in blameworthiness judgments are the differences among the underlying theories that drive these two conceptions of desert and that thereby shape their application. In its most fundamental form, the difference is this: The special value of the empirical conception of desert is its utilitarian effectiveness in crime-control; the special value of the deontological conception of desert is its ability to produce true principles of justice independent of personal or community opinion.

---

281 Those arguing that resulting harm should matter include: Leo Katz, Why the Successful Assassin Is More Wicked than the Unsuccessful One, 88 Cal. L. Rev. 791, 806 (2000) (arguing by hypothetical that principled moral analysis suggests that harm should be considered when assessing blameworthiness); Ken Levy, The Solution to the Problem of Outcome Luck, 24 Law & Phil. 263 (2005); Michael S. Moore, The Independent Moral Significance of Wrongdoing, 5 J. Contemp. Legal Issues 237, 267–271 (1994) (positing that our own experiences—we feel more guilty about our own completed misdeeds than we do about attempts, and we are dissatisfied with reasonable moral choices that produce undesirable consequences—suggest that "results matter" in the moral arena).

However, there is significant disagreement in this arena. See, e.g., Joel Feinberg, Equal Punishment for Failed Attempts: Some Bad But Instructive Arguments Against It, 37 Ariz. L. Rev. 117, 119 (1995); Sanford H. Kadish, The Criminal Law and the Luck of the Draw, 84 J. Crim. L. & Criminology 679, 686 (1994) ("punishing attempts and completed crimes differently makes no sense insofar as the goal of the criminal law is to identify and deal with dangerous offenders who threaten the public."); Stephen J. Morse, The Moral Metaphysics of Causation and Results, 88 Cal. L. Rev. 879 (2000).

282 See, e.g., Robinson & Darley, Justice, Liability & Blame, supra note 223, at 14–28, 181–196 (reporting empirical studies).

283 For community views on a variety of criminal law issues that may conflict with moral philosophers' views, see generally Paul H. Robinson, The Role of Moral Philosophers in the Competition Between Philosophical and Empirical, Desert, Symposium Issue, 48 Wm. & Mary L. Rev. 1831 (2007).

The next chapter examines the instrumentalist crime-control value of empirical desert as a distributive principle, but it may be useful to briefly sketch those arguments to make clear why empirical desert is so fundamentally different from deontological desert. The extent of the criminal law's effectiveness in bringing the power of stigmatization to bear, in avoiding resistance and subversion to a system perceived as unjust, in facilitating, communicating, and maintaining societal consensus on what is and is not condemnable, and in gaining compliance in borderline cases through deference to its moral authority, is to a great extent dependent on the degree to which the criminal law has gained moral credibility in the minds of the citizens it governs. Thus, the criminal law's moral credibility is essential to effective crime control and is enhanced if the distribution of criminal liability is perceived as "doing justice," that is, if it assigns liability and punishment in ways that the community perceives as consistent with its shared intuitions of justice. Conversely, a distribution of liability that deviates from community perceptions of just desert undermines the system's moral credibility and therefore its crime control effectiveness.

While empirical desert has the advantage of crime-control utility, its reliance upon the community's intuitions of justice presents a serious disadvantage. The community's intuitions of justice could be wrong, even if there is a high degree of agreement about them. Empirical desert can tell us only what people think is just; only deontological desert can tell us what is actually just. Like slave owners in the Old South or members of the Nazi party during World War II, one may fail to appreciate the injustice of one's views until later, especially if one's views at the time are shared by a large number of other people. Even a popular liability rule may be unjust. Only deontological desert can spot these justice errors in people's intuitions and provide a conception of desert that transcends time, community, and culture. Only deontological desert can give us the means by which we can tell the truth of what is deserved, insulated from the vicissitudes of human irrationality.

B. Resulting Confusions About the Nature of Deserved Punishment

It is argued here that the failure to appreciate the existence of these three quite different conceptions of desert commonly leads to confusion in the critique of desert as a principle for the distribution of criminal liability and punishment. That is, criticisms of "desert" are sometimes offered without appreciating that the criticism may be valid with regard to one conception of desert but not another, thus leading writers to reject "desert" generally while in fact their criticisms only suggest rejecting one or another specific conception of desert. Further, even when the issue is not the propriety of desert as a distributive principle generally but rather its implications on a specific issue—such as whether it calls for use of prison or the death penalty—the failure to appreciate the existence of these different conceptions of desert leads writers to use arguments based upon an analysis of one conception of desert to draw conclusions that they then apply to a different conception of desert.

Consider the range of criticisms offered against desert.

1. Harsh?

The most common complaint against a desert-based distribution is that it necessarily provides "harsh" or "severe" punishment.

> In practice, . . . retribution is associated with severity. When people think about a punishment policy that gives the criminal his just deserts, they are generally envisioning a situation where that criminal will now serve a full and longer sentence, instead of being given a reduced sentence or paroled before he serves his sentence because of good time credits and the like.[284]

Because vengeful desert focuses primarily on the harm done, with little reference to the offender's situation and capabilities, it is easy to see how the resulting punishment can be perceived as being overly harsh (at least from the perspective of deontological or empirical desert), for it ignores many factors that both moral philosophers and the community would think are relevant in assessing blameworthiness. Thus, while the harshness criticism may seem valid to some people, it is valid only when applied to vengeful desert; it is misguided when applied to deontological

---

284 Edward Rubin, Just Say No To Retribution, 7 Buff. Crim. L. Rev. 17, 58 (2003). Other writers think similarly. See, e.g., Craig Haney, Psychology and the Limits to Prison Pain: Confronting the Coming Crisis in Eighth Amendment Law, 3 Psych. Pub. Pol. and L. 499, 525, 528 (1997) (assuming that desert-based sentencing guidelines necessarily provide "harsh punishment"); Michael Tonry, Theories and Policies Underlying Guidelines Systems, 105 Colum. L. Rev. 1233, 1264 (2005) (desert "calls for the imposition of unduly harsh penalties").

and empirical desert. Indeed, the primary criterion of deontological desert is that the punishment be precisely that which is deserved, no more and no less. Similarly, empirical desert seeks to give an offender exactly what he deserves according to principles of justice derived from the community's intuitions of justice. It would be odd indeed, then, to find substantial complaint that a distribution of liability and punishment based upon empirical desert was judged to be systematically harsh.

Of course, any particular writer may have his or her own peculiar views about exactly what desert requires, views moral philosophers or the community do not share. And often a criticism that "desert" is too harsh or severe (or not harsh or severe enough) is simply a product of that person's particular view. Thus, a writer may believe that "economic, social, cultural, or psychological deprivations" should excuse criminal conduct and therefore may conclude that a criminal justice system that does not embody this view is "harshly punitive."[285] But this kind of criticism must be taken for what it is: not a compelling indictment of deontological or empirical desert as being systematically harsh but simply evidence that this writer disagrees with others about what such desert requires.

In the same vein, another writer attacks desert as being unjust because, he argues, in setting offense grades it distinguishes between an attempt and a completed offense:

> [D]oes the government, in punishing people, really give them what they deserve? Even in our preternaturally punitive era, we decline to punish feckless evil-doers for attempts at the level that we punish their morally equivalent, and only pragmatically superior compatriots for their completed crimes.[286]

But, again, this only illustrates that this writer thinks that doing justice requires a different rule—in this case that it ought not take account of

---

285 David Dolinko, Three Mistakes about Retributivism, 39 UCLA L. Rev. 1623, 1657 (1992):

> The alacrity with which even thoughtful and sophisticated retributivists such as Morse, Morris, and Dressler dismiss suggestions that economic, social, cultural, or psychological deprivations might excuse or mitigate criminal conduct suggests that the harshly punitive attitudes . . . are not misuses of retributivism but its logical outgrowth. Retributivism's inability to specify how much punishment any offender deserves, and its emphasis on the centrality of hatred and outrage, strengthen this suggestion.

286 Rubin, Just Say No To Retribution, *supra* note 284, at 33.

resulting harm. Others, of course, disagree.[287] (In fact, deontologists disagree among themselves about many aspects of what desert requires, the subject of Section B.5. below.) It can hardly be a criticism of deontological desert generally that not all moral philosophers agree with your own view of what such desert requires.

This kind of criticism has no more impact when directed against empirical desert: it only tells us one person's perspective on desert, which may or may not reflect the community's view. Such dissenting views can be a useful piece of data for the social scientists, but only one piece. In the instance of the first example above—the view that "economic, social, cultural, or psychological deprivations" should excuse criminal conduct—the data point is a significant outlier; few people would take this view. Again, it is hardly an indictment of empirical desert that there is not complete unanimity on every principle of justice.

Contrast this with application of the same complaint against vengeful desert. There the complaint goes not simply to a disagreement with one or another liability rule but to the foundational criterion by which punishment is to be distributed: to match the suffering caused the victim. In that context, the complaint may have traction, for the distributive criterion of vengeful desert fails to take account of factors such as culpable state of mind and excusing conditions and thus will regularly and systematically produce punishment that is unduly harsh, at least from the point of view of deontological and empirical desert.

2. Based on Anger and Hatred?

A related complaint against desert as a distributive principle is its "legitimation and even glorification of anger and hatred."[288]

> A theory that legitimates anger and hatred as appropriate responses to crime and proper bases for punishment, and presents the infliction of such punishment as a virtue in itself . . . is a heady, dangerous brew at a time of intense fear and loathing of criminals. Unless carefully qualified, it virtually invites the public and the legal

---

287 *Supra* note 281.
288 Dolinko, Three Mistakes, *supra* note 285, at 1651.

system to indulge the passion for revenge untroubled by moral qualms.[289]

And,

Continued adherence to retributivist modes of thought will encourage even greater vindictiveness and a peculiarly self-righteous and smug indulgence in our society's most punitive reflexes.[290]

Complaint that deserved punishment is necessarily the product, anger and hatred is in some ways similar to the above complaint that deserved punishment is harsh, but the anger and hatred complaint is also different from that above.

One might respond to the two complaints in a similar way: by suggesting that each reveals a confusion between vengeful desert on the one hand and deontological and empirical desert on the other. That is, to the extent that vengeful desert is associated with the special view of victims, it is easy to see how that association might suggest anger and hatred toward the victimizer, a reaction victims often feel. Thus, one might observe that deontological and empirical desert, in contrast to vengeful desert, take no such victim's perspective and therefore this complaint has no application to them. The latter focus on the offender, in particular on his blameworthiness, not on the victim and his injury, and certainly not on the victim's anger or hatred. Indeed, because their goal is to assess as accurately as possible an offender's blameworthiness, it follows that the presence of anger or hatred would be anathema to these conceptions of desert because it risks distorting the accuracy of the blameworthiness judgment.[291] In other words, the complaint that deserved punishment necessarily is the product of anger and hatred reflects a failure to distinguish vengeful desert on the one hand from deontological and empirical

---

289 *Id.* at 1652.

290 David Dolinko, Some Thoughts About Retributivism, 101 Ethics 537, 559 (1991).

291 Feinberg & Coleman, Philosophy of Law, *supra* note 271, at 794: A person is punished in excess of his just deserts if he is punished with greater severity than the blameworthy character of his conduct would justify. A person cannot coherently be held blameworthy for the degree to which he is hated by those wrongs (very blameworthy for injuring thin-skinned victims and minimally blameworthy for injuring stoic victims?), and thus any criminal sentencing that takes account of victim hatred (as any revenge system would have to do) violates a fundamental right, is unjust, and is thus wrong in principle.

desert on the other—a response analogous to the response above to the complaint that deserved punishment is necessarily harsh.

But the complaint that desert is based upon anger and hatred also is problematic for another reason: It is a complaint about *motivation in punishing* rather than about the *distribution of punishment*. Though the complaint is mixed with substantive complaints about lack of justness, it has little to do with justness. A distribution consistent with deontological or empirical desert could be motivated by anger in any particular case or by any particular punisher, but the motivation itself does not make the punishment any more or less just. The same is true of punishment based upon a vengeful desert distribution. If a vengeful desert distribution just happens as a matter of dumb luck in a given case to produce a sentence that exactly matches an offender's blameworthiness, the fact that anger or hatred motivates it does not make the sentence unjust. And conversely, if a vengeful desert distribution produces an unjust sentence (from the perspective of deontological or empirical desert), the absence of anger in its imposition does not make it just. A society has every reason to want its determinations of punishment to be free of anger and hatred for a variety of reasons, but the presence of that emotion itself can be only the basis upon which to criticize the punisher, not the punishment.

3. A Preference for Prison, or Worse?

Desert is sometimes associated with a preference for imprisonment,[292] or worse.[293] For example, in debating the recent proposal to shift the Model Penal Code to a desert distributive principle, one writer explains:

> The Plan for Revision of the Model Penal Code rejects the original Code's choice of rehabilitation as the guiding principle for

---

292 *See*, e.g., Development in Law: Alternatives to Incarceration, 111 Harv. L. Rev. 1967, 1971 (1998) ("In the proretribution culture, incarceration is the punishment of choice. Because the punitiveness of incarceration can be easily adjusted by adjusting the term of imprisonment, incarceration accords nicely with the proportionality premise at the core of retribution."); David McCord, Imagining a Retributivist Alternative to Capital Punishment, 50 Fla. L. Rev. 1, 82 (1998) ("There are two constraints on any efforts to imagine a sufficiently retributive alternative to the death penalty. The first is that any alternative must be based primarily on incarceration.").

293 Rubin, Just Say No To Retribution, *supra* note 284, at 69 (2003) ("the first thing that retribution brings to mind is that the offender should be tortured while in prison.... By torturing the prisoner, society would be 'paying him back' for the wrongs he committed, and would be giving him his just deserts.)

punishment, and proposes to replace it with the principle of retribution. This would be a serious mistake, both for the Code and for the country.

It would be a mistake for the Code because it would align the Code with the worst features of contemporary American penal practice. There is no need to recite the absurdities of this practice at great length; it is well known that the United States has the highest rate of incarceration in the Western world by a factor of five. What is important to recognize is that this trend has been justified, and sometimes exacerbated, by legislation that abandons the goal of rehabilitation and embraces the principle of retribution. If the Code were to embrace this principle as well, it would inevitably be seen as lending its support to all the irrationalities, immoralities, and inefficiencies of our current addiction to incarceration.[294]

If, under the vengeful conception of desert, "the punishment should fit the crime," it might be argued that prison ought to have a preferred place among punishment methods because it best reproduces the victim's suffering, given the limitations liberal democracies place on punishment methods. Any less severe form of punishment would fail to match the victim suffering the offender caused. By the same token, the vengeful conception of desert might logically suggest the death penalty for murder.

However, because neither deontological nor empirical desert has an interest in reproducing the suffering of the victim upon the offender, they have no reason to give special preference to prison or to any other punishment method. Their interest is only in insuring that a certain amount of punishment is imposed—the amount that will put the offender in her proper ordinal rank among other cases according to his relative blameworthiness. Any method or methods of punishment that achieve that result would be fully consistent with the demands of deontological and empirical desert.

Indeed, because their focus is on the amount rather than the method of punishment, deontological and empirical desert can provide greater flexibility in the method by which punishment is imposed than is commonly available today. A sentencing system or sentencing judge could be

---

294 Rubin, Just Say No To Retribution, *supra* note 284, at 17.

allowed complete discretion in fashioning any particular sentencing method or combination of methods for a given case, as long as the total amount of punishment imposed was that deserved given the offender's blameworthiness. All that would be needed would be a table that gave punishment "credit" for each punishment method according to the relative punitive "bite" of that method, as noted previously. Once such a table of punishment equivalencies is established—setting equivalencies between fine, weekend jail, supervised probation, community service, and any other sanctioning method (such tables already exist[295])—a sentencing judge can be left to translate a prison sentence into any other method or combination of methods, so long as the total punitive "bite" totaled the amount deserved. The ideal punishment equivalency table would be one that sets punishment ratios such that an offender and the community are indifferent as to which of the punishment methods is used.[296]

This kind of sentencing flexibility is particularly useful today, at a time when there is interest in promoting nonincarcerative sanctions.[297]

---

295 *See* Harlow, Darley & Robinson, The Severity of Intermediate Penal Sanctions, *supra* note 118, at 71, 85. (displaying a punishment equivalency table); Paul H. Robinson and the University of Pennsylvania Law School Criminal Law Research Group, Final Report of the Maldivian Penal Law & Sentencing Project, Vol. 1, at 14 (2006), *available at* http://www.law.upenn.edu/cf/faculty/phrobins/ ("The table . . . (Punishment Method Equivalency Table) identifies what length or amount of each non-incarcerative method of punishment is equivalent to a given term of imprisonment."); *id.* at 130 (displaying the equivalency table).

296 One might argue that each offender feels punishment differently, therefore, it is impossible as a practical matter to construct a punishment system that gives each offender the punishment he deserves. *See* Michael Tonry, Obsolescence and Immanence in Penal Theory and Policy, 105 Colum. L. Rev. 1264 (2005). In other words, it would be impossible to construct a punishment "equivalency table" because the unique way in which each offender experiences punishment means that the "equivalency table" would have to be different for each offender. While this may be true with regard to deontological desert, which concerns itself with giving each offender the punishment that he personally deserves, the objection is inapplicable to empirical desert. Empirical desert concerns itself with giving not the punishment that each individual offender actually deserves but rather with the amount of punishment called for under the principles that track the community's intuitions of justice—thus, it is the community's perception of the criminal justice system's moral authority that counts, not the transcendent truth of the punishment the offender deserves. Empirical desert calls not for an equivalency table set according to the extent of each offender's reaction to each kind of punishment but rather for an equivalency table set according to the community's collective judgment of the relative punitive "bite" among different punishment methods.

297 For discussion of such sentencing systems generally, *see* Paul H. Robinson, Desert, Crime Control, Disparity, and Units of Punishment, in Penal Theory and

Not only are such sanctions typically much less costly than prison, but they also permit the opportunity to avoid future crime through rehabilitation, incapacitation, or deterrence, without subverting justice.

4. Only Vague Demands?: "Limiting Retributivism" in Setting the Punishment Continuum Endpoint

A primary objection to desert as a distributive principle is what is said to be its vagueness.[298]

> Everyone may agree that five years in prison is unjustly harsh desert for shoplifting, or that a five dollar fine is unjustly lenient desert for rape, but beyond such clear cases our intuitions seem to fail us. Is two years, five years, or ten years the proper sanction for a rape? . . . Our sense of just deserts here seems to desert us.[299]

Practice: Tradition and Innovation in Criminal Justice 93–107 (Andrew Duff et al. eds., Manchester University Press 1994) (discussing a number of nonincarcerative methods and their punitive "bite" and its applicability to both desert and instrumentalist concerns); Paul H. Robinson, A Sentencing System for the 21st Century?, 66 Tex. L. Rev. l, 41–61 (1987) (detailing the idea that taking account of the seriousness of a crime, its quantity, and other relevant judgments and characteristics will produce the relative amount of sanction appropriate for offense and offender, but that various methods (many nonincarcerative) can be imposed in combination to accomplish the appropriate sanction). Other writers have developed the idea in different ways. Norval Morris & Michael Tonry, Between Prison and Probation 73–81 (1990) (outlining the idea of relying on "reasonable interchangeability" of sanctions, including nonincarcerative sanctions to produce a comprehensive sentencing system); Andrew von Hirsch, Martin Wasik & Judith Greene, Punishments in the Community and the Principles of Desert, 20 Rutgers L.J. 595 (1989) (explaining a sentencing grid system which includes incarcerative and nonincarcerative sanctions and introducing three levels of possible substitution between incarcerative and nonincarcerative sanctions).

   Several states have adopted or are testing sentencing systems that rely in part upon nonincarcerative solutions. See, e.g., New Jersey Supreme Court Judicial Conference on Sanctioning and Provision, Report of Committee on Sanctioning (March 1992); Louisiana Sentencing Commission Guidelines, 22 La. Admin. Code tit. 22:IX(1) §403 (revised May 1992); Oregon Administrative Rules §§253-05-011 et. seq. (Nov. 1989).

298 See, e.g., John Braithwaite & Philip Petit, Not Just Deserts: A Republican Theory of Criminal Justice 180 (1990) ("The vagueness of desert . . . masks mistakes."); R.A. Duff, Penal Communications: Recent Work in the Philosophy of Punishment, 20 Crime & Just. 1, 7 (1996) ("It is not enough simply to appeal to the supposedly shared intuition that the guilty deserve to suffer . . . since such an intuition, however widely shared, needs explanation: *what* do they deserve to suffer, and why?").

299 Leo Katz, Criminal Law, in A Companion to the Philosophy of Law and Legal Theory 80–81 (Dennis Patterson, ed., 1996).

Some writers, such as Norval Morris,[300] may be willing to concede that desert is not a hopelessly vague concept, that it has some meaning, but would make a related but slightly different criticism: Desert cannot specify a particular amount of punishment that should be imposed; it can only identify a range of punishment that should not be imposed because it would be a seriously disproportionate. Indeed, this is the underlying assumption of the American Law Institute's recent amendment of Model Penal Code Section 1.02(2)(a), which sets out the purposes of the sentencing provisions and the principles governing their interpretation and application:

> Subsection (2)(a) embraces Morris's observation that moral intuitions about doing justice in specific cases are almost always rough and approximate—and that most people experience them as such. Even if a decision maker is well acquainted with all the circumstances of a particular crime, and has a rich understanding of the offender, it is seldom possible (except in an extreme case) for the decision maker to say that the deserved penalty is *precisely x*. In Morris's phrase, the "moral calipers" possessed by human beings are not sufficiently fine-tuned to reach exact judgments. He postulated instead that most people's moral sensibilities, for most crimes, will orient them toward a range of permissible sanctions that are "not undeserved." At the perimeters of the range, some punishments will appear clearly excessive to do justice, and some will appear clearly too lenient—but there will nearly always be a gray area between the two extremes.
>
> Subsection 1.02(2)(a)(i) codifies Morris's idea of an approximate retributive ballpark when it speaks of a "*range* of severity" of proportionate punishments.[301]

---

300 Morris, The Future of Imprisonment, *supra* note 205, at 75–76 (1974):

> Desert is, of course, not precisely quantifiable. There is uncertainty as to the judge's role in its assessment, argument as to the extent to which he ought to reflect legislative and popular views of the gravity of the crime if they differ from his own. And further, views of the proper maximums of retributive punishments differ dramatically between countries, between cultures and subcultural groups, and in all countries over time. Nevertheless, the concept of desert remains an essential link between crime and punishment. Punishment in excess of what is seen by that society at the time as a deserved punishment is tyranny.

301 American Law Institute, Model Penal Code Amendment (Adopted May 16, 2007), at 8.

If one has in mind the vengeful conception of desert, the claim of vagueness may make sense under the theory that the demand that the punishment be "proportional" to the harm caused leaves a good deal of flexibility in application. That proportionality requirement might be taken to suggest only the need for an approximation. On the other hand, the strict form of lex talionis—that punishment "should correspond in degree and in kind to the offense of the wrongdoer"[302] is not so vague. Admittedly, there may remain some application questions: Exactly how is victim suffering to be measured, and how is it to be reproduced? Doesn't every victim experience a crime differently?

However, the same vagueness complaint is clearly misguided when applied to deontological and empirical desert, with their focus on offender blameworthiness rather than on victim suffering, although the vagueness complaint is made about offender blameworthiness too.

> Insofar as we seek a morally sensitive scale in which to weigh subjective guilt, to classify the individual criminal on the long continuum from unblemished virtue to unmitigated evil, [t]he criminal law is unfitted for such issues. It faces an adequacy of difficulties without addressing such ethical nuances. It is necessarily generalized rather than related to the moral quality of the specific act.
>
> . . . . Questions of guilt will thus be weighed on the imprecise scales of the criminal law which can allow for only a few subjective qualifications to the objective gravity of the crime.[303]

But such complaints are based in part on a failure to appreciate the specific demands of these two conceptions of desert: the demands of ordinal ranking, as opposed to the issue of punishment continuum endpoint, as discussed in Section A.4.a. above. Those who complain about desert's vagueness seem to assume, incorrectly, that deontological and empirical desert seek to provide a universal, absolute amount of punishment as deserved for a given offense.[304] Though this assumption may well

---

302 *See* Robinson, Competing Conceptions, *supra* note 268, at 261.

303 Morris, *supra* note 205, at 74.

304 E.g., consider the following passage, in which the authors think they are revealing a critical flaw in the theory of desert:

> Retributivism cannot tell us what is the right punishment for murder, whether it should be 20 percent higher or twice as high as that for burglary. The eighteenth century judge who sentences the burglar to torture followed by death, the judge

be sound as to vengeful desert, deontological and empirical desert make no such claim for an absolute and universal punishment amount. The primary concern of empirical and deontological desert is to ensure that offenders of different blameworthiness are given different amounts of punishment, each in relation to their relative blameworthiness. That ordinal ranking does not require a specific amount of punishment in a universal sense. It requires imposition of only that specific amount of punishment that will put the offender at her appropriate ordinal rank *given the punishment continuum endpoint in that society.* That is, the uncertainty about deserved punishment amount that Morris and others observe arises not because of any vagueness in the ordinal ranking of offenses according to offender blameworthiness but rather because of differences in the punishment continuum endpoint that a society might adopt. Once that endpoint is set, vagueness in deserved punishment amount disappears.

The project of setting the punishment continuum endpoint might properly include a variety of purposes, including deterrence, incapacitation, or rehabilitation, as well as desert. For example, general deterrence might want to set the continuum endpoint high to maximize deterrence. Thus, torture and cutting off hands might be quite useful from a purely general deterrence point of view. In this context, desert's role may be a limited one, along the lines of "limiting retributivism" in marking out ranges of unacceptable extremes. But, of course, setting the punishment continuum endpoint is not part of the adjudication process—thus not properly part of the distributive principles contained in a criminal code, for example, which is where the Model Penal Code reform attempts to use the concept of "limiting retributivism." In other words, the error of those promoting the concept is only in failing to see that it has application only in this limited role, setting the punishment continuum endpoint, and has no application in the primary function of these conceptions

---

from Alabama who sentences him to ten years, and the judge from Amsterdam who sentences him to victim compensation all pronounce that they are giving the offender what he deserves. There is no retributivist answer as to which judge is right. On the retributivist's view, so long as they are all handing down sentences for burglary that are proportionately more than those for less serious crimes and proportionately less than those for more serious crimes, they could all be right.

Braithwaite & Petit, Not Just Deserts, *supra* note 298, at 178.

of desert in serving as a principle for determining how criminal liability and punishment *is to be distributed along that punishment continuum.*

Deontological and empirical desert may have something useful to say about placing the punishment continuum endpoint, but the nature of their contribution on this point is quite different than when they serve as a distributive principle for punishment: Here they identify only extremes beyond which placement of the endpoint would be problematic.[305] In other words, it is in this limited way that they work as "limiting retributivism" describes them, as establishing only ranges that mark out unacceptable extremes.

For example, the rationale behind empirical desert suggests a limit to the range in which the punishment continuum endpoint should be placed: It should not be placed at a point that is either so low or so high that it will have the effect of undermining the community's collective judgment about whether the criminal justice system is in fact doing justice. Notice that this judgment is one that is necessarily culturally dependent. One community might accept stoning to death as being an acceptable endpoint,[306] while another could reject fifteen years imprisonment as too harsh on endpoint.[307] Moreover, even within a culture, community attitudes toward punishment severity can vary over time.[308]

---

305 For example, von Hirsch argues:

> [H]igh overall severity levels are inconsistent with the moral functions of penal censure. Through punishments' censuring features, the criminal sanction offers a normative reason for desisting to human beings seen as moral agents: that doing certain acts is wrong and hence should be refrained from. . . . The higher the penalty levels rise, however, the less the normative reasons for desisting supplied by penal censure will count, and the more the system becomes in effect a bare system of threats. . . . To the extent this argument is accepted, it points toward keeping penalties at moderate levels.

> Andrew von Hirsch, Proportionate Sentences: A Desert Perspective in Principled Sentencing, Readings on Theory & Policy 174 (Andrew von Hirsch & Andrew Ashworth, eds., 2nd ed. 1998).

306 One of the traditional *hudud* punishments for a married person who commits adultery (*zina*) is stoning to death. Ibn Rushd, The Distinguished Jurist's Primer 523 (Imran Ahsan Khan Nyazee, trans., 1994).

307 E.g., average prison sentences vary widely from nation to nation. American offenders were required to serve an average of 29 months after conviction in 1999. United Nations Survey of Crime Trends and Operations of Criminal Justice Systems at 480. In contrast, the average offender in the Netherlands was released after 5 months (*id*. at 308), while Columbian offenders were not released until a startling mean of 140 months (*id*. at 66).

308 *See*, e.g., Michael Tonry, Sentencing Matters 137 (1996) (noting that the average prison sentence for violent offenses in the United States tripled between 1975 and 1989).

No doubt people within a single community disagree as to where the endpoint should be set, and one approach may be to average these opinions on a proper endpoint to minimize the perceived deviation that would trigger disutility. On the other hand, one might also be able to make the argument that the analysis ought not be symmetrical here. One might argue that more resistance and subversion, for example, would be inspired by an endpoint that is set too high than one that is set too low. This argues in favor of setting an endpoint low enough to avoid the disapproval of most people. That the situation is one of complete asymmetry may not be entirely true, for it is also possible that an endpoint that is set too low may inspire a different kind of subversion. It might promote, for example, the use of extralegal punishment processes such as lynching and vigilantism, overly aggressive prosecution, perversion of the normal investigative, fact-finding, and decision-making process to get the "appropriate punishment" of an offender they fear may get inadequate punishment. Depending upon what research showed, however, one might conclude that the system's moral credibility would be more endangered by setting an endpoint too high than setting it too low.

Returning to the original issue of the vagueness complaint against deontological and empirical desert, the discussion to this point does not fully settle the issue. Some writers argue that even ordinal ranking is something that can be done only in the vaguest terms, that establishing specific rankings is impossible.

> Perhaps, at best, retributivism can determine the roughly appropriate punishment by comparatively ranking offenses in such a way as murder warrants greater punishment than rape, which warrants greater punishment than armed robbery, and so on. But it cannot determine whether rape warrants twenty, thirty, forty years imprisonment. Though retributivism cannot set cardinal or absolute levels of punishment, its advocates insist that they can set ordinal, or relative, levels of punishment (for example, murder warrants greater punishment than larceny). But retributivism cannot even satisfactorily determine degrees of punishment ordinally. For example, even if we assume that, all other things being equal, murder warrants greater punishment than armed robbery, does negligent homicide warrant greater punishment than intentional rape or intentional armed robbery? . . . Retributivism has no answer to the issue of whether greater wrongdoing done with lower culpability (for example, negligence or recklessness) warrants

more or less punishment than comparatively minor wrongdoing with a greater level of culpability (such as intention or purpose). Thus, retributivism can determine neither the ordinal nor the cardinal ranking of crimes and their concomitant degrees of punishment.[309]

Many moral philosophers may have an answer to this challenge and may be able to give a reasoned account of how to make the kinds of judgments called for here,[310] but it is admittedly a problem of sorts that different moral philosophers will have different answers. However, this is not a problem of vagueness but rather a problem of disagreement, which is the subject of Section B.5., discussed immediately below. (This disagreement among moral philosophers may make it difficult to operationalize a criminal justice system based upon the deontological conception of desert, an issue discussed in Section B.8.) However, there is nothing *in principle* to suggest that deontological desert could not produce a principled system for the ordinal ranking of offenses.

When the vagueness complaint is offered against empirical desert, it produces a quite different response. The critics argue that a blameworthiness ranking of offenses is beyond the ability of people's intuitions of justice, that those intuitions are simply too vague to do more than to roughly distinguish between "serious" cases and "not serious" cases and cannot provide the nuance needed to do more. But the empirical studies paint a dramatically different picture.

The evidence comes from a wide variety of empirical studies.[311] In some studies, subjects are asked to put offenses or offense scenarios into one of a set of predetermined categories; in another kind of study, subjects are asked to rank order offenses or offense scenarios; in a third kind

---

309 Russell L. Christopher, Deterring Retributivism: The Injustice of "Just" Punishment, 96 Nw. U. L. Rev. 843, 893 (2002) (footnotes omitted).

310 *See* von Hirsch, Proportionate Sentences, *supra* note 305, at 173–174.

> With respect to comparative rankings, *ordinal* proportionality provides considerable guidance: persons convicted of similar crimes should receive punishments of comparable severity (save in special aggravating or mitiating circumstances altering the harm or culpability of the conduct in the particular circumstances); and persons convicted of crimes of differing gravity should suffer punishments correspondingly graded in onerousness. . . . [T]hey are infringed when equally reprehensible conduct is punished markedly unequally.

311 For a general discussion of these matters, *see* Robinson & Kurzban, Concordance & Conflict, *supra* note 277, at Parts I–III.

of study, subjects are asked to assign numerical values to each of a number of offenses or offense scenarios.[312] The results in all of these studies are consistent: Subjects displayed a good deal of nuance in the judgments they make.[313] Small changes in facts produce large and predictable changes in punishment. Durham summarizes the surveys this way: "Virtually without exception, citizens seem able to assign highly specific sentences for highly specific events."[314] The conclusion suggested by the empirical evidence is that people take account of a wide variety of factors and often give them quite different effect in different situations. That is, people's intuitions of justice are not vague or simplistic, as claimed, but rather quite sophisticated and complex. This suggests that while the vagueness complaint may be valid with regard to vengeful desert, it is misguided when applied to deontological desert, at least in principle, and simply wrong in both principle and practice when applied to empirical desert.

5. Subject to Profound Disagreement?

Another common objection to using desert as a distributive principle for criminal liability and punishment is the concern that, even if individual people may have a clear notion of what desert demands, there is simply no agreement among people. Against this complaint, both vengeful and deontological desert have weak responses. The problem for vengeful desert, at least for its diluted form, arises from the vagueness of its criterion: the vagueness of "proportionality" to victim suffering and the subjectivity inherent in the victim perspective. (Of course, vengeful desert might mitigate this criticism by insisting upon its strict form, of matching the victim's suffering exactly, but this move only aggravates the "harshness" objection to it.)

The problem for deontological desert is slightly different. The focus of its distributive principle is fixed and specific—an offender's moral blameworthiness—but moral philosophers simply disagree about just how this principle translates into specific punishment in a given case. "The Retributivist label . . . might not seem particularly useful, for the differences on particular issues among some retributivists may seem

---

312 *Id.* at Parts I & II.
313 *Id.* at Part I.
314 Alexis M. Durham III, Public Opinion Regarding Sentences for Crime: Does it Exist?, 21 J. Crim. Justice 1, 2 (1993).

greater than the differences between some retributivists and some utilitarians."[315]

The same too-much-disagreement complaint has been made about people's intuitions of justice, which would leave empirical desert in a similar situation. Clearly, it is common wisdom that little agreement exists among people's intuitions of justice.

> There is . . . reason to doubt that anything like a consensus exists on the seriousness of criminal conduct. While there may be some agreement on relative levels of harm, there appears to be great variation in perceptions of the absolute magnitude of harm represented by various criminal acts, and in either the relative or absolute level of culpability represented by various criminal actors.[316]
>
> [E]ven assuming retribution in distribution is appropriate, there is a classic epistemological problem. How do we know how much censure, or "deserved punishment," a particular wrongdoer absolutely deserves? God may know, but as countless sentencing exercises have shown, peoples' intuitions about individual cases vary widely.[317]

But the common wisdom simply does not match the empirical reality. In fact, empirical studies show broadly shared intuitions that serious wrongdoing should be punished and broadly shared intuitions about the relative blameworthiness of different cases, especially for the core of criminality, *malum in se* offenses. The striking extent of the agreement on intuitions of justice is illustrated in a recent study that asked subjects to rank order twenty-four crime scenario descriptions according to the amount of punishment deserved. The researchers found that the subjects displayed an astounding level of agreement in the ordinal ranking of the scenarios, especially for core harms such as physical aggression, taking of property, and deception in exchanges. Subjects agreed with the modal ranking of the group for 96 percent of their pairwise ranking judgments. The most common deviation, as one might guess, was for a subject to "flip" the ranking of two scenarios that were adjacent in the group's modal ranking—for example, a subject might rank order the scenarios as S6, S8,

---

315 Mark Tunick, Punishment: Theory and Practice 107 (1992).

316 John Monahan, The Case for Prediction in the Modified Desert Model of Criminal Sentencing, 5 Int'l J. L. & Psychiatry 103, 105 (1982).

317 Tonry, Obsolescence and Immanence, *supra* note 296, at 1233, 1263.

S7, S9, "flipping" the S7 and S8 scenarios. If these simple "flips" of adjacent scenarios are excluded, the percentage of all rankings that deviate from the group mode rankings is 2.7 percent. In, other words, "flips" aside, subjects agreed with the modal ranking of the group in 97.7 percent of their pairwise judgments.

A more sophisticated statistical measure of concordance is found in Kendall's W coefficient of concordance, in which 1.0 indicates perfect agreement and 0.0 indicates no agreement. In this study, the Kendall's W is .95 for in-person testing and .88 for online-testing (with $p < .001$), an astounding level of agreement. One might expect to get this high a Kendall's W if subjects were asked to judge the relative brightness of different groupings of spots, for example. When asked to perform more subjective or complex comparisons, such as asking travel magazine readers to rank the risk of terror of eight different travel destinations, one gets a Kendall's W of .52. When asking economists to rank the top 20 economics journals according to quality, one gets a Kendall's W. of .095.[318]

Indeed, the high level of agreement in the ordinal ranking of different scenarios according to deserved punishment is generally consistent across demographics, including across cultural differences examined in cross-cultural studies that replicated domestic studies.[319] Typical of the conclusions in these studies, Newman reports that, "it is apparent that there was considerable agreement as to the amount of punishment appropriate to each act"[320] and that looking at relative rankings indicates "general agreement in ranks across all countries."[321]

The level of agreement is strongest for those "core" wrongs with which criminal law primarily concerns itself—physical aggression, taking property, and deception in exchanges—and becomes less pronounced as the nature of the offense moves farther from the core of wrongdoing.[322] But even where disagreement exists, empirical desert offers a ready means by which the disagreements can be resolved: by adopting the majority view. No such means exists to resolve conflicting views for deontological desert. From the perspective of empirical desert, avoiding deviation from

---

318 Robinson & Kurzban, Concordance & Conflict, *supra* note 277, at Parts II.A.,B. and III.

319 *Id.* at Part III.

320 Graeme Newman, Comparative Deviance: Perception and Law in Six Cultures 140 (1976).

321 *Id.* at 141 (*see* Table 12, 142–143).

322 Robinson & Kurzban, Concordance & Conflict, *supra* note 277, at Part IV.B.& C.

community views is best, but where disagreement exists among the community and therefore some deviation from some people's views is inevitable, the law should adopt whatever rule will undermine its moral credibility the least. That commonly will mean adopting the majority rule over the minority rule.

How is it that the common wisdom—the people's intuitions of justice are so different—could have gotten it so wrong? Some sources of apparent disagreement are simply misleading. For example, one may (erroneously) conclude there is disagreement if one fails to distinguish the issue of ordinal ranking from that of setting the punishment continuum endpoint, as discussed in Section B.4: While people may agree on the relative blameworthiness of a set of cases, some people may prefer generally harsher punishments than other people. Thus, people's disagreement on the continuum endpoint masks their agreement on the ordinal ranking of cases along the continuum.

Another source of apparent disagreement arises from different assumptions about the underlying facts in a case. Such differences will predictably underestimate the extent of agreement, rather than overestimate it. When a test scenario is written ambiguously so that different test participants perceive it differently, the existence of shared intuitions of justice itself will predict different judgements among the participants. So too, when a case in the headlines has social or political implications, different people will commonly perceive its relevant facts differently. What one makes of the police testimony in the O.J. Simpson case or the Rodney King case may depend upon how one has come to view police officers from one's daily life experiences. If people draw different conclusions from the testimony, they are likely to have different views of the relevant facts of the case, which would predict different views on the liability and punishment deserved.

The failure to appreciate the high level of ordinal ranking agreement makes sense if people fail to distinguish between the absolute severity focus of vengeful desert and the ordinal ranking focus of deontological and empirical desert. And even in the context of these latter conceptions of desert, it is easy to see how people's disagreements about the proper endpoint for the punishment continuum naturally obscures the existing agreement on the ranking of offenses along that continuum. That is, we are all well aware from news accounts as well as our own personal discussions that we frequently disagree with others and they with us when it comes to deserved punishment for cases in the news. But the point here is that those disagreements often are disagreements not about the relative blameworthiness of this offender as against other offenders but rather disagreements over the general severity of punishment generally or disagreements about the facts of the case.

6. Fails to Avoid Avoidable Crime?

The most fundamental complaint by utilitarians against a desert distributive principle is its disutility.

> Consider the notion of retributive justice that calls for punishment that fits the wrongful act. It is possible that a higher level of punishment would reduce or eliminate the occurrence of wrongs. Presuming that the theory's demand for punishment is motivated by the evil associated with wrongdoing (that is, wrongful acts are themselves unfair), it should be troubling that insistence on fair punishment may result in avoidable wrongdoing.[323]

Such disutility is obviously objectionable to utilitarians, and many would make the claim that it is particularly objectionable in the case of punishment:

> [P]unishment—the intentional infliction of pain—is senseless and even cruel if it does no good, and yet retributivists favor precisely that, i.e., the infliction of pain that need not result in future benefit. Society's goal should be to reduce overall human suffering, not purposely to cause more of it.[324]

Traditionally, the instrumentalist preference has been for distributing liability to optimize deterrence, rehabilitation, incapacitation, or some combination of them.[325] And those consequentialists who seek to minimize future crime would be right to point out that deontological desert as a distributive principle would allow future crimes that could

---

323 Louis Kaplow & Steven Shavell, Fairness Versus Welfare, 114 Harv. L. Rev. 961, 1007 (2001). Similarly, it has been complained that "retributivists would stand idly by even if a just-deserts system of punishment were to drastically increase crime rates or create an interminable line of fatherless families." Luna, Punishment Theory, *supra* note 265, at 221.

324 Joshua Dressler, Understanding Criminal Law 22 (4th ed. 2006).

325 *See*, e.g, Model Penal Code §1.02(1) (1962) (listing the general purposes of the provisions).

have been avoided by an instrumentalist distributive principle, such as one that relied upon these traditional instrumentalist distributive principles.

But of course this classic challenge of utilitarianism to deontological desert does not work against empirical desert because the latter's distribution of liability and punishment is specifically designed to minimize future crime—by harnessing the crime-control power of social influence that comes with building the criminal law's moral credibility. In other words, empirical desert offers a utilitarian, consequentialist rationale for adopting it is a distributive principle. A deontological desert distribution, in contrast, would indeed be ineffective at optimizing effective crime control. Crime-control benefits flow not from "doing justice" in a deontological sense but only from "doing justice" in an empirical desert sense. The community's perception that justice is being done pays crime-control dividends, not the system's actual success in doing justice.

7. Immoral?

Just as the instrumentalist objection of poor crime control has been leveled at a desert distributive principle—with some force when applied to deontological desert but missing the mark when applied to empirical desert—the reverse sort of objection also can be made: that a desert distribution is immoral.[326] Some writers complain of "the injustice of 'just' punishment."[327]

As one might expect, the response to the immorality complaint is essentially the reverse of the response to the disutility complaint above: The objection may have weight against empirical desert but makes little sense with regard to deontological desert. That is, while moral philosophers may well disagree among themselves about how to translate desert into specific principles of justice, all would agree that the primary goal of

---

326 *See*, e.g., Luna, Punishment Theory, *supra* note 265, at 207–208; Dolinko, Three Mistakes, *supra* note 285, at 1635. Dolinko notes that because retributivists cannot specify the amount of punishment due any particular offender but rather can only specify a range, retributivists cannot be said to be acting morally because are no longer giving the offender exactly what he deserves, which is required to treat the criminal as a moral agent.

327 Russell Christopher, Deterring Retributivism: The Injustice of 'Just' Punishment, 96 Nw. U. L. Rev. 843 (2002).

a deontological desert distribution would be to produce criminal liability and punishment that was, above all else, moral.

On the other hand, the criticism is fair when applied to empirical desert: What empirical desert produces is not justice but only liability and punishment consistent with the community's views about what constitutes justice. The community's intuitions of justice could be wrong, even if there is a high degree of agreement about them. At any particular time and place, there may be widespread support for the morality of conduct that only later is revealed to be immoral and unjust, as with slave owning. To protect against this error, to be able to identify when people's shared intuitions of justice are unjust, a system must turn to deontological desert to provide that transcendent check on the justness of its liability rules. It is only deontological desert that can give us the truth of what is deserved, insulated from the vicissitudes of human irrationality and emotions.

But an examination of the modern methodology of moral philosophers suggests that they fail to appreciate the practical importance of the difference between deontological and empirical desert. They commonly rely heavily upon intuitions of justice in their analyses and thereby bias their conclusions in favor of principles of justice that accord with people's shared intuitions. That reduces the extent to which moral philosophy can be relied upon to provide the transcendent check that empirical desert needs.

The current methodology of moral philosophers relies upon intuitions of justice in a variety of ways. A standard analytic form, if not *the* standard form, among moral philosophers today is to test variations in a series of hypotheticals according to philosophers' own intuitions about the proper resolution of each, as in Rawls' "reflective equilibrium."[328] The differences in their judgments about the intuitively proper resolution of different hypotheticals are used as data points, as it were, from which philosophers derive a moral principle, which can in turn be tested and refined by testing that moral principle against the philosophers' intuitions in new sets of hypotheticals.

But the methodological reliance on intuitions of justice creates a bias in favor of moral principles that are consistent with intuitions. Moral

---

328 John Rawls, A Theory of Justice 48 (1971) (explaining that the best sense of justice is one which matches a person's judgments in reflective equilibrium—a state reached after consideration of various conceptions of justice).

principles with principled, reasoned support might nonetheless fail to gain currency among philosophers or might be discarded, simply because philosophers as a group think their results inconsistent with intuitions—a practical veto by philosophers' shared intuitions.[329]

Ironically, the practical effect of this weakness of modern moral philosophy is to make empirical desert somewhat less attractive as a distributive principle. In the absence of a moral philosophy that will identify beforehand the community's shared moral errors, empirical desert is more likely to lead to results later revealed to be unjust. For all its appeal, empirical deserts is not the ideal distributive principle, although it may have fewer disadvantages than the available alternatives.

8. Impractical to Implement?

Writers commonly think it impractical to construct a working criminal justice system based upon desert principles. This was an argument commonly made, for example, in the internal debates among commissioners during the drafting of the United States Sentencing Commission guidelines. "Just desert" could not be used as a basis for drafting sentencing guidelines because of "its impracticability" and because of "its incompatibility with administrative and procedural requirements of sentencing."[330] Yet, as noted previously, the A.L.I. recently adopted desert as the distributive principle for the Model Penal Code's sentencing scheme.[331] Is it, or is it not, possible to implement a distributive principle based upon desert? Again, the answer depends upon which conception of desert one has in mind.

a. Vengeful and Deontological Desert

It follows from what has been said in the subsections immediately above that it would be difficult to produce a system of criminal liability and

---

329 Paul H. Robinson, The Role of Moral Philosophers in the Competition Between Philosophical and Empirical Desert, 48 Wm. & Mary L. Rev. 1831 (2007).

330 Ilene H. Nagel, Supreme Court Review: Foreword: Structuring Sentencing Discretion: The New Federal Sentencing Guidelines New Federal, 80 J. Crim. L. & Criminology 883, 920 (1990).

331 See MPC §1.02 (as adopted on May 16, 2007). Desert here is set as an absolute; other principles can be relied upon only if they work and are not inconsistent with desert.

punishment based upon vengeful desert, at least in the somewhat diluted "proportionality" form that might be politically palatable in a liberal democracy. Vengeful desert fails to provide enough specificity as to the exact criterion for distributing liability and punishment. What exactly is meant by the requirement that the punishment be "proportionate" to the harm of the offense or the suffering of the victim? If proportionality were taken to mean ordinal ranking along a fixed continuum, as in deontological and empirical desert, it could be translated into specific sentences but, by itself, connected only to a concept of extent of victim suffering, it seems to give only general guidance. Perhaps even more problematic is the potentially subjective nature of the criterion. If the offender's punishment is to match the victim's suffering, a determination of the punishment deserved cannot be made upon the objective facts of the offense but requires an examination of how much this particular victim suffered from the offense. These are not unsurmountable barriers, but coming as they are in the context of the serious disagreements over just what vengeful desert requires and in the absence of any authoritative mechanism by which these disagreements can be resolved, it does seem a bit impractical to think that vengeful desert could be used as the distributive principle for the creation and operation of a working criminal justice system.

Nor is it clear that deontological desert can provide the basis for a working distributive principle, such as the one offered in the proposed Model Penal Code section. Deontological desert might in principle be able to provide a specific sentence for each case, but it may not be realistic to rely upon it in practice. The substantial disagreements among moral philosophers about many, if not most, desert issues and the lack of an effective means by which nonphilosophers can reliably choose between these conflicting views, means that though any single moral philosopher might be able to produce a system for distributing punishment, to produce an authoritative deontological-desert-based system may be difficult.

b. Empirical Desert

How does empirical desert fare? Can it be the practical basis for a working criminal justice system? The common wisdom is no because of the concerns about lack of nuance and agreement discussed earlier. For example, Justice Breyer explains in his opposition to basing the United

States Sentencing Commission sentencing guidelines on desert that
desert lacks the required nuance:

> The "just deserts" approach would require that the Commission
> list criminal behaviors in rank order of severity and then apply
> similarly ranked punishments proportionately. For example, if
> theft is considered a more serious or harmful crime than pollu-
> tion, then the thief should be punished more severely than the
> polluter. . . .
>
> Considering the inherent subjectivity of such a trade-off proc-
> ess, the Commission soon realized that only a crude ranking of
> behavior in terms of just deserts . . . could be developed. Although
> guidelines motivated by a just deserts rationale would be cloaked
> in language and form that evoke rationality, using terms such as
> "rank order of seriousness," the rankings would not, in substan-
> tive terms, be wholly objective.[332]

He similarly argues that desert lacks the needed level of agreement:

> [S]ome students of the criminal justice system strenuously urged
> the Commission to follow what they call a 'just deserts' approach to
> punishment. . . . The difficulty that arises in applying this approach
> is that different Commissioners have different views about the cor-
> rect rank order of the seriousness of different crimes.[333]

The average state criminal code distinguishes a dozen grades
of offenses.[334] Modern sentencing guidelines can use several dozen
categories.[335] Presumably, sentencing judges would like to make even more
distinctions in punishment amount. Are the intuitions of laypersons that

---

332 Stephen Breyer, The Federal Sentencing Guidelines and the Key Compromises Upon
    Which They Rest, 17 Hofstra L. Rev. 1, 15–17 (1988) (footnotes omitted). For other
    writers arguing that crimes cannot be rank ordered, see, e.g., Dolinko, Three Mistakes,
    supra note 285.
333 Breyer, The Federal Sentencing Guidelines, supra note 332, at 15–16.
334 See, e.g., Ariz. Rev. Stat. §13-601 (2006) (distinguishing 6 categories of felonies, 3 cat-
    egories of misdemeanors, and 1 category of petty offenses); Colo. Rev. Stat. §18-1-104
    (1999) (listing 6 felony categories, 3 misdemeanor categories, and 2 "petty offense"
    categories); Kan. Stat. Ann. §21-4704 et seq. (1995) (showing 10 felony categories,
    divided into "drug" and "nondrug" offenses and 3 misdemeanor categories); Neb. Rev.
    Stat. 28-105, -106 (1995) (8 felony categories and 7 misdemeanor categories).
335 The United States Sentencing Guidelines represent the far end of this spectrum, with
    43 offense levels. U.S. Sentencing Guidelines Manual §5A (Nov. 2004), available at
    http://www.ussc.gov/2004guid/gl2004.pdf.

support empirical desert nuanced enough to provide this level of specificity? The discussions in Sections B.4. and B.5. make clear that lay intuitions of justice are both nuanced and the subject of substantial agreement, especially regarding the core wrongs that make up the majority of crimes in practice—physical aggression, taking property, and deception in exchanges. From the point of view of empirical desert, that individual sentencing commissioners may disagree is of no significance. It is the community's shared intuitions of justice that should control, not the intuitions of the sentencing commissioners, for it is through building moral credibility with the larger community that the system can enhance its crime control effectiveness.

Existing empirical studies tell us not only that people agree about the relative blameworthiness of different cases but also do much to map for us the contours of people's agreement and disagreement. And they map not only the relative seriousness of different wrongdoing but also the factors that increase and decrease a violator's blameworthiness. One collection of studies reports community views on the liability rules that govern such wide-ranging topics as the objective requirements for attempt, liability for creating a prohibited risk, the objective requirements for complicity, the requirements for omission liability, the use of force in self-defense, the use of force in defense of property, citizens' law enforcement authority, offense culpability requirements, the culpability requirements for complicity, the liability rules that should govern voluntary intoxication, insanity, immaturity, involuntary intoxication, duress, entrapment, the requirements of sexual offenses, the significance of a person's causal connection with the prohibited result (causation requirements), the felony-murder rule, and the rules that should govern the punishment of multiple related offenses.[336]

---

336 Robinson & Darley, Justice, Liability & Blame, *supra* note 223; Linda Drazga Maxfield, Willie Martin & Christine Kitchens, Just Punishment: Public Perceptions and the Federal Sentencing Guidelines, Research Bulletin for the United States Sentencing Commission (1997), *available at* http://www.ussc.gov/research.htm (describing a research project comparing the attitudes of United States citizens on four federal offenses and comparing them with the appropriate sentencing guidelines); Memorandum from Richard A. Conaboy to the United States Sentencing Commission, Public Opinion on Sentencing Federal Crimes (1997), *available at* http://www.ussc.gov/research.htm (reporting the results of a national survey comparing how individuals would sentence a person convicted of a federal crime and comparing the sanction to that prescribed by the Federal Criminal Code).

It is also true, however, that more research is needed. As much ground as the existing studies cover, they each touch only the basics in their specific subject. More importantly, though there is a literature describing the intuitions of laypersons as a group and there is a literature documenting the existence of many areas of high agreement, these two literatures need to be combined. That is, we need to better understand not only the details of the community's shared intuitions on a wide variety of issues but also to understand the contours and demographics of their disagreement.[337]

Where disagreements do exist—and there will be many instances (especially outside the core of wrongdoing) where this is the case—the logic of the empirical desert suggests an obvious mechanism for resolving those disagreements: adopting the principle that reflects the majority view, adjusted as needed to account for a minority's greater strength of feeling on an issue, as discussed above.[338]

c. Deviating from Empirical Desert

Because one could construct a system based upon empirical desert as a distributive principle, it does not follow that one would want to. In any number of instances, one might want the criminal system's distributive principles to deviate from people's intuitions of justice (even if there was no disagreement among intuitions). First, people's intuitions of justice may prove to be immoral, in a transcendent deontological sense, as discussed in Section B.7. Further, clearly a variety of societal interests exist that are sufficiently important to outweigh the crime-control benefits of an empirical desert distribution, such as fair notice, procedural fairness, and the need to control police and to limit governmental intrusion in private lives.[339] Still further, a society may wish to use criminal

---

337 *See* Robinson & Kurzban, Concordance & Conflict, *supra* note 277, at Part IV (discussing the apparent and real sources of disagreements among laypersons' intuitions of justice).

338 *See supra* Chapter 7, section B.5.

339 *See*, e.g., Paul H. Robinson & Michael T. Cahill, Law Without Justice 90, 137, 186 (2006) (explaining instances where societal interests outweigh strict adherence to desert, such as: a case arising that the law could not possibly have anticipated and thus could not provide notice; an instance of the law applied too strictly, resulting in someone being punished for crimes falling outside the law's spirit; the need to promote respect for individual rights through curbing misconduct of criminal justice officials; allowing diplomatic immunity to prevent acts of retaliation against our diplomats

law to change people's intuitions of justice, toward a view seen as more compatible with the societal values to which the community aspires. For example, the community may decide that it wishes to actively change people's existing intuitions about the relative seriousness of drunk driving, domestic violence, same-sex intercourse, insider trading, or Internet-facilitated copyright piracy.[340]

So it is true that in any real world criminal justice system, that the system will in some instances deviate from people's intuitions of justice is inevitable. But the fact that some deviation occurs does not mean that the goal of building law's moral credibility necessarily fails. That is, there is little reason to believe that any and every deviation from a person's intuitions of justice will completely destroy the criminal justice system's moral credibility in that person's eyes. Rather, it seems more likely that the process is one of incremental effects.[341] The better the system does at regularly tracking people's intuitions of justice, the stronger its moral credibility with them. The more it deviates from empirical desert, and the more indifferent it seems to the deviation, the lower its moral authority.

The conclusion here is not that because deviation is necessary there is no value in adopting empirical desert as a distributive principle but rather just the opposite: the system ought not deviate from empirical desert unless the benefits from that deviation are clear and substantial enough to outweigh the cost that flows from undermining the system's moral credibility through this deviation.

---

abroad; and immunity for domestic political officials to guard their ability to perform official duties).

340 Understanding the community's intuitions of justice and their nature may be necessary for such reform programs. *See* Robinson & Kurzban, Concordance & Conflict, *supra* note 277, at 1892–1893.

341 *See*, e.g., Joseph S. Hall, Note: Guided to Injustice?: The Effect of Sentencing Guidelines on Indigent Defendants and Public Defense, 36 Am. Crim. L. Rev. 1331 1364–1365 (1999):

One of the main requirements for this stigmatizing force, however, is that citizens see the law that governs them as basically fair and morally credible. When even small indications of injustice become apparent to a population, the criminal law loses part of its ability to blame effectively. . . . As people's belief that the law was unfair increased, so did their tendency to disregard it.

C. Summary: A More Detailed Account of Three Conceptions of Desert

The previous discussions have been quite detailed in places, and it may be useful to take a step back and revisit the attempt in Section A to sketch an overview of the three conceptions of desert but now including some of the conclusions that have been developed in the intervening sections.

Vengeful desert focuses upon the offense harm and victim suffering and sets the deserved punishment to match that of victim's harm and suffering, preferably imposed through the same or a related method as the offense conduct. In a less literal version, an exact equivalency of method and amount is not necessary for deserved punishment; generally proportionality of amount and comparability of method are sufficient. Typically, this will mean that serious offenses will require prison or something more serious. Often, an exact amount of punishment deserved will not be clear, but only a general range of punishment, that which is generally proportionate and comparable with the victim's harm and suffering. Because of generality of the "proportionality" demand and the uniqueness of each victim's suffering, translating this conception of desert into a workable criminal justice system may be impracticable. Even if it were practical, such a conception of desert would produce common and significant deviations from what moral philosophers and the community would perceive to be just. And such a distribution, therefore, would suffer the crime-control costs of undermining the system's moral credibility by indifferently deviating from the community's perceptions of justice.

Deontological desert and empirical desert differ from vengeful desert in a number of important ways. Their primary concern is to give the offender the amount of punishment that will put him in his proper ordinal rank according to his moral blameworthiness. They have less concern for the absolute amount of punishment imposed. Once the punishment continuum endpoint is set, which all societies must do, the demands of deontological and empirical desert are quite specific. These conceptions of desert also differ from vengeful desert in that their focus is almost exclusively on the amount of punishment not the method by which it is imposed, thus, they have no preference for prison. (These conceptions of desert can play a role in setting the general severity of punishment—in determining the punishment continuum endpoint—but generally only to suggest a range of punishment severity beyond which the endpoint should not be set. In other words, "limiting retributivism" may well make sense in this context, even if it is inappropriate as a distributive principle for punishment.)

Deontological desert differs from empirical desert in that the former offers a transcendent truth about justice, while the latter offers only the community's intuitions of justice. In that regard, deontological desert would seem to provide an advantage over empirical desert because the latter suffers from the fact that people's intuitions of justice may be unjust, in a transcendent moral sense. Unfortunately, deontological desert suffers a number of its own difficulties that empirical desert does not share. There is significant disagreement among moral philosophers about the principles of justice, which makes it difficult to use as the basis for constructing a working criminal justice system. It also may be criticized as failing to avoid avoidable crime. One might be tempted to use it nonetheless, perhaps in conjunction with empirical desert (to provide a transcendent check for moral errors in the community's shared intuitions of justice), but because of modern moral philosophy's heavy reliance upon intuitions of justice, whether it can effectively perform this role is questionable.

Empirical desert distributes punishment according to principles of justice derived from the community's shared intuitions. There is a good deal of agreement on these intuitions, at least regarding those core wrongs that make up the central part of criminal law, and to construct a criminal justice system based upon this conception is practical. Its primary focus is assuring that an offender receives the punishment that will place him at his appropriate ordinal rank according to his blameworthiness. Empirical desert does not suffer the standard disutility objection leveled against deontological desert because it is designed to advance the interests of effective crime control through social influence by building the system's moral credibility with the community. But it is subject to the valid criticism that it may produce results that, while they reflect the community shared intuitions of justice, nonetheless may be unjust in the sense of a transcendent truth of justice.

D. Conclusion

It has been argued here that the failure to appreciate the existence of three quite distinct conceptions of desert—vengeful, deontological, and empirical—commonly leads to confusion in the critique of desert as a principle for the distribution of criminal liability and punishment. Criticisms of desert are commonly offered without appreciating that a criticism may be valid with regard to one conception of desert but not another, thus leading writers to reject "desert" generally while in fact their criticisms only suggest rejecting one particular conception of it. And when desert is adopted as a distributive principle, the failure to appreciate the different conceptions creates confusion as to in its proper operation. Arguments based on one conception of desert are used as to justify applications based upon a different conception. Writers commonly switch between different conceptions of desert during their analysis without acknowledging, or perhaps even realizing, that they are doing so.

Distinguishing the three modern conceptions of desert hopefully may clarify the terms of the debate, but it might not. Consider this: In speculating about the cause of the confusions about desert, it may strike one as an odd coincidence that the modern scholars who make use of the vengeful conception of desert commonly are those who oppose it. It is hard to know whether this is cause or effect. Do they oppose a desert distributive principle because they conceive of desert in the terms described here as vengeful desert? Or, do they treat "desert" in their writings as having the characteristics of vengeful desert because they oppose a desert distribution, and vengeful desert provides the ugliest strawman available to help them rally the opposition they seek? Even if some misunderstandings in the current debate are not accidental, an account of the important distinctions among modern conceptions of desert can at least make it more difficult to mislead.

Whatever the cause of the confusion, it seems clear that distinguishing these three conceptions of desert can only enhance the usefulness of the ongoing debate over desert as a distributive principle. Given the recently increasing popularity of desert, clarification of the debate has not only academic but practical importance.

CHAPTER 8

The Utility of Desert

Chapter 7 distinguishes empirical desert from deontological and vengeful desert, arguing in part that the former has instrumentalist crime-control value that the latter two do not. Several earlier chapters have promised a more detailed account of why there might be utility in such a distributive principle that tracks a community's shared intuitions of justice, and Section A sets out those arguments. The short answer is that a number of specific crime-control powers become available to a system if and only if it earns with the community a reputation as a reliable moral authority. Section B examines how such a reputation can be won and lost. Section C considers how a distributive principle might be constructed that would earn such a reputation for moral credibility and some of the problems that might be encountered in the effort.[342]

A. The Crime-Control Value of Empirical Desert as a Distributive Principle

There is reason to believe that there is great utility in a criminal justice system that distributes liability and punishment in concordance with the

---

342 Much of this chapter is drawn from Paul H. Robinson & John M. Darley, The Utility of Desert, 91 Nw. U. L. Rev. 458 (1997); Paul H. Robinson & John M. Darley, Intuitions of Justice: Implications for Criminal Law and Justice Policy, 81 S. Cal. L. Rev. 1 (2007).

citizens' shared intuitions of justice. Such a distribution may provide greater utility than a distribution following the more traditional instrumentalist approach of optimizing deterrence or incapacitation. The case for this emerges when one considers why most people generally "obey the law" even when law breaking is unlikely to lead to arrest, conviction, and punishment. That is, given the generally weak deterrent threat facing people, examined in Chapter 3, why do the vast majority of societal members still act in a way consistent with the law? Social scientists have two answers to give: people obey the law because (1) they regard the law as representing the principles that moral people adhere to and they are socialized to want to live up to those moral rules, and (2) if the law specifies morally proper conduct, people are naturally inclined to think that the community believes in the "righteousness of the law" and so people fear the disapproval of their social groups if they violate the law. In social science, these two factors are referred to as (1) "internalized behavior" produced by moral standards and rules that have been internalized by the individual, and (2) "compliance produced by normative social influence," generally involving concerns for the social sanctions that others will inflict when one violates the accepted rules of conduct. Criminal law can have influence on people's conduct through both of these mechanisms.

1. Harnessing the Power and Efficiency of Normative Social Influence, Stigmatization

Actors generally feel the force of a social norm as an external force impinging on them. In this, it is not unlike the weight exerted by the general knowledge that a criminal deterrence system has a host of penalties that await transgressors. However, the sanctions feared for social norm transgressions are generally experienced as coming from the community and are not dependent on being caught and convicted.

People obey the social norms of the communities in which they live for a number of reasons. Violating those social norms may involve the loss of one's standing in the community gained from one's past achievements, losing the benefits that flow from valued relationships with others because those bonds are now shattered, and suffering the shunning experienced by those who have become stigmatized within their communities. If one is thought to have done something condemnable, one may lose one's job, ability to borrow money, ability to command trust from others and possible business partners, and diminished marriage prospects.

Other scholars have made similar observations based on the concepts of social capital and reciprocal trust. They have noted that "generalized trust depends on the willingness of individuals to adhere to their community's social norms; moreover, trust and social capital are viewed as products of people's compliance with these social norms."[343] Increasingly, social scientists have come to realize the social value of having a "reputation as trustworthy." An untrustworthy person cannot be counted on to do his share of the countless social exchanges that life in communities depends on. Thus a person seen as not living up to community norms signals, among other things, an unwillingness to live up to the future commitments he would make in exchange for the positive treatments that others might choose to give him in the present. Condemnable behavior, known to the community, even if not resulting in formal criminal liability, is a strong signal that a person is not one in which the community should reside trust or confidence.

Formalizing this general perspective, Eric Posner has created a signaling version of social norm theory. One obeys social norms in the present to signal to others that one will behave cooperatively in future social exchanges, and being included in these exchanges is critically important for one's own benefit. One attempts, in other words, to develop a reputation for normatively trustworthy behavior so that one can trade on or benefit from that reputation in the future.[344]

The core of the argument here is this: People generally do not want to violate social norms, and if they think that legal codes map those social norms, they obey the laws. A good deal of the criminal justice system's power to control conduct derives from the fact that ordinary members of the community will stigmatize violators of criminal laws—with some potential offenders this is a powerful, yet essentially cost-free, mechanism

---

343 Jack Knight, Social Norms and the Rule of Law: Fostering Trust in a Socially Diverse Society, in Trust in Society 354–373 (Karen S. Cook, ed., 2001).

344 Eric Posner, Law and Social Norms 18–27 (2002) (notice the reliance on the motive of self-interest here, which is characteristic of the law and economics movement). Norms, unlike laws, are not published in codified structures, so it is possible to wonder how these apparently invisible social rules get learned. People commonly learn norms from the reactions of observers when a norm is either lived up to or failed. Experienced actors know how to interpret these expressions, and they alter their subsequent behaviors accordingly. Further, observers often deliver not only expressions but also immediate rewards for living up to norms and sanctions for failing to do so. People learn that the likelihood of longer-term sanctions is generally signaled by these immediate cues of distress or disdain when social norms are violated. A good deal of the learning that takes place during childhood socialization lies in learning how to see initial signs of disapproval and modify one's behaviors accordingly.

of behavioral control compared with the financial and social costs of using the criminal justice system of arrest, trial, conviction, and imprisonment.

Notice, however, that this wonderfully efficient power exists only if the community sees violating a legal code as violating a social norm. The system's power of social influence depends upon it having moral credibility with the community. For a violation to trigger stigmatization, the law must have earned a reputation for accurately representing, from the community's point of view, what violations do and do not deserve moral condemnation. Liability and punishment rules that deviate from a community's shared intuitions of justice undercut this reputation.[345]

2. Avoiding the Resistance and Subversion Produced by a System That Is Seen as Not Doing Justice

A second effect of a criminal law that conflicts with the community's intuitions of justice is its tendency to promote resistance and subversion of the criminal justice system. Effective operation of the system depends upon the cooperation or at least the acquiescence of those involved in it—witnesses, police, jurors, prosecutors, judges, offenders, and others. To the extent that people see the system as unjust or failing to do justice, as being in conflict with their intuitions of justice, that acquiescence and cooperation is likely to decline and even disappear. Further, to the degree that the deviations from justice are frequent and morally consequential, active forces of subversion and resistance are generated in the community.[346]

---

345 E.g., in some inner-city communities, in which very high proportions of young African American males have done prison time for actions that the community does not regard as criminal, it may be that being an "ex-convict" no longer stigmatizes the individual in that community. *See* generally Dina R. Rose & Todd R. Clear, Incarcerations, Social Capital, and Crime: Implications for Social Disorganization Theory, 36 Criminology 441 (1998) (Describing social stigma of criminal convictions). *See also* James P. Lynch & William Sabol, Assessing the Effects of Mass Incarceration of Informal Social Control in Communities, 3 Criminology & Pub. Pol. 267 (2004).

346 *See*, e.g., Daniel J. Bell, Family Violence in Small Cities: An Exploratory Study, 12 Police Stud. 25 (1989) (finding empirically that police in small cities are likely to subvert the law regarding domestic violence by not reporting incidents, not arresting violent offenders, or deferring to other agencies; also reporting that police responded in such a manner because they believe domestic violence to be a family matter).

There are, in a broad view, two ways that the criminal justice system may deviate from the community's intuitions about appropriate criminal laws: by failing to punish or underpunishing conduct that the community thinks is morally condemnable and by punishing conduct that the community regards as morally innocent or overpunishing wrongdoing. Depending on which of these intuitions is violated, the community may respond differently. If the law allows conduct that the community regards as condemnable, then in some cases the community will seek to mobilize informal social methods that restrict and sanction this conduct, as with the vigilantism discussed below. If, on the other hand, the law criminalizes actions that the community or segments of the community think are morally acceptable, then it is likely that these actions will continue to be practiced by people but will "go underground." This in turn generates other consequences: the rise of entrepreneurs who profit by facilitating people's indulgence in those activities, venues in which those activities are practiced, pay to authorities willing to overlook the commission of these actions, and so on.

But in addition to these undesirable reactions attempting to engage or escape control mechanisms for these actions, when the criminal justice system is seen as out of tune with community sentiments, a less obvious but more common and troublesome reaction occurs in the loss of moral credibility that the justice system brings on itself. And in general, these reactions can be summed up as the justice system's loss of relevance as a guide to moral conduct. Initially, the reactions may be limited to conclusions about the idiocy of the specific legal rule that offends the community's morality, but as the apparatus of the social control agents of the government, such as police and the courts, are mobilized to enforce the senseless laws, or as those forces seem to stand by passively as moral offenses are committed, a generalized contempt for the system in all its aspects and a generalized suspicion of all of its rules develops.

> Just as the institution of the criminal law may be brought into disrepute by the too easy attribution of criminality in situations where the label criminal is generally thought inappropriate, so also may the institution be undercut if it releases as noncriminal those society believes should be punished. This does not mean that the criminal law may not be a means of educating the public as to the conditions under which moral condemnation and punishment is inappropriate. It does mean that the results

may not depart too markedly from society's notions of justice without risking impairment of the acceptability and utility of the institution.[347]

Responses to what are perceived as failures of the justice system can be widespread. Jurors may disregard their jury instructions and punish or not punish according to their own judgments rather than the legal rules. Police officers, prosecutors, and judges may make up their own rules. Witnesses may lose incentive to offer their information and testimony. And offenders may be inspired to fight the adjudication and correctional processes rather than to participate and acquiesce in them.

Empirical studies support this. Research has found that people are more likely to obey the law when they view it as a legitimate moral authority.[348] In turn, they are likely to regard the law as a legitimate moral authority when they regard the law as being in accord with their own moral codes. As Tyler concludes, "the most important normative influence on compliance with the law is the person's assessment that following the law accords with his or her sense of right and wrong."[349]

As this in turn implies, people who come to believe that the legal codes are importantly deviant from their own moral codes feel lessened concerns with abiding by the law. Two recent experiments provide evidence for the beginnings of this rejection process in individuals who discover contradictions between the legal codes in force and their own moral intuitions of justice. In these studies, participants read about a case in which there was a mismatch between the laws in existence and the moral intuitions of the participants. The mismatch was one that many participants found shocking. It was derived from a real world instance in which one young man dragged a young girl into a semiprivate space and raped and killed her. A friend, aware of the series of actions, took no steps to intervene or report the action to authorities that might have intervened. The watcher and the friend spent the next two days gambling in casinos, and on return home, the watcher bragged to friends about the crime. Because there was no law against the watcher's actions in the state in

---

347 Joseph M. Livermore & Paul E. Meehl, The Virtues of M'Naghten, 51 Minn. L. Rev. 789, 792 (1967).
348 See, e.g., Tom Tyler, Why People Obey the Law 68 (1990).
349 Id. at 64.

question, no legal action was brought against him.[350] Many respondents found the absence of a law criminalizing this conduct unbelievable. In their study of community intuitions of justice, Robinson and Darley found that their respondents generally punished actors who failed in a duty to rescue a person in distress, if the intervention could be achieved without serious inconvenience or danger to the potential rescuer, as it could have been in the case described here.[351]

Participants made aware of this and other unjust cases rated themselves significantly less likely to cooperate with police and less likely to use the law to guide their behavior after reading these intuition-violating cases.[352] More specifically, participants who had read cases in which the legal system behaved in ways counter to their moral intuitions rated themselves more likely to take steps aimed at changing the law (including replacing legislators and prosecutors and breaking the law while taking part in demonstrations), less likely to cooperate with police, more likely to join a vigilante or watch group, and less likely to use the law to guide behavior. Overall, participants appeared less likely to give the law the benefit of any doubt after reading cases where the law was at odds with their intuitions.[353] In another study, learning about a case in which a similar mismatch occurred on one law "caused participants to report a willingness to flout unrelated laws commonly encountered in everyday life as well as willingness of mock jurors to engage in juror nullification."[354]

These studies report the beginnings of the process within individuals of coming into contempt for legal codes when they learn about third-hand examples of the legal system failing to do justice. But the community would also come into contempt for the justice system in the reverse case: where it criminalized actions that the community thought were morally acceptable. The United States "experiment" with the prohibition of the consumption of alcohol in the 1920s demonstrates what can be the

---

350 For a narrative describing the case facts and a discussion of the issues arising in it, *see* Paul H. Robinson, Criminal Law: Case Studies & Controversies, Section 15, "The Act Requirement and Liability for an Omission" (2005).

351 Robinson & Darley, Justice, Liability, and Blame, *supra* note 223, at 4, 42–50.

352 The contrast ratings were provided by control respondents who read similar stories but with endings that they perceived as just. For example, control respondents learned that the watcher was prosecuted as an accessory to the crime and received a one-year prison sentence. Janice Nadler, Flouting the Law, 83 Tex. L. Rev. 1399, 1417 (2005).

353 Erich Justin Greene, Effects of Disagreements Between Legal Codes and Lay Intuitions on Respect for the Law, 64 Sci. & Engineering 2-B (2003).

354 *See* Nadler, *supra* note 352, at 1399 (2005).

end result of a catastrophic mismatch between the legal codes and the moral intuitions of large segments of the population. People continued to wish to drink alcohol, and the institutions that came into being to allow this were, of necessity, illegal. The inadvertent and unforeseen consequences of Prohibition included the rapid development of thriving criminal activity focusing on smuggling and bootlegging and the consequential clogging of the courts with alcohol-associated prosecutions.[355] Crime increased and became "organized," and crime mobs eventually engaged in criminal activities beyond those associated with alcohol consumption. Contrary to Prohibition's goal of eliminating corrupting influences in society, it increased those influences because it brought many persons into contempt for the moral correctness of one law, which generalized to the institutions enforcing this law, and eventually, to the legal code in general.

It has been suggested that the United States Congress has continued in similar "over-criminalization" practices. John Coffee asserts that "the dominant development in substantive federal criminal law over the past decade has been the disappearance of any clearly definable line between civil and criminal law." He also concludes, with a note of anger, that "this blurring of the border between tort and crime predictably will result in injustice, and ultimately will weaken the efficacy of the criminal law as an instrument of social control." This is so because "the factor that most distinguishes the criminal law is its operation as a system of moral education and socialization. The criminal law is obeyed not because there is a legal threat underlying it, but because the public perceives its norms to be legitimate and deserving of compliance."

Coffee cites other scholars who have made similar points. "Our leading criminal law scholars—among them Henry Hart, Stanford Kadish, and Herbert Packer—have periodically warned of the danger of 'over-criminalization'; namely, excessive reliance on the criminal sanction, particularly with respect to behavior that is not inherently morally culpable.... All three agreed that a basic 'method' distinguished the criminal law ... including a close linkage between the criminal law and the behavior deemed morally culpable by the general community."[356]

---

355 Paul L. Murphy, Societal Morality and Individual Freedom, in Law, Alcohol, and Order: Perspectives on National Prohibition 67–80 (1985).

356 John C. Coffee Jr., Does "Unlawful" Mean "Criminal"? Reflections on the Disappearing Tort/Crime Distinction in American Law, 71 B.U. L. Rev., 193, 193 (1991); see also Tyler, Why People Obey the Law, supra note 348 (using survey research to find that

This applies not only to cases where civil law and criminal law have become blurred but also to many "moralistic" criminal prohibitions. In an Op-Ed essay in the New York Times, Charles Murray comments on a recent bill signed into law that "will try to impede online gambling by prohibiting American banks from transferring money to gambling sites." He first comments that this will cost those who passed the law a good many votes from online gamblers who think that what they do is morally allowable, but then he goes on:

> In the long term, something more ominous is at work. If a free society is to work, the vast majority of citizens must reflexively obey the law not because they fear punishment, but because they accept that the rule of law makes society possible. That reflexive law-abidingness is reinforced when the laws are limited to core objectives that enjoy consensus support, even though people may disagree on means.
>
> Thus society is weakened every time a law is passed that large numbers of reasonable, responsible citizens think is stupid. Such laws invite good citizens to choose knowingly to break the law, confident that they are doing nothing morally wrong.
>
> The reaction to Prohibition, the 20th century's stupidest law, is the archetypal case. But the radical expansion of government throughout the last century has created many more. . . .
>
> The temptation for good citizens to ignore a stupid law is encouraged when it is unenforceable. In this, the attempt to ban Internet gambling is exemplary. One of the four sites where I play poker has blocked United States customers because of the law, but the other three are functioning as usual and are confident that they can continue to do so. They are not in America, and it is absurdly easy to devise ways of transferring money from American bank accounts to institutions abroad and thence to gambling sites.
>
> And so the federal government once again has acted in a way that will fail to achieve its objective while alienating large numbers of citizens who see themselves as having done nothing wrong. The libertarian part of me is heartened by this, hoping that a new political coalition will start to return government to its proper

---

the public complies with the criminal law based not on its deterrent threat, but its moral legitimacy).

functions. But the civic-minded part of me is apprehensive. Reflexive loyalty to the rule of law is an indispensable cultural asset. The more honest citizens who take for granted that they are breaking the law, the more their loyalty to the law, and to the government that creates it, is eroded.[357]

The criminal law can most effectively maximize its moral credibility and thereby minimize resistence and subversion by adopting criminal law rules that track shared community intuitions of justice. The danger of failing to harmonize criminal codes with intuitions of justice is that the conflicts may cause the code to lose credibility generally and to thereby jeopardize its effectiveness in broad terms.

3. Avoiding Vigilantism

The most extreme form of response to disillusionment with the criminal justice system is vigilantism.[358] Vigilante justice, descriptively, refers to occasions in which groups of citizens come together to enforce rules that are not otherwise being enforced by the formal forces of the legal system. Historically, vigilante groups often sprang up in newly settled areas without real law enforcement mechanisms. However, vigilante action also occurs even when police and courts are available if citizens perceive that the criminal justice system is failing in its responsibilities to protect them from wrongful acts.

As Peter French points out, three types of mental states drive the urge to action.[359] The first is the deep and personal feelings the citizens have of being deprived, in this case of justice. The second is a long-held feeling of powerlessness, or in this case the shocking powerlessness of the law, that has built over years, to do what is just. Finally, these two feelings generate further feelings of "contempt, hatred, scorn, disdain, and loathing" for the offender.

---

357 Charles Murray, The G.O.P.'s Bad Bet, N.Y. Times, Oct. 19, 2006, at A27.
358 *See*, e.g., Informal Justice 25–40 (Dermot Feeman, ed., 2002) (discussing vigilantism and "informal criminal justice" generally); *id*. at 99–134 (examining vigilantism more specifically in the context of South Africa); Elisabeth Ayyildiz, When Battered Woman's Syndrome Does Not Go Far Enough: The Battered Woman as Vigilante, 4 Am. U. J. Gender & L. 141, 146 (1995) (discussing vigilantism and the place battered woman's syndrome fits into the concept).
359 Peter French, The Virtues of Vengeance 6 (2001).

These are powerful responses, and they motivate equally powerful actions. In the case in which the legal system is tolerating some actions that citizens consider morally wrong, these cognitive/affective appraisals attach themselves differentially to the wrongdoer and the legal system. Hatred and loathing are directed toward the offender, contempt, scorn, and disdain toward the legal system that tolerates the offense. When the system punishes a citizen for some action that the community considers morally acceptable, reactions of sympathy and support are generated toward the unjustly punished person, and again, contempt, scorn, and disdain are generated toward the legal system, along with fear and anger.

Some cases quite vividly make the reader understand the impulses that drive citizens to action. In one case, occurring in 1981 in a small town in Missouri, a man had, for some years, been terrorizing the town, raping young girls, robbing farms for antiques, and blatantly intimidating anyone who accused him of crimes or might testify against him in the various trials in which he was charged with these crimes. (The story includes a lawyer who was constantly manipulating the laws to this person's advantage.) The police in this small town probably also were intimidated but certainly were unable to keep the man from crimes and intimidations. One day the man was standing watch in his truck in front of the place of business of a grocer whom he had threatened with death. This proved to be bad timing on his part. At their wit's end about what to do, the townsfolk were meeting nearby, and a large number of them came out of their meeting to see the man sitting in his truck, intimidating the grocer. He was shot with several weapons and killed.[360] This is a classic vigilante response to an obviously intolerable situation.

Unfortunately, when vigilantism appears. it is not just a symptom of a troubled system but itself a new problem for that system. If the community views the vigilante act as necessary and just, then the system's punishing it will be seen as unjust. However, the system's failure to punish such an unsanctioned killing only adds to the system's reputation as being weak and ineffective. It may have been the lesser of bad alternatives, then, that the system never had to choose whether or not to prosecute in the bully-killing case above. Although the circumstances suggest that killing had been witnessed by many, nobody could be found, then or ever, to

---

360 *See* generally, Harry Maclean, In Broad Daylight (1990).

report what they had witnessed. But even this result is one that silently reinforces the law's alienation from its citizens.

4. Having a Role in Shaping Societal Norms: The Persuasive Power of the Law

Enhancing the power to stigmatize and avoiding resistence and subversion, and especially vigilantism, are important effects of tracking community views of justice, but the greatest utility of an empirical desert distribution may come through a more subtle but potentially more powerful path. As suggested above, the real power to gain compliance with society's rules of prescribed conduct lies not in the threat of official criminal sanction but in the influence of the intertwined forces of social and individual moral control. People's conduct is controlled by the networks of interpersonal relationships in which people find themselves, the social norms and prohibitions shared among those relationships and transmitted through those social networks, and the internalized representations of those norms and moral precepts.

The law is not irrelevant to these social and personal forces. Criminal law, in particular, plays a central role in creating and maintaining the social consensus necessary for sustaining moral norms. In fact, in a society as diverse as ours, the criminal law may be the only societywide mechanism that transcends cultural and ethnic differences. Thus, the criminal law's most important real-world effect may be its ability to assist in the building, shaping, and maintaining of these norms and moral principles. It can contribute to and harness the compliance-producing power of interpersonal relationships and personal morality, but only if it has earned a reputation for moral credibility with its citizens.

In many discussions of the criminal justice system, it is noted that a characteristic that sets it apart from other societal institutions is that it has a monopoly on the legitimate use of force against citizens. This may be true, but the criminal justice system also has the power to persuade. The criminal justice system, as an institution involving legislatures, legal philosophers, various criminological experts, and enforcement agencies, has the power to persuade citizens about the moral appropriateness of some conduct and inappropriateness of other conduct. Social scientists know a good deal about persuasion, both in terms of how it succeeds and how it fails, and applying their theories to the issues can be quite illuminating.

Consider the criminal justice system as a "persuasive source." A large body of research suggests that a source that has certain characteristics has considerable power to persuade people of the correctness of its conclusions. Specifically, a source that is seen as legitimate in its authority, expert in its knowledge, and trustworthy in its motives is highly persuasive.[361] If the criminal justice system, and more generally, the government's criminal liability and punishment rules can be persuasive guides of conduct for citizens, the knowledge of "what the law says" can play a powerful role in the debates among citizens about what the governing social norms should be. As another writer suggests: "[In criminal law enforcement] all is not positivism and command. The criminal law can only truly shape norms if it commands some moral respect. In the absence of a constable on every corner, the mere command of a law that moves too far ahead of existing notions of justice and morality will not succeed in shaping behavior."[362]

5. Gaining Compliance in Borderline Cases

The criminal law also can have effect in gaining compliance with its commands through another, related mechanism. If it earns a reputation as a reliable statement of what the community perceives as condemnable, people are more likely to defer to its commands as morally authoritative and as appropriate to follow in those borderline cases in which the propriety of certain conduct is unsettled or ambiguous in the mind of the actor. The importance of this role should not be underestimated. In a society with the complex interdependencies characteristic of ours, an apparently harmless action can have destructive consequences and thus code drafters may "criminalize" the action. When the legal system criminalizes the action, one would want the citizen to "respect the law" in such an instance even though he or she does not immediately intuit why that action is banned. Such deference will be facilitated if citizens are disposed to believe that the law is an accurate guide to appropriate prudential and moral behavior.[363]

---

361 Richard Petty & John Cacioppo, Attitudes and Persuasion, Classic and Contemporary Approaches 62–69 (1996).

362 Joseph E. Kennedy, 51 Emory L.J. 753, 838–839 (2002) (footnotes omitted).

363 *See also* Kent Greenawalt, Punishment, 74 Crim L. & Criminology 343, 359 (1983) ("[S]ince people naturally think in retributive terms, they will be disenchanted and

Social science research on "persuasion" supports this conclusion and illuminates the mechanisms of thought that bring it about. Lately persuasion researchers have distinguished between two types: one more analytic and direct, the other more peripheral and heuristic.[364] The latter is more relevant to the discussion here. This path often involves giving the person cues that lead her to believe that the action in question should be regarded as wrong or right, criminalized or decriminalized, without presenting the direct arguments why this should be so. It often relies heavily on the person's assessment of the source of the communication. Specifically, if the message comes from a credible and trustworthy source, people are likely to accept the rightness of the communication.[365] This is the immediate acceptance and obedience that Murray referred to as the "reflexive loyalty to the rule of law." It is what the state relies on people giving when, for instance, the state passes laws against "insider trading" of stocks based on news that is not yet known by the public. Without knowing quite why it is that "insider trading" is morally wrong, most of us accept the conclusion that it is wrong because the relevant authorities have thought about it and assert that it is wrong. Or, it is what we all count on when, as we travel down a highway that is new to us, we slow up when we see a sign saying "caution, blind curve" and count on others to slow up as well. It is, in one sense, "blind obedience," but it is extremely socially useful, and it functions based on attitudes of trust toward the source in turn based on past experiences of the source providing messages that turned out to be credible.

That citizens are inclined to regard the law as a credible guide to how they ought to behave is shown by the responses of a random sample of Chicago citizens tested in Tyler's 1990 survey.[366] Eighty-two percent of the sample agreed or strongly agreed with the statement that "disobeying the law is seldom justified," and eighty-five percent agreed or strongly agreed with the statement that "people should obey the law even if it goes against what they think is right." However, it will be remembered that this survey

---

eventually less law abiding if the law does not recognize that offenders should receive the punishment they deserve").

364 Tilmann Betsch, Henning Plessner & Elke Schallies, The Value-Account Model of Attitude Formation, in Contemporary Perspectives on the Psychology of Attitudes 251, 252 (Geoffrey Haddock & Gregory Maio, eds., 2004).

365 Richard Petty & John Cacioppo, The Elaboration Likelihood Model of Persuasion, 19 Advances in Experimental Social Psychology 123–205 (Lennard Berkowitz, ed., 1986).

366 Tyler, Why People Obey the Law, *supra* note 348, at 46.

also revealed that the people Tyler tested assigned a high degree of moral authority to legal codes, and it is this "moral credibility" that gives the law what social science calls its "informational influence;" its power to bring about law-abiding behavior even when citizens are unsure in their own minds about whether behavior is wrong.

6. Conclusion

The extent of the criminal law's effectiveness in all these respects—in bringing the power of stigmatization to bear; in avoiding perversion of the system through resistance and subversion engendered by an unjust system; in avoiding abandonment of the criminal justice system through a resort to vigilantism; in facilitating, communicating, and maintaining societal consensus on what is and is not condemnable; and in gaining compliance in borderline cases through deference to its moral authority— to a great extent depends on the degree to which the criminal law has gained moral credibility in the minds of the citizens it governs. Thus, the criminal law's moral credibility is essential to effective crime control and is enhanced if the distribution of criminal liability is perceived as "doing justice," that is, if the system assigns liability and punishment in ways that the community perceives as consistent with their shared intuitions of justice. Conversely, the system's moral credibility, and therefore its crime control effectiveness, is undermined by a distribution of liability that deviates from community perceptions of just desert.

B. The Determinants of Criminal Law's Moral Credibility

If the criminal law's ability to harness the powers of social influence over the community it governs depends upon its moral credibility with them, then how can the criminal law best earn such credibility? How can such credibility be lost?

Enhancing the criminal law's moral credibility requires, more than anything, that the criminal law makes clear to the public that its overriding concern is doing justice. Therefore, the most important reforms for establishing the criminal law's moral credibility may be those that concern the rules by which criminal liability and punishment are distributed. The criminal law must earn a reputation for (1) punishing those who deserve it under rules perceived as just, (2) protecting from punishment those who do not deserve it, and (3) where punishment is deserved, imposing the amount of punishment deserved, no more, no less.

1. The Detrimental Effect of Blurring the Criminal-Civil Distinction

The single most important structural reform may be a resharpening of the criminal-civil distinction, which has grown increasingly muddled over the past two decades. Civil law has been "criminalized" with the increased use of punitive damages. But, of greater concern, is the "civilization" of the criminal law: the tendency to criminalize conduct that the community does not conceive of as condemnable. As Jack Coffee has noted, there is a strong trend toward the criminalization of regulatory offenses, leading to the astounding number of some 300,000 federal "crimes."[367] The problem is that current law has extended criminalization beyond even the domain of traditional *malum prohibitum* offenses, to criminalize conduct that is "harmful" only in the sense that it causes inconvenience for bureaucrats. Thus, most federal regulations are now routinely converted to federal crimes to give the regulators greater leverage in enforcement. Of similar effect is the increased use of strict liability and vicarious liability, common features of civil law but out of place in a criminal system.

Examples of concrete cases will make the point clear. As is well known, individuals and organizations are required to provide large amounts of information to federal, state, and local governments. Providing false information is sometimes a criminalized regulatory offense. If false information knowingly is supplied to evade pollution regulations, taxes, or safety precautions, then the community will agree that this is conduct worthy of criminalization. However, if erroneous information is provided unwittingly or if such information has little bearing on matters of importance, then the community is not likely to see the action as criminal. Or consider a case in which an employer inadvertently fails to put all required information in a federally required report (as opposed to knowingly putting false information in the report). This may arguably hurt society in some sense, but it is hard to see how; and even if it does, the degree of the injury is so small that no one—even those who have full

---

367 Coffee, Jr., *supra* note 356, at 216 (1991).

information about the need for the reporting requirement—would think that the failure rises to the level of harm that deserves the moral condemnation traditionally associated with criminal conviction. If an adult-appearing twenty-year-old, with high-quality forged ID papers, buys an alcoholic beverage from a harassed bartender, the community has trouble seeing the action as criminal, although a strict liability statute holds the bartender criminally liable and a vicarious liability statute holds the absent bar owner similarly liable.

The law cannot have moral credibility in a system without a clear criminal-civil distinction for several reasons. Principles unrelated to desert govern much of civil law. For example, though there is some disagreement on the issue, one might well justify a tort system that uses forms of strict liability or vicarious liability. A tort system is in the business of allocating a fixed loss as between the party who suffered it or the party that caused it; it is a compensation system. Even if fairness was adopted as the primary distributive principle for tort liability, no one would claim that tort liability ought to be limited to cases where moral condemnation is appropriate.

A mixed criminal-civil system, then, will inevitably have some cases where the result is driven by moral desert and others where it is not. It would be difficult, if not impossible, for such a system to build a reputation with the public as a system devoted exclusively to judging moral blameworthiness. Every instance of liability based upon non-desert criteria would undercut the system's moral credibility, and the "criminal" label could not serve as a clear signal that moral condemnation is deserved. In cases where the criminal system wishes to wave the red flag of moral condemnation, it would have only an ambiguous pink flag at its disposal. The separation of the two systems, into criminal and civil, enables the criminal law to focus exclusively on desert and, perhaps more importantly, to make clear to the public that it is so focused. It allows the "criminal" label to be a red flag.[368]

The current trend toward blurring the distinction is particularly foolish because it can provide little or no long-term gain, even with respect to the very cases brought within the expansion. First, cases of

---

368 *See* Paul H. Robinson, The Criminal Civil Distinction and Dangerous Blameless Offenders, 83 J. Crim. L. & Criminology 693 (1993); Paul H. Robinson, The Criminal-Civil Distribution and the Utility of Desert (Symposium on the Intersection of Crime and Tort), 76 B.U. L. Rev. 201 (1996).

regulatory offenses, strict liability, and vicarious liability are just the cases where the likelihood of a prison sentence often is remote or nonexistent; the sentences typically are fines and restitution, which are the sanctions that are already available at civil law. Thus, by criminalizing such civil violations, we do not effectively access more severe sanctions.

But, of course, access to more severe sanctions is not the reason that many have argued for the extension of the criminal sanction to these cases. More severe sanctions could be provided within the civil system. The arguments for criminal expansion often focus upon the possibility for the moral stigmatization that criminal liability brings that civil liability does not.[369] Given the previous discussion, it is clear that stigmatization can have a substantial effect in shaping the conduct of potential offenders. But this attempted use of stigmatization is likely to be ineffective because it offends rather than educates the moral code of the community. Passing a statute that criminalizes new conduct does not itself cause that conduct to be perceived as immoral. As the previous discussion suggests, law does not create norms but only acts as a participant in the process by which consensuses are built. Making a regulatory violation a "crime" is not in itself likely to do much to cause people to attach stigma to liability for the violation. Making 300,000 regulatory violations "crimes" makes it even less likely that people will take the resulting liability as evidence that moral condemnation is deserved. Similarly, criminalizing actions that are offenses only from a strict or vicarious liability perspective fails to bring the stigmatization of criminality to bear on those violations. Far from being an independent and respected source of moral authority, a collection of laws of this sort becomes a pettifogging caricature.

More important to us, the expansion of criminal law to punish these various violations is not only ineffective but also destructive. The more criminal law's stigmatizing effect is sought to be applied to noncondemnable conduct, the less stigmatizing effect there exists to apply. With each additional nonblameworthy use, the meaning of "criminal" liability

---

369 See John C. Coffee, Jr., "No Soul to Damn: No Body to Kick": An Unscandalized Inquiry Into the Problem of Corporate Punishment, 79 Mich. L. Rev. 386, 424–434 (1981); Brent Fisse, The Use of Publicity as a Criminal Sanction Against Business Corporations, 8 Melb. U. L. Rev. 107 (1971); Ernest Gellhorn, Adverse Publicity by Administrative Agencies, 86 Harv. L. Rev. 1380, (1973). But see Michael K. Block, Optimal Penalties, Criminal Law and the Control of Corporate Behavior, 71 B.U. L. Rev. 395 (1991).

becomes incrementally less tied to blameworthiness and incrementally less able to evoke condemnation. As each strict liability case, or vicarious liability case, or case of innocent or trivial conduct is criminalized—such as the woman charged with a criminal offense for picking an eagle feather from the floor of a cage and using it in a piece of art work that she then sold [370]—more and more people will conclude that the criminal law is being used not to reflect community notions of desert but rather as a tool of a powerful government to intervene destructively in the lives of ordinary people. Expanding the criminal law beyond the bounds of perceived desert initially weakens the stigmatizing effect that that expansion seeks to enlist.

Ultimately, such a practice destroys the stigmatizing effect that it seeks to enlist. Criminal penalties for noncondemnable conduct cause the public to sympathize with the person charged and to despise the legal system that brings the charge. Criminal conviction for a noncondemnable violation undermines not just the meaning of liability imposed for those offenses but also the condemnatory message for all criminal convictions.

2. The Problem of Moral Divisions within the Community

There will be some circumstances in which the law's moral credibility will be at risk regardless of the criminalization policy that it chooses. When a society contains groups with a strong and deeply felt moral disagreement, as ours does at this time on the morality of abortion, for example, the situation is destructive of the law's moral credibility and thus its power to gain compliance. More critically, one side will feel that the law is immoral, either because it criminalizes an innocent act or because it fails to criminalize a morally abhorrent act—in this case fails to criminalize what is seen as a particular kind of murder. The arguments here predict the destructive consequences that this conflict has. Specifically, it suggests that the "losing" side, will lose respect for the legislative process, for the courts that enforce the laws, and, eventually, for the legitimacy of the entire criminal law system.

When one thinks that the law does not prohibit murder, one is inclined to "take the law into one's own hands," and anti-abortion people

---

370 They Swooped, The Economist, Aug. 19, 1995, at 27.

have done this. Note the sequence of steps in what one might call the radicalization of the "pro-life" individual. Perhaps it begins with picketing the abortion clinic and then moves toward more coercive forms of picketing that are arguably legal violations of the rights of others. For some, it moves toward spraying noxious substances into the clinics at night—a line has been crossed to committing an undeniable and more substantial legal offense. The next step is setting fire to the abortion clinic, perhaps at night so "no one will get hurt," but certainly this is an act of arson and possibly life risking. Then death threats and finally the murder of a doctor or nurse who does abortions.

A similar destructive tension exists in Britain at this time. Those who are convinced that animals deserve more humane treatment are outraged at what one is allowed to do to animals under Common Market laws. They protest, seeking to block animal-transporting lorries before they cross the channel. As a recent article comments, for the activists, "the issue is radicalizing . . . It begins as a protest against abuse of animals. But if the law permits outrages, can it claim moral legitimacy? And if the police protect atrocities, are they not complicit?"[371] Again notice the radicalizing dynamic at work. The people in question begin as classically law-abiding citizens, typically middle class, middle aged, conservative individuals, but some become willing to commit illegal acts because they regard those acts as morally required. The process of radicalization occurs most easily and dramatically when there is a group of individuals who are morally opposed to the content of some aspect of the criminal law but also can occur for a single individual who opposes a law.

3. The Generalization of Disrespect

One might discount the danger of such moral disagreements on the ground that people who disapprove of a particular law—be it Prohibition or giving a right to an abortion—can distinguish this "bad" law from the remainder of the system. But the possibility for such compartmentalization of disrespect is limited; more likely than compartmentalization is what might be called "the generalization of disrespect." Consider the psychological processes that are begun when, for instance, a constitutional amendment prohibiting the use of alcohol is put in place. Examine the situation from the perspective of a person whose cultural traditions have

---

371 Also a Part of Creation, The Economist, Aug. 19, 1995, at 21.

a place for alcohol consumption on certain occasions and whose individual opinion supports such use.

A law that criminalizes an activity, such as drinking, that a person considers not immoral, may initially seem to the person to be an isolated and aberrant one, and only the moral validity of that specific law will be denied. However, the person cannot deny that it was a criminalization action taken by the same authorities that produced the entire criminal code, and the person must now be willing to entertain doubts about the moral correctness of the criminalizing of the other activities that those authorities. By a process that is easily understood psychologically, if not logically, when the police apprehend the person violating the drinking laws, the person has a revelatory experience that cancels their previous view that equated all police actions with the apprehension of wrong-doers, and if the court convicts, the hypocrisy that the person sees manifests itself as a candidate for generalization to other courts. If the person becomes aware of another instance of the code violating her moral sensibilities, then all these generalizations, and others, are likely to occur. There is a natural process of spreading generalization of disrespect that the reader can intuit here.

The potential for the generalization of disrespect is even greater where the disapproval does not concern a particular controversial law. Where the system generates objectionable case results because of a highly publicized and controversial position, as with Prohibition or the right to an abortion, there is at least the potential to limit the system's discredit to the controversial law. But much more frequently the case is that the cause of an objectionable result is not so apparent, and in these cases the compartmentalization of disrespect is essentially impossible. The criminal law may conflict with community views in an endless number of ways in its definition of offenses or general principles of liability. An objectionable definition of rape; or a counterintuitive rule governing offense culpability requirements, accomplice liability, or causal accountability for a harmful result; or any of a wide range of the general rules relied upon in most cases can generate an objectionable result. Yet, the specific source of the perceived error will not be apparent to the observer, just the improper result. Without a segregable and visible "bad" law to blame, the observer can do little other than be suspicious of the entire enterprise.

What are the consequences of a generalized discontent with the criminal law and the criminal justice system? Johannes Andenaes remarks that "a certain degree of respect for the formal law is probably essential

for the smooth functioning of society. Where it is lacking, law enforcement agencies play a role similar to that of an occupying army in foreign
territory."[372] World War II helped create a popular view that violently
opposing the rules imposed by an occupying army is not only not
immoral; it is highly moral. A set of laws that is not seen as just is likely to
be seen as unjust. When a criminal law offends the moral intuitions of the
governed community, the power of the entire criminal code to gain compliance from the community is risked.

Given that some unavoidable sources of injury to the criminal law's
moral credibility exist, it follows that it is that much more important that
the criminal law be formulated to maximize its moral credibility in all
other respects that are within the control of law makers, all those respects
in which there is general agreement among the community.

4. Persuasion versus Contempt

It is argued above that sometimes the law can convince persons that they
should respect and obey the provisions of the criminal code and internalize those prohibitions as part of their own moral code. But at other times,
a conflict between the legal code and individual moral intuitions can lead
people to persevere in their own judgements and move toward contempt
for the legal code. What are the conditions under which one or the other
outcome will occur, when the code will be persuasive, and when it will be
rejected? The psychological literature on persuasion and attitude change
provides some insights.

Social science research suggests that two factors are particularly relevant: the credibility of the source that is attempting to persuade the individual who is the target of the message and the certainty or strength with
which the target holds his or her own opinion. Intuition, as well as
research, makes clear that the two factors interact as follows: the higher
the credibility of the source, the more likely the source's message is to
persuade the target;[373] the more strongly or certainly held the original

---

372 Johannes Andenaes, Punishment and Deterrence 34 (1974).
373 In a comprehensive review of the attitude literature, the authors reach the conclusion
      that: "Subjects typically exhibited greater agreement with the beliefs and attitudes
      recommended in persuasive messages when the source of these messages were por-
      trayed as higher in expertise [and] trustworthiness." Alice Eagly & Shelly Chaiken,
      The Psychology of Attitudes 429–430 (1993).

opinion, the less likely the target is to be persuaded to change his or her opinion.[374]

The application of these factors to the present case is fairly direct. The source of the message is the legal code and the intentions and motivations of the drafters who stand behind it. The message is, in essence, that this or that action ought to be criminalized, is wrong, and deserves the specified level of punishment. When will the legal code, as source, be regarded as credible? Much of the argument up to now has been directed to answering this question. One may conclude that the legal code is credible to the extent that it has what is referred to here as moral credibility. For the present discussion, note two components of this credibility. First, the law's credibility is a function of the trustworthiness of its judgement. The code gains trustworthiness by assigning punishment in accord with the principles of justice of the person it is attempting to convince. Second, the law's credibility is a function of its perceived expertise, relevant in this instance when the code asserts that some conduct that is not obviously harmful should be treated as such because the conduct has less apparent but real harmful consequences. The law is saying, in essence, "Trust those of us who drafted the code. We have thought this through. This action is sufficiently harmful or evil that it deserves to be criminalized."

The other factor that influences whether the law will persuade or will draw contempt is the strength of the original opinion on the issue. When are individuals relatively certain of their opinions in the domain of criminal law? People are likely to be certain about the criminality of actions such as killing, arson, and theft—those offenses that historically have been referred to as *malum in se*, "actions that are wrong in and of themselves." Different people may have somewhat different mappings, however, as the nature of the offense moves out from the core, as discussed in Chapter 7, Section B.5. (For example, abortion and animal cruelty are held to be wrong with great certainty by some.) People in general can be expected to be less certain on the actions historically referred to *as malum prohibitum* and may have quite differential certainties produced by past personal histories. A parent whose child has been killed by a drunk driver is likely to hold, with a high degree of certainty, that drunk driving is a serious wrong.

Thus, the social science literature suggests five generalizations, most of which reaffirm conclusions developed in earlier sections. First, the

---

374 Eagly & Chaiken conclude, "we believe that few researchers would disagree with the idea that [the strength of] people's prior attitudes represent an important source of the resistance to attitude change." *Id.* at 589.

credibility of the legal code depends on it being perceived as a trustworthy guide to assigning liabilities according to the community's perception of which actions are moral, which are immoral, and how severely the immoral actions should be punished. Second, the higher the credibility of the code (i.e., the greater its reputation for assigning liabilities according to perceived desert), the more persuasive it will be in convincing people of the correctness of its judgement, and thus, the more they will be inclined to behave in compliance with the code and internalize its judgements as morally appropriate. Third, because people are likely to be relatively less certain about *malum prohibitum* offenses, the code will be more likely to convince people with regard to those offenses. Fourth, when a legal code condemns an action that a person is certain is not morally condemnable or fails to condemn an action that a person is certain is morally condemnable, its credibility is, at minimum, put at risk, normally lowered, perhaps eventually destroyed, by the spreading processes of radicalization noted above. Fifth, when the criminal law, asserting its expertise, criminalizes an act that is not obviously harmful, if people later discover that the act does not lead to the consequences that they generally regard as properly criminal, the law loses credibility, although not as decisively as in the fourth conclusion above.

Suppose that code drafters wish to adopt a specific proposal that is known to conflict with the moral intuitions of the community or a section of the community. They face a difficult but not impossible task; they must convince the community that the community's intuitions are wrong and that distributing liabilities according to the new principle would serve justice better. To be effective, they must engage in this persuasive task directly and forcibly and assess the success of their efforts. If they do not succeed in convincing the community, they then risk lowered credibility if they nonetheless adopt the proposal. When, as sometimes happens, the code provisions are adopted without this sort of educational debate, the potential for community contempt for the code is established, and that potentiality is likely to become an actuality when the first publicized prosecution for violation of the new provision takes place.

5. The Fragility of Reputation: The Costs of Deviations from Desert

Some utilitarians apparently believe that only the threat of punishment or lack thereof determines whether a person will commit an offense.[375] But other utilitarians might agree that personal morality and interpersonal relations have effect and that altering community perceptions of the criminal law's moral credibility can influence the operation of these forces. Nonetheless a system that intentionally and regularly deviates from a desert distribution may tempt them. They might argue that the crime-control value of one or another deviation from desert outweighs the incremental loss in the criminal law's moral credibility.

Such a system of selective deviations would be an improvement over our current state in which little regard is paid to the effect of deviations from desert. Nonetheless, it is suggested that the crime-control utilitarian ought to be cautious here. If we had perfect data on the dynamics of the forces at work and their relative effects, the cost-benefit analysis would be clear. We do not, of course, and are not likely to have even a crude understanding of the dynamics in our lifetimes. We can only speculate about the relative effects.

What conditions determine when the system will be seen as in fact living by the set of rules that it professes, such as doing justice? What will cause it to lose its "reputation" as a reliable moral authority? One concern is whether the deviations are repeated. All of us are aware that a system could occasionally come to a wrong outcome for many reasons; rare deviations do not signify. However, repeated ones do signify, especially when the deviations seem to point to the same underlying cause; regular deviations that fall in a regular explanatory pattern, even if they are minor, could do much to hurt the system's reputation. This would be true even if the number and extent of the deviations were small in comparison with the system's overall output of decisions.[376]

This reflects the fact that a large part of preserving the reputation of a person or an organization is to cause others to see that the person or organization is genuinely motivated to "play by the rules" that it espouses. An error can be forgiven if it is seen as "out of character." This is true of personal reputations; it is also true of the reputations of larger entities.[377]

---

375 See, e.g., Shavell, *supra* note 6.

376 In the case of sentences handed out by the criminal justice system, this process is exacerbated by mass media reports that focus on what they see as system failures. Laypersons tend not to see the larger picture and rarely are able to put mass media reports in perspective. (The more cynical observation is that news is more "newsworthy" when it exaggerates the significance and extent of a failure of justice.)

377 See Bernard Weiner, Judgments of Responsibility: A Foundation for the Theory of Social Conduct 212–214 (1995).

People know that they cannot know what all aspects of the criminal justice system are doing at all times. Their view of the system is likely to be governed by what they think the system is trying to do, by what they see as its *motivation* to do justice. The criminal law's reputation may depend on its public commitment to never *intentionally* deviate from the principles of perceived desert, while conceding that inadvertent deviations are unavoidable. To admit a policy that intentionally authorizes failures in administering only deserved punishment is to render the system suspect in all its workings.

6. Underestimating the Power of Moral Credibility

Not only is it easy to underestimate the detrimental effect of intentional deviations from desert, it also is easy to underestimate the benefit of maintaining the system's moral credibility. Unlike the threat of legal punishment, the sources of compliance discussed here are not dependent on the effectiveness of the system in arresting, convicting, and punishing offenders. The real sources of compliance power—a person's family or friends and the person's own conscience—can know of an offender's violation even if the authorities do not or cannot prove it. Thus, harnessing the compliance powers of social group and personal morality can reduce crime levels even if policing and prosecuting functions cannot be made more effective.

Note as well that these sources of compliance power do not have the staggering costs of the increased enforcement, adjudication, and imprisonment that would be required if reduced crime was to be achieved through deterrence (or incapacitation or rehabilitation). Again, their power comes not from catching and punishing every criminal but rather from the system's moral power in obviously trying to do justice. That educational and symbolic function can be served in the adjudication of whatever cases are brought to the system, even if many are not. Nor does crime reduction through these mechanisms require the increased intrusions of privacy that more effective crime investigation would require or the increased errors in adjudication that easier prosecution rules would require. In other words, harnessing the social and personal forces of compliance offers the possibility of better compliance at lower cost.

It has been argued above that a criminal law based on community principles of perceived desert can enhance the law's compliance power and that a criminal law that is seen systematically to deviate from those principles reduces that power. This account of the role of criminal law assigns it a less powerful role in producing law-abiding behavior than do the traditional theories. One reason for the attractiveness of deterrence theory, for instance, lies in its claims of having great power to autonomously produce compliance. No such claim is made here for the legal code; its role is secondary and contributive rather than primary and determinative of law-abiding behavior. This seems to be an accurate representation of the true state of affairs and, if adopted, might have the useful function of removing from public debate some of the unrealistically high expectations about what the manipulation of criminal liability and punishment can accomplish.

To conclude, there is every reason to think that more than any other body of law, criminal law plays a central role in the creation of new norms and that the criminal law can have a direct effect in gaining compliance when it is seen as a moral authority. And both of these sources of influence by the criminal law—in building and maintaining norms and in gaining compliance through moral authority—depend upon the criminal law's moral credibility with the community. The criminal law's moral credibility with the community requires a distribution of liability that follows the community's perceptions of principles of deserved punishment and requires a separate and distinct criminal justice system, a system which can demonstrate its exclusive focus on blameworthiness and can effectively convey the special condemnation of criminal conviction. This credibility is risked when the legal system criminalizes actions that the community regards as not criminal or does not criminalize actions that the community regards as serious moral violations that deserve criminal condemnation. A society that contains groups in deep disagreement about what should count as a criminal offense is a society in which the moral authority of the criminal law is in tension and at risk, and in such a society, it is that much more important that the law track community views in the areas not subject to such strong dispute.

C. Determining Community Perceptions of Desert

If there is value in having the criminal law track people's shared intuitions of justice, how are such shared intuitions to be determined? First, consider how empirical desert is not determined: not by public reaction to cases in the news, not by operation of the standard processes of American crime politics, as Subsection 1 explains. Nor does empirical desert reduce to the instrumentalists' judgements on optimizing deterrence or incapacitation of the dangerous, as Subsection 2 makes clear. Empirical desert is about doing justice—in a way that will maximize the community's confidence in the justness of the system's criminal liability and punishment judgements. Subsections 3 and 4 discuss what this means in practice.

1. Misconceptions of Empirical Desert as Inevitably Draconian: The Disutility of Injustice

Some resistance to giving empirical desert a role in setting punishment comes from a line of reasoning that goes something like this: (1) I don't like many of the modern crime-control reforms—such as three-strikes statutes, lowering the age of prosecution as an adult, high penalties for drug offenses, the trend toward expanding the scope of criminalization to what had previously been regulatory offenses. (2) These reforms are the product of recent legislative action that reflects the community's views. (3) Giving explicit deference to empirical desert will only increase the influence of an apparent public preference for such draconian measures.

However, such reasoning both misconceives the nature of empirical desert and mistakenly assumes that modern American crime politics track people's intuitions of justice. In fact, empirical desert has little, if anything, to do with people's views on the cases and issues in news headlines and political debate. And modern American crime politics have little, if anything, to do with people's intuitions of justice. On the contrary, the common modern crime-control measures noted above conflict with rather than embody people's shared intuitions of justice.[378]

Empirical desert embodies those principles of justice that people intuitively rely upon in making judgments about blameworthiness, not their announced views on matters of public debate. The most reliable

---

378 See, e.g., Robinson & Darley, Justice, Liability, and Blame, supra note 223, at 139–147 (Study 13 suggests people's intuitions would not support trend toward reducing age of prosecution as an adult), 189–197 (Study 18 suggests people's intuitions would not support three strikes statutes); Paul H. Robinson & John Darley, The Disutility of Injustice (forthcoming 2008) (empirical study showing how modern crime-control policies conflict with lay intuitions of justice).

method for determining people's intuitions of justice is by giving a series of factual scenarios, each a variation on a single baseline story, seeing how the subjects treat the cases differently, then deducing from the differences among the cases the factors that are shaping the person's blameworthiness judgments.[379] The point is, it is how people actually assess blameworthiness that can be trusted, not the abstract rules they may publicly claim they are using. Further, people's political views on criminal law rules or their reactions to cases in the headlines commonly have little to do with their true intuitions of justice. Too often, a political position or a case in the headlines brings with it baggage that colors people's views. Whether one supports or opposes the death penalty, for example, is an issue that people see as placing them in a larger complex of social and political dimensions, which involve much more than their intuitions of justice. The social and political context of the people involved in a case in the headlines, including their race, gender, social status, political views, sexual preference, and so forth commonly colors how a person would sentence that particular case.

Perhaps more importantly, the engine driving American crime politics is not people's intuitions of justice. It is primarily crime-control policies, most notably deterrence and incapacitation, that commonly conflict with desert, deontological and empirical. Three-strikes statutes, lowering the age of prosecution as an adult, high penalties for drug offenses, expanding the scope of criminalization to what had previously been regulatory offenses, and other recent popular reforms are typically justified by their purported ability to reduce crime, not by claims that they are necessary to do justice. The increased criminalization and penalties are justified as needed to produce a stronger deterrent threat, and the longer prison terms are said to more effectively incapacitate persons seen as likely to recidivate. As noted above, empirical studies give grounds to believe that these reforms conflict with people's shared intuitions of justice.

The utility of desert arguments of Section A suggest that these kinds of crime-control reforms are shortsighted and that effective long-term control of crime lies not in trying to maximize deterrence or incapacitation in ways that conflict with people's intuitions of justice but rather in

---

379   For a more detailed description of the methodology of scenario research, *see* Robinson & Darley, Justice, Liability, and Blame, *supra* note 223, at 7–11, 217–228.

doing justice and, thereby, building the criminal law's moral credibility to harness the powerful forces of social influence.

2. Do People Intuitively Assess Punishment According to Desert, or Do They Look to Deterrence or Incapacitation?

One criticism leveled against the utility of an empirical desert distributive principle is that people's intuitions of justice are not distinct from conceptions of deterrence or incapacitation. That is, people making intuitive judgments of justice make them according to traditional utilitarian models and not according to an assessment of the offender's moral blameworthiness. Studies, however, suggest a quiet different view: that people make intuitive judgments of justice based upon desert criteria, not deterrence or incapacitation criteria.[380]

One set of studies explored the intuitive use of just deserts and incapacitation as models for judgements about justice. Participants were given ten short descriptions of criminal cases, which were generated by combining five levels of moral seriousness, "case seriousness" (theft of a CD, theft of a valuable object, assault, homicide, and assassination), with two levels of perpetrators' criminal history, "case recidivation" (no prior history, history of conduct consistent with the crime committed). Participants read each scenario separately and after reading were prompted to rate the case on two scales: first a 7-point scale of the severity of the punishment that should be imposed, ranging from "not at all" to "extremely severe"; and second a 13-point scale of criminal liability, ranging from "no liability" to "death penalty." After submitting their liability judgments on these scales, participants were asked to reconsider the scenarios and assign punishments from a just deserts perspective and from a incapacitation perspective, respectively. The just deserts standard was described as assigning "the just punishment that the criminal *deserves* for the wrong he did," while for the incapacitation standard, participants were instructed to assign "a sentence long enough to protect society from further harms by this person."[381]

---

380 *See* Darley, Carlsmith & Robinson, Incapacitation and Just Deserts as Motives, *supra* note 207, at 659; Kevin M. Carlsmith, John M. Darley & Paul H. Robinson, Why Do We Punish? Deterrence and Just Deserts as Motives for Punishment, 83 J. Personality & Soc. Psychol. 284 (2002).

381 Incapacitation and Just Deserts, *supra* note 380, at 681.

The results showed that participants were more responsive to case seriousness than to case recidivation. More importantly, participants' punishment assignments based on just deserts were closely aligned with their original intuitive decisions, while the punishments they assigned using the incapacitation model were not. "What this suggests is that the default perspective of sentencing is indistinguishable from the just deserts perspective, but that both are significantly different from the incapacitation perspective."[382]

Another set of studies explored participants' reliance upon a just deserts model as against one of deterrence. In three studies, participants were given criminal scenarios that varied on a 2 by 2 format: The scenarios included high and low desert situations (severity of offense, extenuating circumstances) and high and low deterrence factors (detection rate, publicity). Different variations of deterrence and desert factors were used and participants were asked to rate the scenarios based on the same scales described above, along with study specific questions including: whether they endorsed or rejected general statements about the two theories; the moral acceptability of the crime committed; and how much resources should be expanded to either catch the perpetrator or prevent future occurrences.

The results of these studies reinforce the notion that people's intuitive default for assigning criminal liability is consistent with a just deserts model. Although participants endorsed abstract deterrence justifications for punishment, in practice they meted out sentences "from a strictly deservingness-based stance."[383] All three studies indicated that people assign punishment in relation to an actor's deservingness rather than out of concern for deterrent effect on future offenses. Though participants support the concept and goals of deterrence, that support does not translate into differential assignments of punishment.

Finally, in a third kind of experiment, the researcher used a "judgment tracing method" to examine whether punishment intuitions were based on just deserts considerations.[384] In this method, respondent is initially told only, for instance, that an offender has embezzled a certain amount from his employer. It is the respondent's task to determine the

---

382 Deterrence and Just Deserts, *supra* note 380, at 295.
383 *Id.*
384 Kevin M. Carlsmith. The Roles of Retribution and Utility in Determining Punishment, 42 J. Experimental Soc. Psychol 437 (2006).

appropriate sentence by examining, in an order that the subject selects, various pieces of information about the crime. The researcher then examines the order in which the subject acquires the information, inferring that the most important information is acquired first. The information "bits" used in the study were either relevant to just deserts issues, incapacitation, or deterrence. Results showed that participants initially requested information related to desert considerations. Only later did some seek information relevant to incapacitation and rarely sought deterrence-relevant information.

Subjects were asked their level of confidence in the punishment judgement at each point in their acquisition of information. Increments in the respondents' confidence in their proposed sentence for the crime was most influenced by the just deserts information. This effect could have occurred because the just deserts information was acquired first, when the respondents' uncertainly would have been maximal. However, in a follow-up study, this confound was removed, and it continued to be the case that the desert information was the most effective in increasing the confidence of the respondents in their sentencing assignments.[385]

These studies, taken together, provide support for the conclusion that intuitive judgements about punishment are based primarily on just deserts considerations.[386]

3. Using Community Principles of Justice to Draft Criminal Codes and Sentencing Guidelines

It should be clear, then, that basing the criminal law on community standards does not mean resolving individual cases as the public or press sees them in the heat of the moment. Nor do the arguments here support legislators' hastily passing laws driven by public reactions to some recent court case that outrages public opinion.

The proposal envisions commissions of lawyers, criminal law experts, and social scientists drafting criminal codes and sentencing guidelines. They would seek community input by means of research studies in which respondents make judgments of sets of cases that elicit their intuitive

---

385 Id. at 447.
386 Further research that demonstrates that citizens' judgments on crime sentences are
     strongly affected by their perceptions of what is justly deserved for the crime can be
     found in Norman J. Finkel. Commonsense Justice: Jurors' Notions of the Law (1995).

principles for the just distribution of liability. Community judgments on the minimal requirements for criminalization, on the justification of otherwise criminal conduct, on the conditions under which wrongful conduct should be excused, and on the relative grading and sentencing of offenses would, at a minimum, have claims on the drafters' attentions. The drafters would incorporate such shared community intuitions into the code or guidelines, unless they had well-worked-out reasons not to do so. If they had such reasons, they would make clear what they were and attempt to educate the community on their validity. The commission's deliberations would be public, and the maximum attention of the community would be sought. The output of the commission, of course, would be submitted to the legislature, which is the institution to which our constitutional system grants standing to make criminal laws.

Many if not most of the commission's recommendations would be noncontroversial, especially because they will generally track community views. But where the community disagrees, the commission will have no consensus to report, and it will be in these instances of disagreement that the commission will have to make its best judgement about which alternative positions or formulations would do the least damage to the criminal law's moral credibility. Often this will mean following the majority view over the minority view. At other times, if the minority view is strongly held and the majority view is not, this might mean adopting the minority view. In any case, empirical research can be helpful in this regard, taking account, for example, of the lessons social science has learned about what is more likely and what less likely to undermine the criminal law's reputation, as discussed in Subsections B.4. and B.5. above.

In any case, the moral intuitions of the community ought to be a valued beginning for the drafters, followed by a process of debate and analysis done in public with an eye to educating and involving the community. The establishment of public understanding of the criminal law provides the best chance of a criminal code or sentencing guidelines gaining the respect of the community and surviving the occasional case of deep community disagreement.

It is admittedly a complex a task to determine liability rules that will capture shared community intuitions of justice. But, as has been shown by past research, it is a feasible undertaking given the state of current social science methodology,[387] and it is also an important undertaking.

---

387 Robinson & Darley, Justice, Liability, and Blame, *supra* note 223, at 217–228 (1995).

Over the long term, by this means the system will earn its moral credibility with the community.

4. Community Principles of Justice versus Current Law

If that is the process by which a criminal code or sentencing guidelines should to be drafted, what if anything can be said about what such a process would produce? Based on existing research, a community-based criminal code or sentencing guidelines would retain many if not most of the foundational principles on which traditional criminal law doctrine is based: a focus on a person's level of culpability, the extent of the harm attempted or risked, the degree to which that harm actually comes about, and the presence of any justifying or excusing conditions. Nevertheless, in many respects, the research may suggest changes or refinements in existing law. Consider a few examples.

There seems a strong consensus, for example, that the degree of an offender's liability should follow to a considerable degree the person's level of culpability toward the conduct constituting the offense. However, for most offenses other than homicide, current criminal codes set a minimum level of culpability, frequently recklessness, and assign a constant degree of liability once that minimum level is reached. The respondents in the research studies generally impose higher degrees of liability as the culpability level of the offender increased above the minimum required for liability. A person who commits a crime purposefully, rather than recklessly, receives a stiffer prison sentence from the respondents.[388] And this sees to be true generally, not just in homicide cases. A criminal code that wanted to enhance its moral credibility would recognize culpability level differences in a wider range of offenses.

Research also suggests, for another example, that respondents recognize and grant validity to many of the excusing conditions that are recognized in criminal law. Specifically, they judge that the effects of mental dysfunction could exculpate a person, and they base their judgments of whether to grant an insanity defense on the degree of cognitive and control dysfunction, as do most (but not all) legal codes.[389] The respondents similarly recognized and gave validity to the broad notion of justification

---

388 *Id.* at 169–170.
389 *Id.* ch. 5.

defenses—defenses that approve of and therefore exculpate a person for normally unlawful conduct in certain circumstances, such as self-defense or citizen's arrest to prevent commission of a crime.[390]

The research suggests, however, that a community-based code would differ from current codes in some other important respects. For example, the respondents in the research disagreed with the treatment of rape offenses based upon the Model Penal Code. For instance, where forcible rape has occurred, the Model Code gives a mitigation to the rapist if the victim had been "a voluntary social companion" of the rapist who had "previously permitted him sexual liberties" or if the victim is the rapist's spouse.[391] The respondents do not.[392] For a final example, the respondents do not agree with the Model Code's assertion that a substantial step toward committing a crime alone ought to be sufficient grounds for punishment. And, even for very advanced attempts, they disagree with the Code's grading attempts the same as the completed offense.[393]

The law's moral credibility also may depend upon procedural and institutional reforms. To give a few illustrations of changes to current practice or trends that one might imagine: one might increase the criminal justice system's moral credibility with the community by less use of the exclusionary rule to exclude reliable evidence, by less plea bargaining based upon reasons unrelated to genuine factual disputes, by less restriction on police power where affected citizens want more, and by insistence that while nonincarcerative sanctions are appropriate, they ought to have sufficient punitive bite to inflict the amount of punishment deserved. On the other side, the system might increase protection of inmates against prison violence, decrease the use of dangerousness as a criterion in setting prison terms and increase more vigorous police training, discipline, and leadership to bring greater respect and restraint by police in dealing with citizens. Of course, there are commonly interests other than crime control that a society must consider as well, and the trade-offs with these interests are not always easy to make.[394]

---

390   *Id.* ch. 3.
391   Model Penal Code 213.1(1), .1(1)(d)(ii).
392   Robinson & Darley, Justice, Liability, and Blame, *supra* note 223, at 160–169.
393   *Id.* Study 1.
394   *See* Paul H. Robinson, Moral Credibility and Crime, The Atlantic Monthly, Mar. 1995, at 72; Paul H. Robinson & Michael T. Cahill, Law Without Justice: Why Criminal Law Doesn't Give People What They Deserve (Oxford 2006).

The larger point is that every deviation from an empirical desert distribution can incrementally undercut the criminal law's moral credibility, which in turn can undermine its ability to help in the creation and internalization of norms and to gain compliance through its moral authority. Thus, contrary to the apparent assumptions of past utilitarian debates, deviations from desert are not cost free, and their cost must be included in the calculation when determining which distribution of liability and punishment will most effectively advance society's greatest interests.

D. Summary and Conclusion

The evidence is reasonably clear that the power of interpersonal relationships and internalized norms to prevent crime is dramatically greater than that of the threat of official sanctions. The ability of the law to harness these forces is less clear. Studies suggest that increasing the law's moral credibility can enhance its compliance power, but the studies are preliminary and many important questions remain unanswered. Will further research confirm the apparent mechanisms described here by which a morally credible criminal law can increase compliance? Will further research confirm the analyses here about the practices that will most undermine the system's moral credibility and those that will most enhance it?

It will take some time for social scientists to conclusively answer these questions, but one need not wait for those answers before one can make changes in what we now do. Most importantly, it is clear that a instrumentalist calculus in determining the rules for the distribution of criminal liability and punishment must take account of real-world costs that come from deviating from the community's principles of deserved punishment. The costs and benefits of moral credibility may be difficult to measure, but ignoring the risks renders the cost-benefit calculation meaningless.

While one cannot know with certainty the degree of importance of the criminal law's moral credibility, one can be reasonably sure that it has some. Thus, a corollary is that one ought not tolerate any deviation from empirical desert or any other practice that may undermine moral credibility, without a clear and significant benefit from such deviation. And even then, it is wise to counsel a close examination of long-term as well as short-term effects. This suggests a number of reforms; examples have been mentioned above.

Where does this leave the long-running debate between desert and utilitarian principles for the distribution of criminal liability and punishment? The analysis offered here uses essentially utilitarian reasoning to argue for a desert-based system of criminal law. More specifically, it argues that people obey the law not so much because they are fearful of being apprehended by the criminal justice system, but because they care about what their social group thinks of them and because they regard obedience as morally appropriate. Criminal laws based on community standards of deserved punishment enhance this obedience. One may conclude that a desert distribution of punishment happens to be the distribution that has the greatest crime-control utility. Thus, utility theorists ought to support punishment assigned according to such a desert-based system.

If these arguments are accepted, then they have, in some sense, united two groups of criminal justice theorists who have characteristically been thought to be at hopeless odds. Desert-based punishment proponents assert that what matters in liability and sentencing is doing justice; utilitarians require an analysis of the consequences of a liability assignment system to justify it, characteristically a showing of how the system is maximally effective in avoiding crimes in the future. While these two sides do not agree on the reasons for imposing punishment, if they agree with the analysis offered here, they can, incredibly enough, agree on how punishment should be distributed.

While liability and punishment should be distributed according to desert, the traditional desert advocate may not be entirely pleased by this. The proposed empirical desert system is importantly different from the traditional deontological one. In the latter, what a criminal deserves is derived from some underlying systematization of moral principles. Empirical desert is not derived from any philosophically based, coherently-reasoned systematization but rather is patterned on the principles the community uses in assessing blameworthiness. It does not de justice in a transcend sene; it only does what is perceived as justice by the community.

Has the utilitarian won the battle if empirical desert is adopted as the system's distributive principle? In one sense, yes; utilitarian arguments are used to justify desert-based liability and sentencing. However, the results of that analysis install the kind of liability distribution system that the utilitarians have argued against for decades. Worse, from their point of view, they cannot reject the empirical desert distribution, as they have rejected deontological desert arguments in the past. If the power claimed here for the law's moral credibility is confirmed, it makes a compelling utilitarian argument for the adoption of a desert-based criminal law.

If an empirical desert distributive principle is adopted, the utilitarian criminal justice system is constrained in its workings as compared with its past practices. In other ways, however, it is freed from constraint. During the past decades of the traditional utilitarian approach, some criminal justice systems and institutions have had their charters set to a strictly utilitarian purpose, which seemed to exclude considerations of desert.[395] The offered thesis suggests that a charge to prevent crime is, as a practical matter, a charge primarily to do justice—to consider just desert—for that will reduce crime more than distributive criteria that ignore desert. Thus, the thesis allows these systems and institutions to look to desert without violating their charters. Indeed, their charters now demand it.

The central point offered here is this: there is practical value, not just "philosophical" value, in maintaining the criminal law's focus on doing justice. What in the past has been taken to be instances of injustice imposed on some individual, when the just desert principle is violated, can be understood now as instances of injustice of sorts imposed on all of us because each such instance erodes the criminal law's moral credibility and, thus, its power to protect us all.

---

395 See, e.g., Alaska Const. art. I, 12; State v. Chaney, 477 P.2d 441 (Alaska 1970); G.A. Res 152, U.N. GAOR, 46th Sess. Supp. No. 49, at 12, U.N. Doc. A/152 (1992) (establishing UN Commission on Crime Prevention).

CHAPTER 9

"Restorative Justice"

S trictly speaking, "restorative justice," as its academic originators call it, does not offer a distributive principle but rather a distributive process. There are no articulated criteria by which punishment is to be determined but rather a process, such as victim-offender mediation, sentencing circles, or family group conferences, to name just a few.[396] The result will depend not upon any articulated rules but rather upon the intuitions and preferences of the particular people involved in the process at hand.

Such restorative processes have some interesting similarities and differences to empirical desert. Part of the attraction and success of restorative processes derives from the fact that they seem to give the participants

---

396 *See*, e.g., Leena Kurki, Restorative and Community Justice in the United States, 27 Crime & Just. 235, 280–281 (2000) (explaining that sentencing circles involve victim, offender, key community members; that they are also open to the public; and that the agreements reached in the circles are either recommendations for the judge or the final sentence); Ilyssa Wellikoff, Note, Victim-Offender Mediation and Violent Crimes: On the Way to Justice, 5 Cardozo Online Journal of Conflict Resolution 2 (2004) (explicating that for victim-offender mediation the victim is able to question his or her offender and discuss how the crime affected his or her life). Other mechanisms include conferencing, victim assistance, ex-offender assistance, restitution, and community service. *See* Restorative Justice Online—Introduction, *available at* http://www.restorativejustice.org/intro; Paul H. Robinson, The Virtues of Restorative Processes, the Vices of Restorative Justice, Symposium on Restorative Justice, 2003 Utah L. Rev. 3.

what they want, and in that way they reflect a recognition that lay perceptions can be important, a theme underlying empirical desert as a distributive principle. Indeed, one might even speculate that given that there
is much agreement among laypersons about principles of justice the dispositions agreed upon in restorative processes may well naturally track
those shared intuitions of justice, in other words, may track an empirical
desert distribution.

On the other hand, because the participants include the victim and
offender and commonly their family and friends, the biases that would
naturally inhere in being in such a relationship may deflect one's views
from the justice principles that one would normally apply to other cases
in which one had no partiality (or, if not deflecting from principles of
justice, at least altering one's perception of the relevant case facts). Thus,
while a disposition may satisfy the participants at hand, it may well seriously conflict with the notions of justice of the community at large as
occurs in some reported cases. In other cases, however, the potential distortions of empirical desert are held in check by the presence of participants with allegiances to each side of the case, potentially cancelling out
one another. It is possible, then, that the results in restorative processes
may operate like a de facto empirical desert principle and track the community's shared intuitions of justice. This is ironic given that, as Section
B explains, an antidesert agenda in large part motivates the academic
originators of the "restorative justice" movement. As Section C explains,
restorative processes are not necessarily incompatible with a system of
doing justice. Certain restorative processes will be more likely to do justice better than others—in particular, those with more participants rather
than fewer—and justice is more likely where restorative processes are
used as an integral part of the criminal justice adjudication process rather
than as a wholesale substitute for it.

Ultimately, it is argued here that restorative processes can be used in
ways entirely consistent with doing justice, that they can and should be
used more widely, and that the best thing for the restorative processes
movement would be to publicly disavow the antijustice agenda of the
"restorative justice" movement.[397]

---

397 This chapter is drawn primarily from Paul H. Robinson, The Virtues of Restorative
     Processes, the Vices of Restorative Justice, in Symposium on Restorative Justice, 2003
     Utah L. Rev. 375; Paul H. Robinson, Restorative Processes and Doing Justice,
     Symposium Issue, 3 Univ. St. Thomas L. Rev, 421 (2006).

A. The Virtues of Restorative Processes, the Vices of "Restorative Justice"

Restorative processes include a wide variety of mechanisms that can be quite valuable in helping both victims and offenders, providing something that nothing in the traditional criminal justice can. For offenders, the processes can provide a better understanding of the real effect of their offenses and can put a human face on their victims. They also can give offenders an important insight into the norms they violated: during the process they see people who they know and respect openly expressing disapproval of their conduct. As Chapter 8 suggests, the potential influence of this kind of social interaction should not be underestimated.

Restorative processes also have a special benefit for victims. Consider the case of an elderly woman who had her house burglarized by a neighborhood youth.[398] The emotional cost to her was devastating. She was afraid to go out, yet afraid when she stayed in. The incident turned into a generalized fear of everything around her. As part of the offender's reparations, the youth agreed to do some household chores for her and, by design, came to know her better and her him. That contact let the victim to better understand what had happened and how, and with that understanding, her generalized fear faded.

But one may quarrel with some of the "restorative justice" advocates who see these benefits as the only relevant effects. Victims and offenders are not the only people who have a stake in how we deal with wrongdoing. The adjudication of criminal wrongs is not a private affair, which is why criminal cases are treated as state prosecutions and not civil disputes. Important societal interests are at stake. Consider one case example to help bring the issues into focus. In *Patrick Clotworthy*,[399] a New Zealand case about which John Braithwaite, one of the major proponents of "restorative justice," speaks in admiring terms,[400] the defendant stabbed

---

398 *See* Kathy Elton & Michelle M. Roybal, Restoration, A Component of Justice, 2003 Utah L. Rev. 43, 53 n.57 (2003) (citing Mark S. Umbreit with Robert B. Coates & Boris Kalanj, Victim Meets Offender: The Impact of Restorative Justice and Mediation 160 (1994)) (highlighting the case of an elderly woman whose home was burglarized by a neighborhood youth as one where restorative processes were used appropriately and successfully).

399 The Queen v. Clotworthy, T.971545 (D.C. April 24, 1998) (N.Z.), *available at* http:// www.restorativejustice.org.nz/Judgements%20Page.htm (follow "Sentencing Notes" hyperlink). But *see infra* note (reversing disposition in Clotworthy).

400 John Braithwaite, Restorative Justice: Assessing Optimistic and Pessimistic Accounts, 25 Crime & Just. 1, 87–88 (1999).

the victim six times during a vicious robbery, puncturing the victim's lung and diaphragm and seriously disfiguring his face. It was the disfigurement that had the most devastating effect on the victim, for the result was sufficiently repulsive to people that it interfered with the victim's normal social interactions. In the mediation session, it was agreed that Clotworthy would not go to prison but, instead, would work to earn money to pay the $15,000 needed for the surgical operation to diminish the victim's disfigurement. Braithwaite thought this a wonderful disposition, an example of a restorative success. One might offer this an example, however, of what is wrong with his vision of "restorative justice."

One can understand why the defendant would agree to such a disposition: he was desperate to reestablish his appearance of humanity and thereby his social relationships. And one can understand why Clotworthy thought this a great disposition: it was as if he was just paying civil compensation with no punishment for his attack (and not even fair compensation at that, because there was no compensation for the horrors that the victim had been put through). But the victim should never have been put to a choice of getting justice or getting his life back. To take advantage of his desperate situation to get him to agree to such a disposition is simply to victimize him again—this time with official institutions approving the dirty deed.

The result is objectionable; to approve it as a desirable disposition, as Braithwaite does, is even more so. It illustrates how unfortunately indifferent the "restorative justice" proponents can be to the importance of doing justice, important not just to victims but to the rest of society. Society has an important interest at stake here—doing justice—and dispositions such as *Clotworthy* undermine that interest. A justice disposition would have Clotworthy stay out of prison long enough to make the money needed for the operation, then go to prison or to suffer whatever additional punishment was deserved.[401]

As Chapters 7 and 8 reviewed, the society's interest in doing justice can be both deontological—the transcendent moral value of justice—and practical—doing justice avoids future crime by enhancing the criminal law's moral credibility. Adopting dispositional rules that let wrongdoers

---

401 For an account of how "restorative justice" can conflict with desert, *see* David Dolinko, Restorative Justice and the Justification of Punishment, 2003 Utah L. Rev. 319, 331–334; Stephen P. Garvey, Restorative Justice, Punishment, and Atonement, 2003 Utah L. Rev. 303, 306–308.

such as Clotworthy get off with paying their victim's medical bills would seriously undermine the system's moral credibility with the community, with all of the resulting damage to crime control that would follow. Perhaps for this reason, the "restorative" decision in *Clotworthy* was overturned by the supervising court in favor of a prison sentence.[402]

B. "Restorative Justice" and Doing Justice

For the academic supporters of "restorative justice," it may be the potential to undermine deserved punishment that makes restorative processes attractive. Many of these advocates use the term "restorative justice" as if it were interchangeable with restorative processes, but the literature make clear that a system based upon "restorative justice" ideally would ban "punishment," by which is meant, apparently, banning punishment based on just deserts. Though in practice participants in restorative sessions commonly bring to bear their own intuitions of justice in sorting out an acceptable disposition, the advocates concede, the "restorative justice" ideal nonetheless is forgiveness, not deserved punishment. Bowing to what they see as the crime-control demands of reality, the "restorative justice" advocates reluctantly direct the use of deterrence mechanisms if restorative processes fail and incapacitation mechanisms if deterrence fails,[403] but giving offenders the punishment they deserve is rejected as never an appropriate goal.

The centrality of this antijustice view is expressed in the movement's name, "restorative justice." The point of the naming exercise is to present restorative processes as if they were a form of doing justice. But, of course,

---

402 The Queen v. Clotworthy, CA 114/98 (C.A. June 29, 1998) (N.Z.), *available at* http://www.restorativejustice.org.nz/Judgements%20Page.htm (follow "New Zealand Court of Appeal" hyperlink).

403 *See* John Braithwaite, A Future Where Punishment is Marginalized: Realistic or Utopian?, 46 UCLA L. Rev. 1727, 1746 (1999) (classifying restorative justice as competing with punitive justice); Burt Galaway & Joe Hudson, Criminal Justice, Restitution, and Reconciliation 1–2 (Burt Galaway & Joe Hudson eds.,1990) ("The central notion [of restorative justice] is to reject traditional justifications, both retributive and utilitarian . . . and to suggest that the purpose of state intervention in criminal matters should be to bring about peace among the participants and restore loss."); Howard Zehr, Changing Lenses: A New Focus for Crime and Justice 209–210 (1990) ("If there is room for punishment as a restorative approach, its place would not be central."); *see also* Steven P. Garvey, Punishment as Atonement, 46 UCLA L. Rev. 1801, 1843–1844 (1999) ("Put bluntly, restorativists really don't much care for punishment. . . . Missing from [their] agenda . . . is the idea of punishment as moral condemnation.").

such word games only work so far. Calling something "justice" does not make it so. The term "justice" has an independent meaning and a common usage that cannot so easily be cast aside: "reward or penalty as deserved; just deserts."[404] (In this text, the term "restorative justice" is used to include the more ambitious, antijustice agenda, and the term "restorative processes" to refer to just the processes themselves.) The naming move can create confusion, and perhaps that is all the leaders of "restorative justice" want at this point: time to get a foothold in common practice before it becomes too obvious that their "restorative justice" program is in fact antijustice. But such word trickery is not likely to be sufficient for gaining longer-term or wider support. For that, they must face the antijustice issue squarely and persuade people, if they can, that people ought to no longer care about doing justice. There are good reasons to think that such a task is not possible.

That "restorative justice" adds this anti-desert agenda to restorative processes is somewhat odd and unfortunate. It is odd because, as noted previously, there is every reason to believe that it is the shared intuitions of justice of the persons participating in the restorative process that is shaping its disposition. In other words, group restorative processes are empirical desert in action. As social science research reported in Chapter 8 has confirmed, the criterion that drives people in assessing appropriate punishment is desert, an offender's blameworthiness.[405] Thus, when members of a sentencing circle are sorting out an appropriate disposition for a case, what is driving their thinking is in large measure their intuitions of justice—in other words, desert. As Chapter 8 also makes clear, the studies suggest that these intuitions are quite strongly held and widely shared. It seems quite odd, then, that the "restorative justice" proponents approve of restorative processes that commonly run on the participants' shared intuitions of justice, yet at the same time claim that desert is to be opposed as a basis for assessing punishment.

---

404 Webster's New World Dictionary of the American Language 766 (1970).

405 *See*, e.g., Kevin Carlsmith, John M. Darley & Paul H. Robinson, Why Do We Punish?, *supra* note 380, at 284. (concluding that laypersons are highly sensitive to factors uniquely associated with just desert principles and that their individual sentencing decisions are exclusively driven by just desert concerns); Darley, Carlsmith & Robinson, Incapacitation and Just Deserts as Motives, *supra* note 207, at 659, 676. (deducing that just desert was the primary sentencing motive since research participants increased punishment as the seriousness of the offense increased and did not alter punishment based upon variations in the likelihood of committing future offense).

Nor is desert as a distributive principle inconsistent with the use of nonincarcerative sanctions that are encouraged in restorative processes. Distributing punishment consistent with the degree of an offender's blameworthiness can be done through punishment in any form. Prison is one possibility but there are many other possibilities, including the full range of things that restorative processes might agree upon for an offender. As Chapter 7 makes clear, all that desert demands is that the sum total of all punishment add up to a total that matches the amount of punishment that the offender deserves according to the degree of his or her blameworthiness. So, for example, a prison term of X amount might be "converted" into a fine of Y amount or Z hours of community service, and so forth. The goal in these efforts is to provide as much flexibility as possible in the selection of sentencing method, while at the same time ensuring that offenders get the amount of punishment they deserve, no more, no less.

One may wonder why, if there is nothing in restorative processes that is inconsistent with desert, Braithwaite and other "restorative justice" proponents are so opposed to desert? One might speculate that they misconceive modern desert as being what Chapter 7 terms "vengeful desert." This is certainly consistent with how they speak of desert.[406] On the other hand, as the conclusion to Chapter 7 hints, the cause and effect may be reversed: they may adopt "vengeful desert" as their conception of desert because it makes the easiest strawman to attack.

C. Using Restorative Processes More Widely and in More Serious Cases

The opposition of the "restorative justice" academics to desert is not only odd but also unfortunate because it inevitably produces both political and public resistance to restorative processes. The anti-desert stance associates restorative processes with a failure of justice, which translates into political opposition. Despite the wonderful things that restorative processes can do, today they typically remain limited in use to cases of juveniles and minor offenses.[407] In contrast, evidence suggests that their

---

406 *See*, e.g., Braithwaite & Petit, Not Just Deserts, *supra* note 298, at 178.
407 *See* Paul H. Robinson, Virtues of Restorative Processes, *supra* note 397, at 384–385 (reviewing the scope of present programs using restorative processes); Kurki, *supra* note 396, at 240 ("[R]estorative justice initiatives in the United States are typically

greatest benefits may be found in their use in the more serious cases,[408] where more is at stake for both for victims and offenders. But it seems clear that restorative processes will never get the chance to be used in these serious cases as long as they are trapped by the anti-desert agenda of their academic proponents.

Can restorative processes be used in a way that would permit expansion to serious offenses? There is reason to believe so. First, if the seriousness of the authorized dispositions by restorative processes is increased, the kinds of cases dealt with could be widened. Some people will be hesitant to give serious sentencing authority, such as imprisonment, to a restorative process body, no matter what an offender's veto power. But one can conceive of versions of restorative processes that include judicial participation and/or include guidelines that structure the exercise of discretion.

A second point may be the most important for expanding restorative processes. As Chapter 7 discusses, justice cares about *amount, not method* of punishment. Thus, one could impose deserved punishment through any variety of alternative methods without undercutting justice—fine, community service, house arrest, curfew, regular reporting, diary keeping, and so forth—as long as the total punitive "bite" of the disposition (the "punishment units") satisfies the total punishment the offender deserves, no more, no less.

This characteristic of justice has two important implications for restorative processes. First, because all forms of sanction can give rise to "punishment credit," good-faith participation in restorative processes itself can count toward satisfying the required punishment, at least to the extent of the personal suffering that produces in the offender. No doubt there can be discomfort in attending a meeting where family and friends have gathered to discuss one's wrongdoing. Second, the restorative processes may provide an effective means for sorting out just how the total punishment units called for are best "spent"—that is, they may be a particularly effective means of fashioning a disposition from among the wide

---

used as diversion programs for juveniles in minor, nonviolent, and nonsexual crimes").

408 *See* Heather Strang & Lawrence W. Sherman, Repairing the Harm: Victims and Restorative Justice, 2003 Utah L. Rev. 15, 40 (mentioning recent studies which indicate that restorative justice is more effective in reducing violent crime than property crime).

variety of available methods that will best advance the interests of restoring the victim, the offender, and society.

Finally, limitations on the dispositional authority of restorative processes are a problem only where such restorative processes are used as the sole dispositional process—that is, where they are substituting for the criminal justice system. However, where such processes are only complementary to the criminal justice system—where they operate in parallel to or as an integrated part of the criminal justice system—there is no practical limit on the available dispositions and no reason to impose any such limit. For example, if the criminal justice system remains available to review the fairness and justice of dispositions proposed by restorative processes, then the full range of dispositions, including the most serious, can be made available.

Ideally, we ought to use restorative processes whenever we think such processes can give benefit and make available a wide range of sanctioning methods, including serious sanctions. Unfortunately, the broader use of restorative processes may never have a chance as long as restorative processes are sold as "restorative justice," with its agenda of undermining justice rather than of achieving it for all parties.

CHAPTER 10

The Strengths and Weaknesses of Alternative Distributive Principles

The previous chapters have separately examined each alternative distributive principle. This chapter reviews those earlier discussions and draws from them a summary of the strengths and weaknesses of each.

A. General Deterrence

What can we say about the strengths and weaknesses of general deterrence as a distributive principle? On the one hand, under the right conditions, it can avoid future crime. Indeed, it has the potential for enormous efficiency. For the cost of punishing just the offender at hand, one can deter thousands, even possibly millions, of others who hear about the case and heed its warning. (This, however, can raise ethical objection to the fact that the process of general deterrence relies on treating the person being punished as a mere instrument by which to influence the conduct of others.)

On the other hand, it may well be that general deterrence will be effective in only a limited number of instances. As Chapter 3 explains, for it to work, three prerequisites must be satisfied. First, a deterrence-based rule can deter only if the intended targets are aware of the rule, directly or indirectly. Second, even if the target audience knows of the deterrence-based rule, a deterrent effect can come only if the targets have the capacity and inclination to rationally calculate what is in their best interest. Finally, even if the targets know of the deterrence-based rule, are able to rationally calculate their conduct, and do in fact make such a calculation, the rule will deter only if a person concludes that the costs of committing the offense exceed its anticipated benefits. As Chapter 3 concludes, it may be rare that these three prerequisites are satisfied, thus casting doubt on the ability to realize the potential benefit of deterrence.

The first prerequisite requires that the potential offender be aware of the deterrence-based rule. However, evidence suggests that this commonly is not the case. For example, a primary justification for the felony-murder rule—treating even accidental killings during a felony as murder—is its presumed deterrent effect on potential felons. But few felons are likely to know whether their jurisdiction has such a rule or what its terms might be.

Studies suggest that most people assume the criminal law tracks their intuitions of justice. Therefore, deterrence will have its greatest difficulty in cases where it deviates from what empirical desert would dictate because it is in these cases of conflict between the two where people are the least likely to know what the law requires of them (and without this knowledge cannot be deterred). Yet, these are the very cases upon which general deterrence must rely to provide greater deterrent effect than that inherent in a desert distribution. Thus, it is in just the cases where it might be able to offer more deterrence than would desert that a deterrence distribution performs at its worst.

Further, even in cases where the potential offender knows of the rule intended to deter, the second prerequisite, he must be able and inclined to do the balancing of costs and benefits that deterrence relies upon. Again, evidence suggests that this commonly is not the case. Potential offenders as a group are less inclined than most people to think carefully about the future consequences of their conduct and are more likely to be under the distorting influence of drugs, alcohol, or mental illness.

The last prerequisite encounters a similar problem: even if a potential offender knows the deterrence-based rule and is able to calculate his best interests, a variety of factors commonly lead potential offenders to conclude that the perceived benefits of committing a crime outweigh its perceived costs. In fact, capture and punishment rates are exceptionally low for most offenses. Even if they were not, a deterrent effect depends not upon the reality of the deterrent threat but rather upon its perception. Thus, even if the deterrent threat were real, deterrence may fail if the intended targets do not fully appreciate the likelihood of punishment or its effect. For example, people show a natural tendency to discount a future detriment just as they discount a future benefit.

In sum, for general deterrence to effectively achieve its aims, the three prerequisites must be satisfied. Yet satisfying each prerequisite encounters its own challenges, which general deterrence may have difficulty overcoming. And, even if the prerequisites are satisfied and some general deterrent effect results, the crime-control cost that results from being in conflict with community intuitions of justice may outweigh the crime-control benefit of the effect. The distributive criteria for general deterrence—such as adjusting punishment according to the capture rate for the offense or the news worthiness of a case—ensure that a general deterrence principle will conflict with desert. Thus, the cases in which general deterrence can provide greater deterrence than a desert distribution—cases where it deviates from desert—are just the cases where it has its most difficult time showing a crime-control gain.

B. Special Deterrence

Under the right conditions, a special deterrence distributive principle can avoid future crime, although it lacks the potential for the enormous efficiency of general deterrence. It works only through the offender at hand. As with general deterrence, special deterrence will not work unless the prerequisite conditions exist—knowledge of the deterrence-based rule, the capacity and inclination to rationally calculate what is in one's best interest, and a perception that the costs of a crime exceed its benefits— which, again, commonly do not exist. (However, the chances the subject will know the deterrence-based rule are at least greater in cases of special deterrence than for general because the intended target is the offender before court. He or she can have the rule specially explained if needed for future use.) Finally, as with general deterrence, a distributive principle of special deterrence seems destined to distribute punishment in ways that conflict with both deontological and empirical desert, the latter conflict producing crime-control costs that may outweigh any special deterrence crime-control benefits.

C. Rehabilitation

Rehabilitation, if successful, can avoid crime by the offender at hand. On the other hand, as Chapter 5 makes clear, the potential for crime-control benefits from a rehabilitation distributive principle are limited. It does not share the enormous potential efficiency of general deterrence to effect others beyond the offender at hand. More importantly, the success rate of rehabilitation programs is typically quite modest and commonly limited to a narrow range of offenders and offenses.

Finally, a rehabilitation distributive principle, like deterrence principles, is destined to distribute liability and punishment in ways that conflict with both deontological and empirical desert. If rehabilitation is possible, minor offenses may require long terms of rehabilitation, and serious offenses may require only short terms. If rehabilitation is not possible, and if rehabilitation is the sole principle for distributing punishment, then the offender must be released. (To avoid simply releasing offenders who cannot be rehabilitated, it might make more sense to combine rehabilitation with another distributive principle, such as incapacitation, which would mean that if a person could not be rehabilitated, then the person would be incapacitated for as long as the person remains dangerous. Such hybrid distributive principles are the subject of the next chapter.)

It can be argued, however, that rehabilitation may have a value beyond simply its effect in avoiding crime. It may bring a sense of personal satisfaction and self-actualization to the person and a better life to the person's family and friends. Because of this, some people may see rehabilitation as having a transcendent component—as being a value in itself that ought to be pursued even if it does not produce less crime. Of course, if rehabilitation rarely is achievable, then achieving this value will be equally rare. On the other hand, some people may argue that forcibly changing a person's nature raises ethical questions, for it suggests a serious intrusion by the state into personal autonomy, an intrusion more serious than the simple forced suffering of punishment.

One may conclude that it is not necessary to adopt rehabilitation as a distributive principle to achieve much of the rehabilitation objective. One might adopt instead a practice of taking every opportunity to rehabilitate amenable offenders during whatever sentence is determined by another distributive principle. In other words, one might get as much as is to be gotten in terms of rehabilitation with a minimum of cost by adopting it not as a distributive principle but as a practice of correctional administration. The criminal justice system might rehabilitate offenders as much as is possible but not use rehabilitation as the basis for determining the length of a person's punishment term.

D. Incapacitation

Like special deterrence and rehabilitation, incapacitation can have a crime-control effect only on the offender at hand. It lacks the enormous potential efficiency of general deterrence. However, while there are serious concerns about the crime-control effectiveness of the other traditional instrumentalist distributive principles—general deterrence, special deterrence, and rehabilitation—no similar doubts exist for incapacitation as a distributive principle. Incapacitation can reduce crime by the person detained even if he or she does not calculate cost-benefit analysis and is not amenable to rehabilitation.

The weaknesses of incapacitation as a distributive principle reside primarily in the inefficiency and unfairness of its administration, as Chapter 6 discusses. For incapacitation to be effective as a distributive principle, one must be able to identify persons who will commit offenses in the future, preferably with a minimum of "false positives" (persons predicted to be dangerous who in fact would not commit an offense). Presently, however, the behavioral sciences have only a limited ability to make such predictions accurately. "False positives" commonly exceed "true positives." This is especially true where the criminal justice system does not look directly to the dangerousness of the offender at hand but instead, in its attempt to "cloak" its preventive detention as criminal justice, uses prior criminal record as a rough "stand in" for future dangerousness.

The system's high false-positive rate means a large amount of resources are wasted on detaining nondangerous persons, to say nothing of the serious and unjustified intrusions upon their personal liberty. Further, like the other instrumentalist distributive principles described above, incapacitation as a distributive principle will distribute liability and punishment in ways that conflict with empirical and deontological desert, which will bring both moral violations and crime-control costs.

As Chapter 6 suggests, one might achieve the preventive detention goal with greater accuracy, thus producing less unjustified intrusion on liberty, and avoid having the criminal justice system regularly conflict with desert by relying instead upon an open civil preventive detention system as currently exists to civilly commit persons who are dangerous because they are mentally ill, have a contagious disease, or have a drug dependency. If preventive detention can be more effective when performed apart from the criminal justice system, and if such separation avoids the crime-control cost of conflicts with empirical desert, it seems difficult to justify using incapacitation as a distributive principle for criminal liability and punishment.

E. Empirical Desert

Empirical desert as a distributive principle would track the community's shared intuitions of justice. It is by definition the distributive principle that the community sees as most reliably doing justice. As has been argued in Chapter 8, this increase in the criminal law's moral credibility is likely to enhance the criminal justice system's long-term crime-control effectiveness in a variety of ways. Greater moral credibility will reduce the resistance and subversion of the criminal justice process, among witnesses, police, prosecutors, jurors, and offenders, that a system seen as regularly doing injustice would provoke. Similarly, it will reduce the vigilantism that a system seen as regularly failing to do justice would provoke. The system's greater moral credibility also can increase the stigmatizing force of criminal violations. The better the system's reputation for "getting it right" in imposing criminal liability, the more criminal liability is likely to provoke moral condemnation. Greater moral credibility also is likely to gain greater compliance in grey-area cases, where people may be unsure as to whether conduct is only technically prohibited or is truly condemnable. Imagine, here, cases of insider trading and downloading music from the Internet. Finally, and perhaps most importantly, greater moral credibility gives the criminal law greater influence in the public conversation by which societal norms are shaped and reinforced. A society's ability to change norms—such as those regarding domestic violence, drunk driving, or date rape—is at its greatest when it has criminal law as a tool in its arsenal to shape people's views on the condemnability of the conduct at issue.

The central weakness of empirical desert as a distributive principle is its potential to do injustice that is not apparent to the present community.

The community's shared views of justice may simply be wrong. Consider the lessons of slave-holding Southerners before the Civil War and the views and treatment of Jews and Gypsies in prewar Germany. Only a transcendent notion of justice, derived independently from principles of right and good—deontological desert—can give true justice.

A second objection to empirical desert as a distributive principle might be voiced by instrumentalists who argue that such would pass up attractive crime-control opportunities simply because they would require punishment that might seem unjust to the community—for example, in instances where the prerequisites to effective general deterrence really do exist. Such a greater crime-control opportunity may not arise often—an empirical desert distribution of punishment will itself provide some deterrent effect, some opportunity to rehabilitate, and some incapacitative effect—but it seems likely that some such opportunities will arise. If the crime-control benefits of deviating from empirical desert would be so great as to exceed the crime-control costs of undermining the criminal law's moral credibility, then the good utilitarian will want to deviate from empirical desert.

F. Deontological Desert

The obvious strength of deontological desert is that it does justice—and true justice, not just the community's perception of justice as relied upon by empirical desert. As Chapter 7 discusses, however, such a distributive principle would encounter serious practical difficulties. First, moral philosophers famously disagree among themselves about most issues. How could code or guideline drafters know which position to adopt. Further, there is danger that moral philosophy, in relying as it commonly does upon shared intuitions of justice in its modern methodology, may construct principles of justice biased toward accepting as just those rules that are consistent with peoples' shared intuitions of justice. Thus, even if moral philosophers did agreed among themselves regarding a rule, the bias renders the resulting deontological desert principles less reliable as the transcendent justice check that empirical desert requires. Possibly, an awareness of the danger among moral philosophers might help minimize the difficulty.

The more obvious weakness of deontological desert as a distributive principle is that it fails to prevent avoidable crimes. It would distribute liability and punishment in ways that ignore the crime-control opportunities of the instrumentalist distributive principles. Deontological desert conflicts not only with the more traditional instrumentalist mechanisms of deterrence, rehabilitation, and incapacitation but also with empirical desert. For example, laypersons nearly universally believe that resulting harm is important in assessing blameworthiness, yet moral philosophers are very much split on the issue. Because deontological desert as a distributive principle may ironically undermine the criminal law's moral credibility, it may produce the costs—resistence, subversion, vigilantism—and fail to provide the benefits—stigmatization, gaining grey-area compliance, influence in shaping norms—that such moral credibility can bring.

G. Conclusion

One may conclude that none of the alternative distributive principles examined in the previous chapters provide the ideal distributive principle. Each has strengths but also weaknesses, some of which seem disqualifying. But a principled criminal justice system must have an articulated controlling principle, and if forced to pick one of the above, one could weigh the strengths and weaknesses of each and come to a conclusion as to which, on balance, seems less problematic than the rest.

Luckily, we are not forced to this hard choice. As the next chapter discusses, it is possible to construct a principle that relies upon more than one principle, which may provide a principle's benefits without suffering its costs. How might one construct such an articulated hybrid distributive principle?

CHAPTER 11

Hybrid Distributive Principles

Chapter 10 suggests that each alternative distributive principle has both strengths and weaknesses. Might one be able to build on the strengths and minimize the weaknesses by combining principles in some way? Section A below explores some of the ways in which this might be done in a principled way, by articulating a hybrid distributive principle.

Chapter 2, Section C documents the problem of the unarticulated hybrid distributive principle: the failure to define the interrelation among alternative distributive principles provides only a facade of principle over a reality of unconstrained discretion. A decision maker can select a result for any, even elicit, reasons then choose that distributive principle or combination that will produce that desired result. The problem is not insurmountable. As Section A explains, a variety of mechanisms exist by which one can define the interrelation among multiple distributive principles.

The American Law Institute's recent adoption of a revised Model Penal Code Section 1.02 provides an interesting attempt at constructing an articulated hybrid distributive principle. Unfortunately, the proposal contains both structural and policy flaws, as Section B explains.[409]

---

409 Much of Section A of this chapter are derived from Paul H. Robinson, Hybrid Principles for the Distribution of Criminal Sanctions, 82 Nw. U.L. Rev. 19 (1987).

A. Alternative Approaches to Constructing an Articulated Hybrid Distributive Principle

When alternative principles conflict, a principled hybrid must define which of the competing principles is to be followed. This might be done in any of a variety of ways.

1. Relying upon the Principle with the Greatest Punishment

Some writers have suggested in the context of sentencing that after determining an appropriate sentence under each alternative distributive principle, one should impose the highest of those sentences, under the theory that the highest sentence will assure that all of the principles are satisfied.[410] Thus, if desert requires seven years, deterrence five years, and incapacitation one year, this approach generates a sentence of seven years. If deterrence requires seven years, incapacitation five, and desert one, seven years is again appropriate. The same process can be used for the selection of criminal law rules and doctrines: after formulating a rule or doctrine using each of the principles separately, one can simply adopt the formulation that gives the broadest liability to assure that all of the principles will be satisfied.

However, this approach assumes, incorrectly, that to give a sentence higher than a principle calls for is to satisfy the principle. In the context of formulating doctrinal rules, such an approach assumes, equally incorrectly, that a formulation that imposes broader liability than a principle requires satisfies that principle. The truth is that "satisfying" a principle sometimes requires limiting the punishment or extent of liability. In the first hypothetical above, the seven years desert requires is apparently an inefficient waste of punishment according to deterrence and

---

Section B is derived from Paul H. Robinson, The A.L.I.'s Proposed Distributive Principle of "Limiting Retributivism": Does It Mean In Practice Pure Desert?, Symposium Issue, 7 Buff. Crim. L. Rev. 3 (2004).

410 P. O'Donnell, M. Churgin & D. Curtis, Toward a Just and Effective Sentencing System 109 (1977) ("The length of the sentence of imprisonment imposed on the defendant by the court shall be the longest of the four sentences derived in accordance with subsections (d)(1),(2),(3), (4) [which govern the determination of a sentence solely for the principle of deterrence, incapacitation, rehabilitation, and denunciation, respectively].") (section 2302(d)(5) of their proposed statute). For an illustration of how the proposal would be applied, see id. at 52.

incapacitation principles.[411] In the second hypothetical, the seven years deterrence requires not only violates a principle of efficient incapacitation but also is grossly undeserved. Such a sentence does not satisfy desert; it violates it.

The same conclusion applies to doctrinal formulations. One might, for example, use desert arguments to impose liability on the host for the drunk driving of an intoxicated guest (where the host knew of the intoxication). If general deterrence suggests even broader liability—say liability for homicide caused by the drunk-driving guest—it does not follow that this broader liability also would satisfy a desert principle. The broader liability might further a deterrent principle yet violate desert.

In the end, then, a hybrid principle that follows the principle with the highest sentence or broadest liability is not a defensible hybrid. It neither minimizes crime nor advances noncrime-prevention goals like deontological desert or rehabilitation. Its attractiveness rests upon a failure to appreciate that giving more punishment than a distributive principle calls for can be as damaging as giving less. And the point is not limited to the natural tension between crime prevention and desert. Even among pure crime-control principles, money wasted on greater punishment than a principle calls for is money that could have been spent to reduce crime in instances where it would be more effective.

2. Establishing Priorities

A less result-driven approach is to establish ex ante a priority scheme that will determine which principle is to control when principles conflict. Under what might be called a "simple priority" approach, whenever Principle A (the principle of highest priority) supports a doctrine or sentence different from that supported by another principle, Principle A shall govern. To the extent that Principle A is indifferent as to which of two doctrines or sentences is adopted, but Principle B supports one and Principle C the other, then Principle B (the second highest priority principle) shall be followed, and so on. Under such an approach, the principle

---

411 A sentence higher than an instrumentalist principle calls for may be an inefficient sentence. To the extent that liability is justified by a deterrence utilitarian calculus—a comparison of the social cost of imposing liability and the social benefit that is projected to flow from the future crimes deterred by imposing such liability—the imposition of liability in a given situation may create more social cost than benefit.

selected as primary is given greater weight than in any other approach of lesser priority. The principle of higher primary controls whenever it makes a difference.

Somewhat more sophisticated is a "contingent priority" approach. It sets priorities, as in a simple priority approach, but it also sets conditions assuring that a principle is given priority only in those cases where, for example, a defined level of reliability or effectiveness is present. Thus, for example, incapacitation might be given first priority but that priority can be exercised only if, for example, the data shows that the reliability of the dangerousness prediction exceeds a minimum level in that situation.[412] Or, general deterrence might be given first priority, contingent upon the existence of conditions assuring that the prerequisites for deterrence discussed in Chapter 3 are satisfied. Under this approach, the decision maker would follow the principle with the highest priority that satisfies its contingent criteria. The virtue of such an approach is that it permits a principle to control only to the extent that the assumptions underlying the effectiveness or accuracy of the principle are true.

3. Distinguishing Determining Principles from Limiting Principles

The priority approaches generally assume that a particular principle will call for a particular doctrinal formulation or a particular sentence. Some principles, however, might be used to limit rather than to determine the distribution of punishment. That is, their effect may be to exclude a formulation or sentence rather than to recommend one. A limiting principle cannot determine the distribution of punishment; it can only operate to bar some part of a distribution suggested by another principle, a determining principle.

Some commentators suggest that just deserts is properly treated as such a limiting principle, as discussed in Chapter 7, Section B.4. Under this conception, it is assumed that desert makes relatively imprecise demands—it conceives of just punishment as simply prohibiting certain "unjust" formulations or sentences—and does not require specific results.

---

412 John Monahan has proposed an incapacitation-desert hybrid of this sort. Monahan, The Case for Prediction in the Modified Desert Model of Criminal Sentencing, 5 Int'l J.l. & Psychiatry 103 (1982).

As discussed in Chapter 7, modern desert theory, neither deontological and certainly not empirical desert, take this form. Both take seriously the ordinal demands of desert—that cases of greater blameworthiness receive more punishment than cases of less blameworthiness—which necessarily translates into a specific amount of punishment (that required to get a case's ordinal rank correct), not just a wide range of permissible punishment.

On the other hand, the notion of a limiting principle might well be useful for several of the traditional instrumentalist principles. For example, one might set deterrence as a limiting principle to exclude sentences or formulations that would miss out on deterrent opportunities of a certain crime-control benefit. In this role, deterrence would set an upper limit on the disutility that society is willing to suffer for the sake of deontological desert, for example. Use of deterrence as a limiting principle might result in a formulation that was less just but significantly more efficient than a pure desert formulation.

In practice, however, the operation of a determining-limiting approach is in many respects similar to a contingent priority approach. The difference between the two is partly formalistic and partly real. Under a contingent priority approach, the first priority principle is presumed to control as long as the contingencies concerning its effect and reliability are met. Under a determining-limiting approach, the limiting principle has first priority but is presumed *not* to control *unless* the limitation criteria of the principle are violated.

The more significant difference between the two approaches is that under a contingent priority approach, a principle falls from priority only because of its own shortcomings—failing to meet the criteria that assure that it will do what it claims it will do. Under a determining-limiting approach, a determining principle may be operating as promised, but the punishment or scheme it dictates nonetheless will be rejected if it violates the limiting criteria of another principle. A contingent priority approach maximizes reliance upon a single primary principle so long as the principle works effectively. Where it is not possible to achieve the goal of the primary principle, it is hardly a sacrifice of that principle to turn to another principle. Under a determining-limiting approach, by contrast, a determining principle is indeed sacrificed where it sufficiently conflicts with a limiting principle.

Lastly, the differences created by choosing a determining-limiting approach also vary based on the principle doing the limiting. If a principle can effectively do what it promises across the full range of cases, as some may think is true in the case of desert, the principle will have greater effect as the primary principle under a contingent priority approach than under a determining-limiting approach. If a principle has proven effectiveness in a more limited range of situations, as is frequently the case with deterrence and rehabilitation, the principle is more likely to have influence as the primary principle under a determining-limiting approach.

One last point regarding limiting principles is worth emphasizing: one cannot construct a workable distributive principle for a criminal justice system using only a limiting principle. For example, Chinese scholars are in the midst of the important task of developing a criminal law theory upon which a new criminal code can be based. One of the proposals urges a "human rights theory of criminal law."[413] As admirable as it may be to give such a central role to human rights, such a theory, by its nature, can only place limits on what a criminal justice system can do; it cannot provide the substantive content to liability and punishment rules. Human rights simply do not have enough to say about what criminal liability and punishment *should* be. With some exceptions, human rights operate only to say what such rules should not be.

4. Combining Principles: Deferring to the Greatest Utility

Rather than choose a hybrid in which one principle is furthered at the expense of another, one could instead formulate an approach by which principles are combined to give a result influenced in part by all principles. Indeed, such an approach seems ideal; it seems to further all and sacrifice none. Unfortunately, while the concept seems perfect, the extent of its realization is limited. The combination of principles is feasible only if the principles to be combined same ultimate goal, for example, efficient crime prevention. And they must be measurable in a common currency, for example, the "costs" in monetary terms of avoiding or not avoiding certain crimes.

Not all principles of liability or sentencing share a common goal of crime prevention or a common currency of monetary cost and benefit.[414]

---

413 *See* He Bingsong, Qu Xinjiu and Lu Min, The New Theoretical System of Criminal Law in the Age of Globalization (2007).

414 As the Model Penal Code commentary suggests:

It is also recognized that not even crime prevention can be said to be the only end involved. The correction and rehabilitation of offenders is a social value in itself,

Because deontological desert and the instrumentalist distributive principles focus on different goals—doing justice versus avoiding crime—it would be impossible to construct a hybrid that gives deference to both. The same problem may exist when trying to combine rehabilitation with another instrumentalist principle. Though some suggest that the principle of rehabilitation is primarily instrumentalist crime prevention, others see it as having a value in itself, which may not easily be traded for crime prevention effectiveness.

The combined-principle approach, however, does offer a means of constructing a hybrid among instrumentalist efficient crime-control principles. For example, it can generate a principle that directs that, when instrumentalist distributive principles conflict, follow the principle that has the greatest crime-control efficiency for the cases at hand. Consider, for example, the combination of general deterrence and incapacitation. Assume that from a general deterrence perspective, doctrinal formulation or sentence A costs 10 units to gain a crime-control benefit of 15 units, producing a net societal benefit of 5, while formulation B costs 15 to save 15, for a net benefit of 0. In this situation, general deterrence as a distributive principle would prefer formulation A. Assume that incapacitation finds that the same formulation A costs 20 to avoid a harm of 15, for a net loss of 5, while formulation B costs 10 to avoid an injury of 15, for a net gain of 5. Thus, incapacitation as the distributive principle prefers formulation B. This would be an instance where the two principles conflict and where any of the previously described hybrid approaches might be used to choose between the two conflicting principles depending upon which has priority.

But the dilemma can be resolved without giving absolute or conditional priority to one principle. Because the two principles have the same goal (efficient crime prevention) and a single currency, the costs and benefits of each formulation may be determined for both principles and these totals for each formulation may be compared to select the best formulation. Thus, if the incapacitation principle is significantly increased by a formulation that only minimally hurts the general deterrence principle in comparison to an alternative formulation, that difference in

---

as well as a preventive instrument. Basic considerations of justice demand, moreover, that penal law safeguard offenders against excessive, disproportionate or arbitrary punishment.

Model Penal Code §1.02 commentary at 4 (Tent. Draft No. 2, 1954).

magnitude of effect might be enough to justify following the incapacitation formulation. The example above generates the following combined analysis:

	Formulation A	Formulation B	
Deterrence	-10	-15	
	+15	±15	
	+5	0	Deterrence prefers Formulation *A*
Incapacitation	-20	-10	
	+15	±15	
	-5	+5	Incapacitation prefers Formulation *B*
Combined Assessment	0	+5	Combined principles prefer Formulation *B*

Thus, by combining the costs and benefits of both principles one can determine that formulation *B* will best further the common goal of efficient crime prevention.

One serious difficulty, of course, is that the effective operation of such a principle would require a level of knowledge and sophistication about the effect of these distributive principles in the real world that does not now exist, as Chapters 3, 4, and 6 have shown.

5. Distinguishing Liability Assignment and Amount of Punishment from the Method of Punishment

While the combined-principles approach combine deontological and instrumentalist principles, one aspect of the natural conflict between the two might be accommodated.[415] This is possible because distributive principles must resolve a range of distinguishable issues in the distribution

---

415 The distinction discussed above, in A.4., concerns that between deontological desert and all of the instrumentalist principles. Only the latter can be combined in the manner described. The distinction at issue here, in A.5., is between both kinds of desert, both deontological and empirical, on the one hand, and nondesert principles, on the other.

of liability and punishment: Who should be punished? How much punishment should they receive? How should the punishment be imposed? The first issue is one of liability assignment—who should be held criminally liable. The second issue—how much punishment—goes both to liability rules (i.e., what grade or degree of offense is appropriate for certain conduct) and to sentencing practice (e.g., how long a sentence or how great a fine is appropriate in a particular case). Together, these two issues govern the quantitative distribution of punishment—who will receive how much. The third issue, concerning the method of punishment, is distinguishable from the distribution of amount. Under some distributive principles, two offenders may merit the same *amount* of punishment (e.g., equally blameworthy or equally dangerous) yet different *methods* of punishing may be suitable for imposing that amount. These two issues—how much for whom and what method—might properly be governed by different rules within the system's distributive principle.

And different distributive principles may have quite different things to say about these two issues. For example, one may seek to optimize efficient crime control by manipulating rules governing both of these issues—by setting both the amount of punishment and the method of punishment. In contrast, as Chapter 7, Section 4 explains, satisfaction of desert concerns depends almost exclusively on the amount issue—achieving a proper ordinal ranking of offenders by overall blameworthiness. As long as the ordinal ranking is correct, the *method* by which the amount of punishment is imposed is not relevant to desert. If one month in state prison is the punitive equivalent to five months of weekends in the local jail, then desert is satisfied even if the more blameworthy offender gets probation, with a condition of six months of weekends in jail, while the less blameworthy offender goes to prison for one month. Or, if the punitive "bite" of a fine of 15 percent of a business offender's assets is equivalent to one week in jail, then desert is served if the more blameworthy offender is fined an amount equal to 25 percent of assets, while the less blameworthy is sentenced to jail for one week.. It is critical, of course, that the punishment equivalencies be properly set. Empirical research has been done on perceptions of relative seriousness of different punishment methods.[416]

---

416 *See*, e.g., Harlow, Darley & Robinson, The Severity of Intermediate Penal Sanctions, *supra* note 118, at 71, 85. (displaying a punishment equivalency table). For an example of a practical application, *see* 1 Paul H. Robinson and the University of Pennsylvania

Equipped with an estimate of equivalencies, one can construct a sentencing system that allows independent determination of the amount and method issues. The principles governing the "amount" issue can generate total "punishment units" for each offender, which can then be allocated to a particular punishment method or combination of methods according to a different set of "method" principles. As long as the issues can be effectively segregated in practice, one can develop a hybrid distributive principle for governing the amount of punishment that is different from the principle used to determine the method of punishment. One could, for example, emphasize desert in determining the amount of punishment but ignore it in determining the method. The selection of method could be made to maximize traditional utilitarian concerns without infringing desert interests—a precious no-loss, all-win opportunity.

As Chapter 7, Section B.8. hints, the separation of amount and method issues has other important collateral advantages. For example, unwarranted disparity in sentencing primarily concerns disparity in amount rather than disparity in method. Thus, one might significantly reduce judicial sentencing discretion on the amount issue, in order to reduce disparity among judges, yet maintain broad judicial discretion on the method issue. As long as the total "punishment units" for an offender are satisfied and the punishment equivalencies are properly set, it does not matter what method or methods an individual judge selects; the punitive "bite" will be the same.

B. The A.L.I.'s Distributive Principle of "Limiting Retributivism"

For the first time since its promulgation in 1962, the American Law Institute has approved a revision to the Model Penal Code: a new formulation of the Code's distributive principle in Section 1.02(2), which is set as the basis for the exercise of discretion by sentencing judges. The amendment is certainly an advance over the 1962 formulation, which offered the standard "litany" of principles and failed to define the interrelation among them. The new provision offers a true articulated distributive

Law School Criminal Law Research Group, Final Report of the Maldivian Penal Law & Sentencing Project at 14 (2006), *available at* http://www.law.upenn.edu/cf/faculty/phrobins/ (a UNDP sponsored project incorporating a punishment equivalency table).

principle that tells decision makers with greater clarity what criteria should guide their judgements.

The new provision sets desert as the primary distributive principle and allows reliance upon deterrence, rehabilitation, incapacitation, restoration, and reintegration to the extent that they are shown to be feasible and to the extent that they do not conflict with desert.

The provision reads:

(2) The general purposes of the provisions on sentencing, applicable to all official actors in the sentencing system, are:

  (a) in decisions affecting the sentencing of individual offenders:

    (i) to render sentences in all cases within a range of severity proportionate to the gravity of offenses, the harms done to crime victims, and the blameworthiness of offenders;

    (ii) when reasonably feasible, to achieve offender rehabilitation, general deterrence, incapacitation of dangerous offenders, restoration of crime victims and communities, and reintegration of offenders into the law-abiding community, provided these goals are pursued within the boundaries of proportionality in subsection (a)(i); and

    (iii) to render sentences no more severe than necessary to achieve the applicable purposes in subsections (a)(i) and (a)(ii); [417]

The new distributive principle might be outlined this way:

In determining punishment, look primarily to the extent of the offender's blameworthiness (including the seriousness of the offense conduct), and:

reliance upon the traditional principles of rehabilitation, general deterrence, and incapacitation of the dangerous, as well as restoration and reintegration, is permitted:

  (A) where those goals can effectively be achieved;

---

417 American Law Institute, Model Penal Code Amendment (Adopted May 16, 2007), Section 1.02(2) ("Purposes...").

    (B) but not if it would produce punishment in conflict with
        the offender's degree of blameworthiness.[418]

The drafters imagine that both desert and the traditional instrumentalist crime-control mechanisms will have influence under this hybrid distributive principle, which they term "limiting retributivism." For the reasons set out below, however, it seems likely that in practice, if the A. L.I.'s principle commitment to desert is taken seriously, it will in fact produce a pure desert distribution of punishment. That is probably not what the drafters anticipate nor what rational policy would want.

1. The Effectiveness Requirement

Reliance upon non-desert principles will be seriously limited, first, by the fact that those principles commonly cannot effectively be achieved, as discussed in Chapters 3 through 6, and thus are excluded from use by the feasibility requirement of paragraph (2)(a)(ii). Consider each of the traditional instrumentalist principles in turn.

As Chapter 5 documents and as the A.L.I. Report concedes,[419] there are limits to the effectiveness one can expect from rehabilitation programs. As Chapters 3 and 4 have shown, our realistic expectations for the effectiveness of deterrence also are fading. Potential offenders commonly do not know the legal rules, either directly or indirectly, even those rules that have been explicitly formulated to produce a deterrent effect. Even if they know the rules, the cost-benefit analysis potential offenders perceive—which is the only cost-benefit analysis that matters in deterrence—commonly leads to a conclusion suggesting violation rather than compliance, either because the perceived likelihood of punishment is so small, or because it is so distant as to be highly discounted, or for a variety of other reasons. And, even if they know the legal rules and perceive a cost-benefit analysis that urges compliance, potential offenders commonly cannot or will not bring such knowledge to bear to guide their conduct in their own best interests, such failure stemming

---

418 The provision also requires that a sentence be no more severe than is necessary to achieve the applicable principle, but this is inherent in the requirement of fixing punishment according to an offender's blameworthiness and inherent in the efficient achievement of the instrumentalist principles.
419 American Law Institute, Model Penal Code: Sentencing, Report 129 (April 11, 2003), at 28–31.

from a variety of social, situational, or chemical influences. Even if no one of these three hurdles is fatal to law's deterrent influence, their cumulative effect typically is fatal.

As to incapacitation of the dangerous, it is true that incapacitation undoubtedly works to prevent future crime. Prison terms, for example, do prevent offenders from reoffending, at least against the unimprisoned population. Thus, unlike rehabilitation and deterrence, incapacitation might actually qualify for use under paragraph (2)(a)(ii). But it, along with the other non-desert principles, will be excluded from use because of the demands of the dominant desert principle, discussed in Subsection B.3. below. Before taking up that issue, consider a problem with the new hybrid principle that is illustrated by its effort to incorporate incapacitation of the dangerous and other crime-control principles into the hybrid principle.

2. The Problem of Countervailing Criminogenic Effect

As Chapter 6 argues, while incapacitation works, it also incurs serious costs, including costs in effective crime prevention. Using the criminal justice system for such preventive detention, rather than providing such detention in a more open and explicit civil preventive detention system, produces both unnecessarily ineffective prevention and subverts justice. Using it as a principle for distributing criminal liability and punishment can produce frequent conflicts with desert, thereby undermining the system's moral credibility and its long-term crime-control effectiveness.

The principle of restoration and reintegration present a similar situation. As Chapter 9 explains, there is evidence that "restorative" processes, such as sentencing circles, victim-offender mediation, and family group conferences, do work in the sense that they can help "restore" victims and communities and can have a modest effect in reducing crime by the same offenders in the future. But, depending on how they are used, restorative processes also can produce more future crime. For example, they may produce results that seriously deviate from shared community intuitions of justice and, thus, can undermine the criminal law's moral credibility and thereby its power to gain compliance as a moral authority that can harness social influence.

The incapacitation and "restoration" principles reveal a weakness in the Report's distributive principle: it does not take into account the *costs* of advancing a principle—for example, its crime producing effects—that may outweigh its benefits. The A.L.I. text authorizes reliance upon one of the enumerated principles when it is feasible to serve the goals. Thus, as long as the goal is being satisfied, the A.L.I. principle would authorize reliance upon it *even if such would seriously increase future crime* because of its other effects.

A second, related flaw in the Code's distributive principle is its failure to give guidance in selecting among the enumerated principles when more than one of those principles meets the "realistic prospect of success" test and each suggest a different distribution. If both incapacitation and "restoration," for example, have a "realistic prospect of success" but suggest different sentences, as they commonly would, which principle should be advanced? The provision fails to tell us, thus essentially leaving it to the unbridled discretion of the sentencing judge, with all of the potential for abuse and disparity in treatment of similar cases that such discretion brings. In other words, though the new Code provision is a more articulated hybrid than the original, it remains open to some of the same criticisms: a failure to provide guidance when alterative principles conflict, thereby allowing unguided discretion dressed up as principle.

For reasons explained in the subsection below, in practice the effect of these flaws in the Code's distributive principle may be limited due to a different and more serious flaw in the new provision.

3. The Nonexistent Range and Desert's Ordinal Ranking Demands

The limitation on the use of any non-desert distributive principle noted in Subsection B.1.—deriving from the difficulty in showing that such principles can be effectively—may be dwarfed in effect by a second, more serious limitation on non-desert principles: The drafters appear to assume that giving priority to desert will have limited effect because they assume desert is only a limiting principle—"limiting retributivism"— while in reality a desert principle is quite specific and demanding in its resulting distribution, leaving little or no room under the A.L.I.'s provision for non-desert principles to ever operate.

The original advocates of "limiting retributivism" assumed that desert provides only vague outer limits on punishment.[420] That is, they

---

420 *See*, e.g., Morris, The Future of Imprisonment, *supra* note 205, at 75–76.

believed that desert was only a limiting principle not a determining principle. However, as Chapter 7, Section B.4. makes clear, desert is not so vague. A desert distributive principle produces a specific amount of punishment not a range, driven in large part by desert's demand for proper ordinal ranking. A desert distributive principle requires that a case of greater blameworthiness receive greater punishment than a case of lesser blameworthiness. Given the limited range of punishments a liberal democracy typically is willing to inflict and the vast number of cases of distinguishable blameworthiness (on either deontological or empirical grounds), each case will fall at a particular point on the punishment continuum. There will be no substantial "range" of deserved punishments along which the non-desert principles can freely operate, as the A.L.I. drafters seem to assume.

This characteristic has important implications for operation of the Code section: even where the enumerated non-desert principles pass the provision's effectiveness test, the nondesert principles will rarely be used because such use would commonly conflict with desert. Where they do not conflict—where they give the same result as a desert distribution—they are irrelevant. That is, as earlier chapters have noted,[421] non-desert principles can provide crime-control effectiveness (in excess of that inherent in a desert distribution) only to the extent that they deviate from desert. Yet, by its explicit rule, the Code's provision expressly forbids such deviation!

There may be instances where a non-desert principle can have an effect. Most importantly, desert generally cares about punishment amount not punishment method, as noted previously. Thus, once the punishment amount is determined, one could look to non-desert principles to determine how that fixed amount of punishment is to be imposed. One might look to the special circumstances of each case to determine whether the punishment method should maximize incapacitation or restoration, or even rehabilitation or general deterrence if the special circumstances exist that make achievement of such principles possible. (Of course, there remains the troublesome failure of the principle to articulate which among the enumerated non-desert principles is to be served when more than one of the principles can be effective but where the different principles suggest different methods of punishment.)

---

421 Most notably in the context of deterrence, in Chapter 4, Section B.2&3.

The method of punishment issue aside, the A.L.I.'s distributive prin-ciple, with its bar to any conflict with desert, will produce an almost exclusively desert distribution of liability and punishment. While desert is an attractive distributive principle, for the reasons set out in Chapter 8, a criminal justice system may well have instances where a deviation from it would be desirable. The next chapter proposes a hybrid distributive principle that shares many features with the A.L.I. provision. It begins with desert—specifically empirical desert (the A.L.I. provision never makes clear which conception of desert it has in mind)—but tries to avoid the A.L.I. problems discussed here.

CHAPTER 12

A Practical Theory of Justice: Proposal for a Hybrid Distributive Principle Centered on Empirical Desert

Chapter 10 reviews the strengths and weaknesses of each of the alternative distributive principles. Chapter 11 examines how multiple principles might be prioritized or combined to provide a principled hybrid. With this foundation, what hybrid might one best construct?

Admittedly different value judgments can suggest different hybrids, although some hybrids will be difficult to defend under any set of values. Set out in Section A below is the hybrid distributive principle that all things considered, it is argued here would seem to represent the most defensible principle on current evidence. Later sections of the chapter consider the implications of such a hybrid principle for criminal justice reform.

A. A Proposed Distributive Principle

The core of the proposal might be summarized this way:

1. *Primary Principle of Empirical Desert.* Formulate criminal liability and punishment rules and the exercise adjudication discretion to most effectively build the criminal justice system's reputation within the community for being just. That is, distribute liability and punishment according to the relative blameworthiness of an offender based upon principles derived from the shared intuitions of justice of the community that is to be governed by that law— empirical desert. Deviation from empirical desert is permitted in the three instances set out below.

2. *Inconspicuous Deviations.* Liability and punishment may deviate from empirical desert in order to advance any important societal interest if the deviation is sufficiently small that it will go essentially unnoticed and therefore will have little or no effect on the criminal justice system's moral credibility.

3. *Deviations to More Effectively Control Crime.* Taking full account of the difficulty in repairing damage to the system's justness reputation caused by deliberate injustice or deliberate failure to do justice, liability and punishment may deviate from empirical desert if (1) the crime-control benefits from the deviation outweigh the crime-control costs, and (2) no nondeviation means of obtaining the crime control is possible. If more than one crime-control opportunity justifies deviation, liability and punishment should be distributed according to the opportunity with the greatest crime-control effect. (This justification for deviation is available to rule-making bodies, such a sentencing guideline drafters, but should be used only cautiously by individual sentencing judges.)

4. *Deviations to Advance Interests Other than Crime Control.* Liability and punishment may deviate from empirical desert in order to advance an important societal interest, such as fairness, limitation on governmental power, privacy, or proper allocation of governmental authority, if the interest is more important than the resulting loss of effective crime control and if there is no other reasonable nondeviation means to advance it. (This justification for deviation is available only to rule-making bodies.)

5. *Method of Punishment.* The previous paragraphs concern primarily the amount of punishment to be imposed, rather than the method of its imposition. The punishment method used should be the one that will most efficiently avoid future crime. Sentencing judges may be allowed discretion to determine the method that will optimize crime prevention, as long as the punitive bite of the punishment method or combination of methods selected equals that called for by the paragraphs above.

A few comments and explanations regarding the proposal:

1. Paragraph 1. Primary Principle of Empirical Desert

Empirical desert seems an attractive centerpiece for a distributive principle in part because it offers an accommodation of sorts between the forever-conflicting goals of doing justice and reducing crime. As for doing justice, one can argue that empirical desert is likely to mimic a deontologically just distribution of liability and punishment more closely than any other instrumentalist distributive principle. As for reducing crime, empirical desert is likely to have good long-term crime-control potential because of its ability to harness the enormous power of social influence and internalized norms.

Further, the punishment imposed under an empirical desert distribution inherently provides some deterrence and some opportunity to rehabilitate and incapacitate. If these alternatives mechanisms were used as distributive principles, they could provide greater crime control than empirical desert only where they deviate from it, and it is this deviation—doing injustice or failing to do justice, in the community's view—that undermines the system's moral credibility and thereby its crime-control effectiveness, perhaps impeding crime control more than promoting it. In other words, empirical desert provides the most efficient starting point from which crime-control costs and benefits can be tallied.

2. Paragraph 2. Inconspicuous Deviations

As Chapter 7, Section B.4. makes clear, empirical desert requires a specific amount of punishment, not a range. Given the limited continuum of punishment possibilities that liberal democracies permit and given the wide variety of cases among which laypersons can distinguish blameworthiness, any given case will require a specific amount of punishment, not because there is some magical connection between that offense and that amount of punishment but rather because that specific amount of punishment is required to place the case in its appropriate ordinal rank among the large number of distinguishable cases.

Nonetheless, as Paragraph 2 acknowledges, in the practical application of empirical desert as a distributive principle, there is a "fudge" range within which punishment may vary yet people will not notice that the amount of punishment puts the case slightly out of order. The existence of such an "inconspicuous deviation" range occurs in part because in today's world cases tend to come to public attention individually rather than as part of a collection, and this makes comparative disparities less obvious. (It follows that the permissible "fudge" range may be greater for some offenses and offenders than others.)

On the other hand, the "inconspicuous deviation" range may decrease as people's knowledge and expectations of the criminal justice system increase, as has been the historical trend. On the structural side, the ad hoc creation of common-law rules gave way to demanding legality requirements in the construction of modern criminal code liability rules. More recently, unfettered judicial discretion in sentencing gave way to sentencing guidelines. It may be that a march toward greater transparency, predictability, and sensitivity to justice is inevitable. As it proceeds, the range of "inconspicuous deviation" may narrow.

3. Paragraph 3. Deviations to More Effectively Control Crime

Empirical desert as a distributive principle is ultimately instrumentalist in its justification; it would have law track shared intuitions of justice because doing such enhances the criminal law's moral credibility and thereby its crime-control effectiveness. It should be no surprise, then, that the proposed distributive principle takes seriously opportunities to more effectively control crime than a pure empirical desert principle would provide. Paragraph 3 explicitly recognizes the possibility that a system might more effectively control crime, even in the long term, by permitting certain deviations from empirical desert where a great crime-control opportunity presents itself.

Of course, it may be that these opportunities will be rare. Rehabilitation and special deterrence opportunities might offer opportunities to prevent recidivism in the individual offender at hand. However, the focus on the individual offender reduces the likelihood that either principle will offer such striking gains as to outweigh the detrimental effects of undermining the system's moral credibility brought on by deviations from desert. By focusing only on the offender at hand, both principles are likely to present only a modest effect on crime as a whole, as compared with the cost to the system's reputation in deliberately doing injustice or failing to do justice. Nonetheless, a good instrumentalist would not want to foreclose the possibility. (Note that these mechanisms may still be used in determining the *method* of punishment, as per Paragraph 5, and may operate within the "inconspicuous deviations" of Paragraph 2.)

Incapacitation of the dangerous may be more likely to present substantial crime-control opportunities because it is so effective at preventing future crimes by the individual offenders detained. But again, it does not follow that these opportunities will regularly justify deviation from empirical desert. Aside from the standard problem of undermining the criminal law's moral credibility, such preventive detention faces a different hurdle in Paragraph 3. A deviation from empirical desert can be justified only if the crime control it offers cannot be achieved through a nondeviation means. In this instance, the possibility for *civil* preventive detention of dangerous persons, which indeed may be more fair and effective and less costly, means that incapacitation cannot justify undermining the moral credibility of the criminal justice system.

General deterrence, which can have effect upon an entire population of potential offenders, may be the more likely alternative distributive principle to present opportunities that would justify a deviation from desert. This is so because deviation from desert in a single case or a small group of cases might be enough to send an effective deterrent message to a very large group of potential offenders. On the other hand, it is likely that one or more of Chapter 3's three prerequisites for a deterrent effect will be missing, thereby subverting the possibility of such striking gains. Nonetheless, it also seems likely that there will be some instances in which the prerequisites will be satisfied and striking gains will be possible.

It should be cautioned, however, that satisfaction of the deterrence prerequisites is not itself enough to justify a deviation from desert. As Paragraph 3 makes clear, a deviation is justified only if the general deterrent effect would be so great as to outweigh even the long-term detriment to the criminal justice system's moral credibility that would result from such a deliberate choice to do injustice or to fail to do justice. As seen in

Chapter 8, Section B.5., even a single well-publicized case (and recall that well-publicized cases are often the most useful for general deterrence) that conflicts with community intuitions of justice can have a serious detrimental effect on the criminal justice system's reputation because the deliberateness of the deviation reveals the system's lack of full commitment to doing justice. Thus, the opportunities for a deviation from desert based on general deterrence, while likely to exist, may not be as frequent as one might expect.

The proposal expresses a preference for limiting such justifications for deviation to rule-making bodies, such a sentencing guideline drafters, urging that it be used only rarely and cautiously by individual sentencing judges. The point is that such deviations have system-wide effect in undermining moral credibility, and generally it ought not to be for an individual judge to decide whether the benefit outweighs that systemwide cost. On the other hand, one would not want to foreclose the possibility if a special opportunity presents itself and the balance in favor of deviation is clear to all.

4. Paragraph 4. Deviations to Advance Interests Other Than Crime Control

Though debates about criminal law and punishment theory tend to focus on the interests of crime control and doing justice, clearly other important societal interests exist. Paragraph 4 acknowledges this and gives several examples. It is not just the end result of the criminal justice process but its fairness in reaching that result that can be important to society. Similarly, liberal democracies place a high value on limiting the power of government to intrude in the lives of its citizens. Privacy interests have come to stand on their own as a societal interest worth respecting. A society also may have strong interests in whom within government exercises governmental power. For example, the legality principle reflects our preference for the most democratic branch of government, the legislature, rather then either the judicial or executive branches, to make criminalization and punishment rules.

Of course, articulating beforehand exactly which of these interests will trump doing justice and its crime-control benefits is an enormous project. It is a significant portion of the agenda of moral philosophy, constitutional theory, and political theory. The point here is not to presume to make some contribution to those debates but only to acknowledge that those debates are indeed relevant to the distribution of criminal liability and punishment.

The existence of a competing interest will not necessarily justify deviation from empirical desert, but the possibility must be examined. Nor does the existence of even a compelling competing interest necessarily justify deviation. Injustices or failures of justice are justified under the proposal only if there is no reasonable nondeviation means by which the compelling interest can be as effectively advanced. More on this in Sections B and C below.

The proposal limits this justification for deviating from desert to decisions by rule-making bodies, such a sentencing guideline drafters. It is not available to individual sentencing judges. The range of possible "interests other than crime control" is so numerous and the potential for mischief and disparity in application is so great that the proposal adopts a fixed bar rather than a mere preference, as it did in Paragraph 3. Thus, it is for criminal code commissions and sentencing guideline commissions to wrestle with the societal interests that compete with effective crime control. Individual case dispositions are all bound by the same balance of interests, that balance struck by the rule-makers.

5. Paragraph 5. Method of Punishment

While Paragraph 4 puts its justification for deviation from desert out-of-bounds for individual sentencing judges, Paragraph 5 moves in the opposite direction, to create a source of broad discretion for them.[422] The demands of the hybrid distributive principle described in the first four paragraphs operate primarily to determine the amount of punishment. Paragraph 5 directs that the punishment method be that which will most efficiently avoid future crime. In this, judges may be allowed a wide range of discretion in determining the method or combination of methods and may select among a wide range of intermediate and nonincarcerative options—fines, treatment programs, weekend jail, house arrest, community service, restorative processes, intensive probation, and anything else

---

422 For a more detailed account on why sentencing judges ought to be relied upon to make some kinds of decisions but not others, *see* Robinson & Spellman, Sentencing Decisions, *supra* note 1, at 1124.

that would seem to advance the societal or individual interests in the case at hand—as long as the punitive bite of the total of all punishment equals that called for by the distributive rules contained in the previous paragraphs. Before such discretion can be allowed, however, the system must adopt a punishment equivalency table that rates each punishment method according to the extent of its punitive bite as perceived by the community, as Chapter 11 discusses.

6. Weakness of the Proposal

The greatest weakness of the proposal may be its failure to solve the problem of community blindness to injustice. It would be tempting to add deontological desert as a check on empirical desert to identify such moral errors by the community, but deontological desert is not given such role for two reasons: First, as discussed in Chapter 7, Section B.7., the state of and methods of current moral philosophy—in particular its tendency to give deference to philosophers' shared intuitions of justice—leaves it poorly equipped to effectively perform this transcendent moral check on community intuitions. Second, even if it could be relied upon in performing this function, the high level of disagreement among moral philosophers, the lack of consensus on many foundational issues (even something so basic as whether resulting harm should be significant in assessing liability), and the absence of any apparent mechanism by which one could authoritatively select among conflicting views, means that reliance upon deontological desert within a distributive principle for liability and punishment would create serious practical problems.

The best solution to the problem, an admittedly unsatisfactory one, may be to simply signal the existence of the problem and to urge a vigilant inquiry by the community and its leaders into the possibility of such moral errors, perhaps encouraging them to consult with moral philosophers, who in fact have thought a good deal about the issues, and to see if that discipline can contribute useful insights to the public debate.

B. Deviations from Empirical Desert

The hybrid distributive principle set out in Section A might be used much as Model Penal Code Section 1.02 is used, to guide the exercise of discretion by judges in interpreting the criminal code's provisions and in sentencing individual offenders. But it also has broader and more important implications for those who design the criminal justice system, its criminal code, and sentencing guidelines.

Under the proposal, it is easy enough to know the primary criterion for constructing a system: adopt rules that will most enhance the system's reputation for doing justice as perceived by the community it governs, as Paragraph 1 provides. More complex is the task of sorting out the justified deviations from desert, under Paragraphs 3 and 4. Under the current system, a wide range of rules and practices may seem to regularly and intentionally deviate from empirical desert. This section offers a catalogue of illustrations of those deviation doctrines and their common justifications.

A close inspection reveals that some of the apparent deviations from desert are not in fact a rejection of doing justice as the primary goal but rather are practical attempts to achieve justice in a complex world, as discussed in Subsection 1 below. Other deviation rules, however, openly sacrifice doing justice to promote another interest, and these doctrines, described in Subsection 2, will require close scrutiny under Paragraphs 3 and 4 of the proposal.[423] Section C below discusses the kinds of systemic reforms that may be required to avoid unjustified deviations from desert.

1. Promoting Justice in a Complex World

Some rules that deviate from desert are adopted out of fear that a more desert-based rule would be subject to easy manipulation and abuse, which ultimately would produce less justice, not more. To give a few examples: The law typically rejects a defense for a reasonable mistake of law. Some states reject an insanity defense or limit its availability to a set of cases more narrow than community views would support. It also is common for states to ignore the individual characteristics of a defendant in making liability judgments, as in judging provocation or negligence, including ignoring the person's incapacities that make it difficult if not impossible for the person to have avoided the violation.

---

423 For general review of current deviations from desert and their justifications, *see* Robinson & Cahill, Law Without Justice, *supra* note 394, at Parts I & II.

A rule that deviates from desert also may be adopted because a more desert-based rule would encounter evidentiary problems that would reduce the reliability of the liability and punishment judgment. Thus, statutes of limitation were adopted to avoid the dangers of stale evidence. Strict liability is imposed in cases where culpability may be difficult to prove but is likely to exist. And coerced confessions and uncounseled lineups are excluded to avoid false recriminations.

Finally, a deviation rule may be adopted because, while it fails to do justice in one case, it allows justice to be done in many other cases or in another more important case. Most notably, plea bargains and witness immunity are granted, even for quite serious offenses, if the cooperation thereby gained will allow the successful prosecution of even more serious offenses by others.

It must be acknowledged that these deviation rules risk undermining the system's moral credibility and that they ought to be maintained, as the proposal suggests, only if there is no other, nondeviation means of achieving the objective. Under that principle, many of these deviation rules will fall.[424] Some of these apparent deviation doctrines may be maintained, however, in part because the system can defend its reputation for doing justice by explaining why the apparent deviation in practice does greater justice overall. Recall from Chapter 8, Section B.5., that good intentions count a good deal in setting reputation. Thus, it is meaningful that by these apparent deviations from desert, the system is *trying* to do justice, as best it can in a complex world.

2. Sacrificing Justice to Promote Other Interests

In other present doctrines that deviate from desert, it is apparent that the deviation does sacrifice desert, typically to pursue some other interest thought to be important. The most obvious example of this to the reader will be those doctrines discussed in Chapters 3 through 6—distributing criminal liability and punishment to optimize deterrence, rehabilitation, or incapacitation of the dangerous—that deviate from desert to advance a traditional crime-control program, even where such a distribution conflicts with the community's shared intuitions of justice.

Other deviations from desert are justified on the grounds that they advance interests other than crime control. The legality principle bars

---

424 For a more detailed account, *see id.*

conviction for offense conduct that was not specifically described in a previously existing prohibition (even if most people, including the offender, believed that the conduct was prohibited). The flipside to this commitment to "living by the rules" is hesitation to excuse an actor who has violated an important prohibition, especially if the prohibition is one presently in need of reinforcement.

Other deviation doctrines are designed to control police and prosecutors. The exclusionary rule may bar the use of clearly reliable evidence to discourage police from engaging in unauthorized searches or seizures, even if such exclusion lets a clearly guilty offender go free. Speedy trial rules, designed to discourage prosecutorial delay, can have a similar effect. The bar against "double jeopardy" operates to limit prosecutorial abuse through repeated prosecutions, even if it means that clearly guilty offenders will escape the punishment they deserve. Similarly, the entrapment defense is designed to discourage overzealous proactive crime control strategies by police; many state formulations give a defense even if the offender is a career criminal looking for an opportunity to commit the offense.

Still other deviation rules are justified on grounds unrelated to criminal justice or the operation of the criminal justice system. Defenses such as diplomatic and official immunity are recognized promote larger international and national governmental interests. Thus, the diplomat deserving punishment goes free, but his immunity is thought to promote the establishment of effective diplomatic relations between nations. The same advancement of noncriminal-justice interests is at stake where the unique condemnatory power of criminal conviction is enlisted to boost the prohibition of minor regulatory violations.

Though each of these deviation rules may have some justification, there is also reason to believe that each incurs a cost to the criminal justice system's long-term ability to control crime by undermining its moral credibility. As Paragraphs 3 and 4 suggest, each may merit re-evaluation to determine whether the benefits derived from the deviation rule outweigh the costs to the law's moral credibility and whether nondeviation means are available to advance the interest. Section C considers the kinds of reforms to which such a re-evaluation might lead.

C. Strategies for Avoiding Deviations from Empirical Desert

Some of the deviations from desert described above may be justified under the terms of the proposed distributive principle, while others may not. This section offers a brief sketch of the kinds of reforms the proposal might suggest, both for practices within the criminal justice system and outside of it.[425]

1. *Criminal Justice Reforms*

Some deviation doctrines may be no longer valid on their own terms. For example, regarding statutes of limitation, there may have been a time when the trial process was inadequate to exclude evidence that was unreliable because it was too old. But now that modern trial procedures give defense counsel good opportunity to expose the weakness in the prosecution's evidence, a need for statutes of limitations seems less obvious. For a long time, however, there was little need to abandon such rules. The burden of proof was on the prosecution beyond a reasonable doubt, and the strength of a prosecutor's case tended to degrade over time, hence prosecutors have little interest in pursuing old cases. Modern developments, however, including advances in crime investigation techniques such as DNA analysis, have increasingly created situations in which compelling reliable evidence is available but the statute of limitations bars prosecution.

For other doctrines of deviation, an awareness of their potential costs suggests that they simply be narrowed in some way or that their objectives be achieved in a way that does not deviate from community notions of desert. For example, rather than rejecting a mistake excuse for a reasonable mistake of law or permitting the use of strict liability, the system can limit the potential for abuse and manipulation by simply shifting the burden of proof to the defendant. Similarly, rather than rejecting legitimate excuse defenses out of fear that an acquittal will muddle the clarity of a prohibition, the system can create a verdict system that distinguishes between an acquittal that condones the defendant's conduct and an acquittal that condemns the conduct but excuses the actor. And of course, rather than imposing punishment that conflicts with community views of justice in order to deter, rehabilitate, or incapacitate, the system can impose the amount of punishment that is deserved but select a punishment method for doing so that best advances these other crime-control mechanisms.

---

425 For a more detailed analysis, *see id.* at chs. 9 & 10.

2. Employing Civil Rather Than Criminal Processes

Paragraphs 3 and 4 admonish against deviations from desert where the interest at issue can be as effectively advanced by a nondeviation means. This sometimes will mean looking to the civil rather than the criminal system to advance the interest at stake. For example, given that the penalties imposed by the criminal justice system for regulatory violations typically are only fines, there is little to gain by using the criminal justice system for such cases, and much to lose. By using criminal conviction in cases devoid of morally condemnation conduct, such convictions dilute the condemnatory effect of criminal liability. In other words, the criminalization of regulatory violations undermines that very characteristic of criminal liability, stigmatization, that such regulatory criminalizations seek to harness.

An even more important reform may be to use civil rather than criminal methods to control overzealous police and thereby avoid the costly deviations that arise from excluding reliable evidence because of police error or that arise from giving an entrapment defense to a career criminal looking for a crime opportunity. Administrative sanction of offending officers by citizen review boards or quick, easy, and substantial compensation for citizens whose rights are violated, or both, can provide a more effective means of controlling police than our current system of letting blameworthy offenders (and offending police) go unsanctioned.

Another important reform of this sort is the subject of Chapter 6, Section D, which urges moving away from using the criminal justice system as a mechanism of preventive detention and to shift this function to an open and explicit system of civil commitment. The current practice is problematic, recall, because by preventively detaining dangerous offenders while cloaking it as deserved punishment for a past offense, we end up both undermining the criminal justice system's reputation for doing justice and relying upon a preventive detention system that is both unfair and ineffective.

The larger point here is that, once it is understood that deviations from empirical desert have crime-control costs, the system ought not permit such deviations unless it is clear that they provide some greater benefit, in promoting crime control or some other core interest, that cannot be promoted through a nondeviation means.

D. The Limits of Criminal Law's Distributive Principle

In closing, this study of distributive principles requires one final admonition: While criminal law's distributive principle is important, it is not the only means or even the most efficient means of reducing crime. When a society thinks about controlling crime, it should understand that there are more avenues to reducing crime than by manipulating the criminal law's liability and punishment rules.

Changes in procedural rules or in the allocation of criminal justice resources often can control crime more effectively than manipulating liability and punishment. Perhaps more importantly, programs outside of the criminal justice system may be able to do more to control crime than would criminal justice reform. Education and training programs, drug treatment programs, and job creation programs, to name an obvious few, all may have good crimecontrol potential. Further, it may be that nongovernmental institutions, such as churches, social groups, extended families, and social reform movements, have as great or greater potential for reducing crime than anything the government to do. The point is, it would be a mistake to rely on the principles for the distribution of criminal liability and punishment as the only means by which crime can be controlled.

INDEX

Note to index: An "n" following a page number denotes a footnote on that page.